ANTHONY MUNDAY
AND CIVIC CULTURE

FOR MY PARENTS

ANTHONY MUNDAY AND CIVIC CULTURE

Theatre, history and power in early modern London

1580–1633

TRACEY HILL

MANCHESTER UNIVERSITY PRESS
MANCHESTER AND NEW YORK

distributed exclusively in the USA by Palgrave

Copyright © Tracey Hill 2004

The right of Tracey Hill to be identified as the author of this work has been asserted by her in accordance with the Copyright, Designs and Patents Act 1988.

Published by Manchester University Press
Oxford Road, Manchester M13 9NR, UK
and Room 400, 175 Fifth Avenue, New York, NY 10010, USA
www.manchesteruniversitypress.co.uk

Distributed exclusively in the USA by
Palgrave, 175 Fifth Avenue, New York NY 10010, USA

Distributed exclusively in Canada by
UBC Press, University of British Columbia, 2029 West Mall, Vancouver, BC, Canada V6T 1Z2

British Library Cataloguing-in-Publication Data
A catalogue record for this book is available from the British Library

Library of Congress Cataloging-in-Publication Data
A catalog record for this book is available from the Library of Congress

ISBN 13: 978 0 7190 6383 1

First published in hardback 2004 by Manchester University Press
This paperback edition first published 2009

Printed by Lightning Source

Contents

List of figures—*page* vi

Acknowledgements—vii

Introduction
'Londons Offspring, though the meanest'—1

1 'Are ye a dweller in this citie, pray?'
Munday's London milieu—19

2 'I purposed nothing, but found it to my profit'
The writer in the marketplace—44

3 'I must needes be derided'
Munday and his contemporaries—69

4 'Plaiers can not be better compared than to the Camelion'
Munday and the theatre—106

5 'The Mother of authenticke memory'
Munday and civic history—144

Bibliography—193

Index—210

List of figures

1 The church of St Giles Cripplegate, with part of London Wall—9

2 The lemon tree and pelican device from *Chrysanaleia* (1616)—23
(Reproduced with kind permission of the Fishmongers' Company)

3 'The Fishmongers Esperanza, or Hope of London' device from *Chrysanaleia* (1616)—95
(Reproduced with kind permission of the Fishmongers' Company)

4 The arms of the Corporation of London, from *A second and third blast of retrait from plaies and Theaters* (sig. A1^v)—108
(By permission of the British Library. BL shelfmark 641.a.40)

5 Map of 'The Cittie of London' (undated), showing the Fortune playhouse—128–9
(Reproduced with the permission of Guildhall Library, Corporation of London)

6 Map of the parish of St Giles Cripplegate Without from John Stow, ed. Strype, *A Survey of the Cities of London and Westminster* (1720)—181
(Reproduced with the permission of Guildhall Library, Corporation of London)

Acknowledgements

I am indebted to various people's generosity with advice, encouragement, comments on drafts, sharing work in progress, pdf files, extensive knowledge of livery company history and numerous other things that helped me write this book. I would especially like to thank the following: Gavin Cologne-Brookes, Richard Dutton, Erica Fudge, Ian Gadd, Graham Holderness, Janelle Jenstad, Steve Longstaffe, Kym Martindale and Jan Richards, Helen Moore, Liz Oakley-Brown, Richard Rowland, Mark Treanor, Richard Wilson, and Jo Wyborn. I am also grateful to the School of English and Creative Studies at Bath Spa University College for financial support. The librarians at Bath Spa University College deserve special thanks for dealing with my interminable inter-library loans with speed and good humour. I am grateful for all their help to Jim Sewell and his colleagues in the Corporation of London Records Office, to the staff at the Guildhall Library and the British Library, to David Beesley, Librarian of the Goldsmiths' Company, to Penny Fussell, Archivist of the Drapers' Company and to Raya McGeorge, Archivist of the Fishmongers' Company. Finally, I would like to thank my cats, who did everything they could to impede my writing, and Leon, for believing (despite all evidence to the contrary) that I am a genius and for reminding me that there is a world apart from Anthony Munday.

In this city everything connects.
(Peter Ackroyd, *London: The Biography*)

Introduction

'Londons Offspring, though the meanest'[1]

ANTHONY MUNDAY's importance to an understanding of the society and culture of early modern London has long been underestimated. Posterity has for the most part treated him with condescension or neglect: only one full-length study of Munday has ever been published (Celeste Turner's rather speculative biography, back in 1928), there is no collected edition of his numerous works, and although he is often mentioned in passing he is rarely given sustained attention.[2] Indeed, his work is usually cited, if it is cited at all, as an indicator of how far his contemporaries' achievements surpassed his own. The massive dominance of Bard-centred criticism has had an even more inhibiting effect. This study of Munday will demonstrate that exploring only canonical texts and writers can never provide a complete account of a culture of so much dynamism and diversity as that of early modern London.

Then as now, London (along with Westminster) was England's chief city, its cultural and its political capital, and Munday busied himself in all the major literary forms of his day. The cultural history of the metropolis during this important period can only be enhanced by paying closer attention to Munday and his works than is usually the case. By putting Munday centre-stage for once, I will show how deeply embedded he was in London's cultural life for over fifty years, for Munday was born only two years after Elizabeth's accession and died less than ten years before the outbreak of the first Civil War. His lifespan therefore covered the majority of Elizabeth I's reign, the entirety of James's, and almost half of the Caroline period. Munday's perpetual reputation as the 'Elizabethan' hack writer *par excellence* has constrained not only his own extraordinarily various literary productions but also the opportunity to read Munday in a wider context. His very versatility is almost always represented as signalling his status as a 'hack writer'. 'Hackdom' has become a kind of prison both for Munday and for critics: the common assumption is that we do not have to explore the works of a writer such as Munday because we already 'know' what they are like – they are not worth exploring. In fact, we can reclaim Munday as a writer essential to an understanding of the culture of early modern London.

Munday played a ubiquitous role in the culture of his day, as even those who consider his works to be of little interest are prepared to admit. In this respect Thomas Seccombe's view in the *Dictionary of National Biography* is typical. He writes that:

> Munday was in his versatility an epitome of his age ... ready to turn his hand to any occupation, he was as a man of letters little more than a compiler, destitute of originality or style ... [however] there are few Elizabethan writers who occupied a greater share of public attention, or contributed more largely to popular information and amusement.[3]

The comments about Munday's literary shortcomings echo those he himself had combated throughout his career, to which I shall return. As Seccombe does concede, a large proportion of Londoners would have experienced some aspect of Munday's activities during his long life. Munday's contemporaries had countless opportunities over some forty years to attend his successful plays at the Rose, the Theatre, or the Fortune, to read one of his numerous translations (some of which were still being republished regularly after the Restoration), to watch as a bystander on the city streets or the riverside as one of his many spectacular civic entertainments passed by, or indeed to witness him haranguing Catholic prisoners at that other great London stage, Tyburn. His texts and his audiences were therefore numerous and various, and comprehensively represented the range of London's culture. This alone, in my view, makes it all the more imperative that Munday should finally be given the attention he deserves.

As William Ingram has written in his contextualised biography of Francis Langley (a man whose career had a number of similarities to Munday's), Langley's 'life is important precisely because of what it tells us about his social milieu. He was in many ways the embodiment of his times: not of the aspirations of the times ... but of the actualities.'[4] One can profitably relate Ingram's point to Munday. Arthur Pennell remarks too that 'Munday is hardly a distinguished writer but this very fact, his mediocrity, may increase his historical significance; for it is usually the case that the less dramatic, everyday facts are the ones that lend solidity to our view of the Elizabethan stage'.[5] I would dispute Pennell's claim about Munday's 'mediocrity' but it is true to say that he was an 'everyday' writer. From what we know of his personal history and despite his often-vaunted piety, he seems to have been a very pragmatic, even unpleasant individual. As with Munday, Ingram writes: 'that [Langley] was unscrupulous and opportunist few would deny, [but he] was not ... very much worse than most of his colleagues in the attitudes and activities that engaged them all'.[6] Although one certainly sometimes feels repelled by what Munday's more controversial texts reveal of the man himself and what he was prepared to do to seek and retain patronage from the powerful (such as on occasion betraying to the Elizabethan authorities some of his Catholic patrons and associates) there is undeniably a fascination in studying a writer who was involved in so many of the literary forms of his day. Munday was first and foremost a writer who was both acutely aware of others' perceptions of his talents and personality flaws and prepared to rebut these perceptions publicly.[7]

Although it has elements of such a genre, this book is not, however, a straightforward biography. I would not wish to replace the omission of Munday from cultural history with an equally misleading exclusively personal focus: Munday is important and interesting primarily *because of* the numerous contexts within which he can be placed. What I am attempting here, then, is a form of recovery, or reorientation, in much the same fashion as Garrett Sullivan, who by focusing on Munday's erstwhile collaborator, Thomas Heywood, seeks not only to explore 'once-ignored texts' but also, and more widely, to rediscover what Sullivan calls 'lost epistemologies'.[8] Munday's 'way of seeing', in Sullivan's phrase, offers us the opportunity of witnessing a quotidian London and its 'everyday practices' which a concentration on major canonical works and writers would circumscribe, if not deny us altogether. It may not be a London that we would empathise with, it might be a London more alien than we might expect, but it *is* a London that was meaningful to a large proportion of its anonymously ordinary inhabitants and for that reason worth the study.[9] Avoiding non-canonical writers prevents us from accessing that ubiquitous if unglamorous urban culture that has been retrospectively degraded by its association with the London commonalty. Hiving Munday off into some cultural ghetto called 'Minor Elizabethans', 'Lesser Elizabethan

Dramatists' or even, ironically, the 'Popular School', traduces not only the writer himself but all those connected with his output, from patrons to audiences to readers.[10] As Kathleen McLuskie writes in relation to Dekker, 'his work illustrates the eclecticism of a professional career which followed the shifting commercial opportunities, crossing the boundaries between elite and popular'.[11] McLuskie has argued further that recent 'radical criticism [is] less comfortable with citizen values' as expressed by writers such as Dekker and Munday.[12] Discomfort notwithstanding, their works *are* part of the picture. This book intends to put centre-stage those aspects of London culture that are so regularly overlooked and underestimated precisely because they can so easily be denigrated, both then and now. As Margot Heinemann writes, much supposedly 'popular' work is in fact *un*popular with contemporary criticism; it is paid scant attention because 'the ideas, beliefs, expression, and culture of ordinary people in the past ... fail to coincide with our own'.[13]

Such preconceptions are so omnipresent that they often appear to be involuntary. Modern-day critics sometimes cannot help themselves unquestioningly inheriting what McLuskie has called the 'scorn and condescension' directed by self-nominated elite writers such as Jonson towards contemporaries such as Munday.[14] As a case in point, one can see how, in his edition of plays by Marston, Middleton, Jonson and Massinger, Gāmini Salgādo underplays the very real connections between these writers and their contemporaries such as Munday. He regards the former writers' work as qualitatively different to that of Dekker and Heywood, for instance, with whom Munday also co-wrote. The words Salgādo uses in his otherwise judicious discussion, such as 'simple' and 'naïve', to characterise the latter type of writer are very revealing of his unspoken assumptions. He states that their 'dramatic objectives ... are as simple and straightforward as the responses they wish to evoke' (here the supposed 'simplicity' of the putative audience is bracketed with that of the dramatists); that they 'celebrate the honest tradesman ... with simple relish'; and that the (limited) social satire in their plays is presented 'in a spirit of naïve hyperbole'.[15] In contrast to this often unthought bias I want to show how despite – or perhaps, paradoxically, *because of* – his dogged ordinariness, his moralising and his nostalgia, Munday managed to express the quotidian voice of the early modern London citizenry: active, individualistic, opportunistic, *modern*. This can stand as a description of Munday himself, from what we know of his life and personality. He is a remarkable admixture of the omnipresent and the elusive. Although there is no extant physical image of the man, his voice comes across to the reader so strongly, particularly when he is talking about himself (one of his favourite topics) that the gap of four hundred years almost disappears. He has many voices, too: he speaks sometimes querulously, sometimes ingratiatingly, sometimes authoritatively; at times he is inadvertently comic and he is often tedious. However, one of the most intriguing and consistent features of his literary work – especially his prose, which in my opinion is his forte – is its directness. His willingness to tackle his detractors and to address a multiplicity of audiences and readerships gives his writing a strikingly modern flavour which presents a challenge to our ideas about early modern authorship. This element in his work derives in the main from the fact that his personal history is rarely far from the surface. It is this interrelationship between the man and the multivarious works that anchors this study in Munday's milieu and moment.

As revisionist historians as well as some new historicist critics have discovered, 'local knowledge' of the kind that I employ throughout this book renders up insights often overlooked when one focuses on the 'big picture' rather than its complicated, if not contradictory, detail. This study therefore sits within an emerging trend of attention to the materiality of culture in this period. Paying attention to one individual's work and experience serves to produce a human dimension to the 'dry facts' of theatre and civic history, and to find a place to ground what the larger socio-economic transformations of the early modern period 'felt like' to those who lived through them.[16] Although, as David Mann has pointed out, 'reconstructing Munday's career is fraught with difficulties', following the outlines of Munday's lifespan can establish a chronology for the cultural history of London from the 1580s onwards.[17] Munday's life and work can thus help us to recover what Barbara Freedman calls 'the lived experience' of early modern theatre.[18] My approach in this book, rather than using the quasi-metaphorical uses of terms such as 'exchange' and 'circulation' as employed by Stephen Greenblatt, for instance, is more concerned for what Ingram calls 'discrete analyses ... biographies [and] particularized evidence'.[19] To the characteristic generalities of much new historicism I wish to counterpose a more genuinely 'local' sense of 'local knowledge', one which is grounded more in material reality. The 'locality' for my analysis is provided partly by Munday himself and partly by his city.

This work, then, will pose often unasked questions about Munday's role in London culture, including: 'why did he stop writing for the stage just when he was at his most successful as a playwright?', 'what relationship did *he* perceive, if any, between his work as a pursuivant for governmental agencies and his literary endeavours?', and 'what was the most important identity for him: being free of the Drapers' Company or writing for the Admiral's Men?' Munday can profitably be considered one of Ingram's exceptions to the rule of the invisibility of the quotidian theatre man: 'on rare occasions ... we are allowed a glimpse of something richer and more ambiguous, full of the qualities of a good text'.[20] If Munday is our 'text', then I will begin by unpicking the connections that serve to make him so interesting; as the next section of this introduction demonstrates, some of those connections are geographical as much as personal.

PLOTTING THE CITY

Within London and its immediate environs Munday's connections were manifold. Tracing these connections reveals a great deal, not only about our protagonist but also about the diverse range of people and institutions with which he came into contact. I will also demonstrate the extent to which Munday's literary output became more closely associated with London itself as his career progressed. According to Franco Moretti in his innovative work *Atlas of the European Novel*, 'placing a literary phenomenon in its specific space – mapping it – is not the conclusion of geographical work; it's the *beginning*'.[21] I aim to transpose the insights of Moretti's pioneering study of the eighteenth- and nineteenth-century novel into an earlier period, and focus more precisely than he does on one writer in one city. Some of the texts to which I resorted constantly when writing this book were Kingsford's magisterial edition of Stow's *Survay* with its indispensable map of London c.1600, the wonderful *A-Z of Elizabethan London* and, to trace the persistence of Munday's city, the *A-Z of contemporary London*. I can now tread what remains of the streets of Munday's London with some confidence since the City's ancient outline still largely persists, as well as some of its features such as Munday's own parish church of St Giles Cripplegate. The amalgam of the old street-plan and the perpetually noisy and chaotic building site that is contemporary London brings to mind Jonson's perceptive description of the Jacobean city in *The Devil Is an Ass*: 'stranger, and newer, and chang'd every hour'.²² Within that restless modernity, however, we can find elements of early modern civic culture (the livery company halls, for example) that still appear in some ways to inhabit that ancient London of such longevity. As Andrew McRae has written: 'at the outset of the seventeenth century the predominant conceptions of space in London were torn between tradition and nascent modernity [where] the demands of the former constructed spaciality upon accretions of memory and localized mythologies'.²³ Hence, as we will see, the recurrent nostalgia of many of Munday's civic texts, together with his conscious use of locality and of the city's self-mythologising cultural traditions.

Even today London still is, in many ways, the city of 'Antiquity, Increase, and Moderne Estate' that Stow and then Munday anatomised some four hundred years ago. An attention to literary geography in a specific, detailed manner makes it possible, for example, to understand more about the vexed early history of the Fortune playhouse which is discussed in Chapter 4. I *know* how close the limit of the City's jurisdiction is to the theatre's location because I have stood on Golding Lane and looked back towards the City across where the boundary lay. It certainly has proved to be the case that a cartographical approach, as Moretti claims, 'bring[s] to light relations that would otherwise remain hidden … It poses new questions, and forces you to look for new answers.'²⁴ These 'relations' take the form of what might otherwise be perceived as accidents or coincidences of geography, like Munday's proximity to the Fortune in his house in Cripplegate, or as transhistorical phenomena like the concentrated accretion of diachronic and synchronic forces that is the Standard on Cheapside (further discussed below), or even as individuals embodying something of the varied geography of a city, like Munday himself over the long course of his life.

The 'literary geography' (in Moretti's term) of Munday and his texts takes a twofold form. First, Munday moved around the City itself and also back and forth from his home on the edge of the City to the other political powerhouse that was Westminster. He would have regularly crossed the river to the Rose in the 1590s, and in the Jacobean period he would have trodden a well-worn path between Cripplegate and the Guildhall and its associated livery company halls in search of civic patronage. He also, notoriously, journeyed through France to Rome during 1578/9, went to the Low Countries in 1595, and travelled widely inside England as part of his work as a pursuivant. He then made use of his personal geographical experience in a variety of broadly cultural ways via his political pamphlets (especially those trading on his trip to Rome), his translated continental romances and, closer to home, his two editions of Stow's *Survay of London*. London thus impacted on his work in two reciprocal ways: it was represented in his texts and it affected the writing of these same texts; thus, as Moretti writes, literary geography can illustrate both 'space in literature [and] literature in space'.[25]

There are also recurrent localities as well as movements in Munday's life and writings. These localities, which exemplify Munday's embeddedness in so many areas of his city's life and which highlight his own sense of belonging, constitute the diachronic rather than the synchronic dimension of this study. Like his parish church, St Giles Cripplegate, which still sits today only yards away from the City wall, Munday's location for most of his long life was established on the margins of the City; within its boundary of jurisdiction, but also 'Without', close to places which were only contingently tolerated such as the Fortune playhouse. Perhaps playing its part in prompting Munday's lifelong interest in history, St Giles also bore (and bears) permanent reminders of London's even more ancient past in the form of the remains of the Roman and medieval City wall.

As we will see, in relation to his employers and patrons from the Privy Council to the City Corporation, as well as to a number of his fellow writers, Munday occupied a marginal position that was not solely geographical. For most of his adult life he worshipped at St Giles, which is a City parish church, but one outside the City walls and close to the Fortune, and thus a place that symbolises Munday's complex relationship to City and theatre.[26] He had been baptised in October 1560, however, in the parish of St Gregory's by St Paul's in the heart of the City.[27] In his later years he moved to the Moorgate area until his death and he was buried in August 1633 at the church of St Stephen on Coleman Street, safely within the walls of the City, just across the way from the Guildhall.[28] It seems appropriate that he should be buried at St Stephen's rather than in Cripplegate, since his association with the theatre was long past by the 1630s; his civic work, in the form of his pageants and editions of Stow, had dominated the latter decades of his life. However, the parish of St Stephen extended outside the walls of the City, as did Cripplegate, and Munday may have lived near Moorgate in the 1620s–30s. In addition, the theatres with which he was most frequently involved were the Rose on Bankside and the Fortune at the outer reaches of the parish of

Cripplegate. Munday's lifelong habit, it seems, was to live and work on and across boundaries, leading those who study him today in turn to question those very boundaries.

Local knowledge again proves to be crucial. As Freedman has argued, 'the reconstruction of cultural histories ... [is] more politically aware at the level of local interests and London typography – streets running parallel, forming junctions, neighbourhoods and antagonisms'.[29] The nexus of power, history and culture formed by Munday

1 The church of St Giles Cripplegate, with part of London Wall

himself is like the intersection of locales of particular interests and forms of power, or of strange, unlikely or unexpected neighbours. As we will see below, Munday is like the Standard on Cheapside, a cross pointing towards these disparate but linked aspects of early modern London. In his role as nexus, he resembles too London itself, as described metaphorically by another of its inhabitants, Thomas Milles: 'all our creeks seek to join one river, all our rivers run to one port, all our ports join to one town, all our towns make but one city ... which the world calls London'.[30]

Civic culture has a spatial, or synchronic, as well as a historical, or diachronic, dimension. The diachronic register can manifest itself as a historical accretion of meanings relating to a place or a locale, overlaid with consecutive re-use. London's topographical features can be seen to have cultural meaning. An example of the kind of accretion I mean here is the 'Evil May Day' riot of 1517, which becomes both a historical and cultural 'event', retold successively in a variety of media: historical accounts such as Holinshed and Hall report it, these chronicles are used as a 'source' by Munday and his collaborators for the *Sir Thomas More* playtext and by John Stow's *Survay*, Munday then greatly expands on Stow's account of these events in his editions of the *Survay*. The diachronic scale of this event and the way in which it is remade is complex, even dialectic. It is not even simply chronological, like an archaeological record – it is more like a spiral, a vortex, a helix.

Focusing on the material conditions of Munday's literary and non-literary careers reveals their interconnectedness. This book's epigraph from Peter Ackroyd's *Biography* of London therefore suggests connections of spatial and geographical as well as personal kinds. Munday's range of intersecting interests and loyalties have proved to be particularly productive. As Leah Marcus argues, local reading 'should be a process of continual negotiation between our own *place* ... and the local *places* of the texts we read'.[31] A local reading is in addition related to, although not identical to, notions of 'topicality' but it goes beyond a simple search for contemporary referents to uncover 'broader ways in which the text can be seen to function if those [local] details are taken as central to meaning instead of marginal'.[32] For this study, Munday himself stands as a hitherto marginal local context newly brought to the fore. There are more texts (and their writers) available for a 'London' reading than *Measure for Measure*.

'SOME CONVENIENT SCAFFOLD'[33]
THE STANDARD AND ITS MEANINGS

To illustrate my sense of Munday's connections, and to bring into view many of this book's concerns, I will now turn for a while to examine the wide-ranging significance of one particular feature of London topography, the Standard on Cheapside. The Standard acts here as a kind of pointer to those parts of the City that were important to Munday, particularly as reflected in some of his most London-focused texts such as *The Booke of Sir Thomas More*, his civic pageants and his editions of *The Survay of London*. Cheapside, the street on which the Standard stood, was for early modern London both a marketplace and a thoroughfare.[34] Jean-Christophe Agnew has discussed the ways in which the notion of 'market' in the early modern period referred as much to a *place* as it did to a practice: 'markets were, in every possible sense of the term, *situated* phenomena ... they were assigned to precise sites – in space and time'.[35] Munday himself, like Cheapside and its Standard, can be seen as a metaphorical 'thoroughfare' or intersection of interests, and, as we will see, his habitual attitude to his texts was that of a salesman appealing to a variety of potential cultural markets.

The Standard was a place with a variety of functions in early modern London: it has been described by Martin Holmes as being 'like a market cross, a central landmark and the natural place for proclamations, executions and the burning of condemned documents', and it was also used as a public water conduit.[36] As a feature of London's major thoroughfare, Cheapside, one of the City's most celebrated shop windows, the Standard would have had a visibility to citizens and visitors alike which other sites such as Tyburn, out on the margins of London, did not. The Standard 'was in the form of a pillar with a dome-shaped top; statues adorned its sides, and a figure of Fame, blowing a trumpet, stood on the summit'.[37] 'Fame' is a common emblem in early modern culture, one often associated with power. With her trumpet she forms part of a woodcut illustration in Munday's 1580 work *Zelauto*, which itself is subtitled 'The Fountaine of Fame', alluding unconsciously to the Standard's function as a conduit.[38] Fame also holds the 'most eminent place' in Munday's 1618 Lord Mayor's Show *Sidero-Thriambos*, where she is depicted with 'her Golden Trumpet, the Banner whereof, is plentifully powdred with Tongues, Eyes and Eares: implying, that all tongues should be silent, all eyes and eares wide open, when Fame filleth the world with her sacred memories'.[39]

For Munday, Fame is 'more morrall and significant' than the other devices because she stands for 'a modell of Londons happy Governement'.[40] In Dekker's 1612 mayoral pageant *Troia Nova Triumphans*, written for John Swynnerton, the Merchant Taylor (of whom more below), the Standard marks the place in the procession of 'the House of Fame', the final device on the procession.[41] Reiterating the association of the Standard and social control, Middleton's 1613 Show *The Triumphs of Truth* uses the Standard as the site where Error temporarily threatens Truth: 'about which place, by elaborate action from Error, [the mist] falls again, and goes so darkened till it comes to St Laurence Lane-end'.[42] The Standard is also connected indirectly to another of Munday's civic texts. The Goldsmiths' Company used 'standards' to assay the quality of gold coin, and the purity of coinage was tested in an ancient annual ceremony called 'the Trial of the Pyx', presided over by the Queen's Remembrancer.[43] Owing to the fact that in 1611 this Goldsmiths' ceremony had been given especial prominence by presence of the King, in his Goldsmiths' pageant of the same year Munday highlights this process of testing: Leofstane says that 'to preserve those pure refined bodies from base adulterating, the *Essay-Maister* or absolute *Tryer* of eythers vertue, makes proofe of them in his Furnaces, and of their true worth or value'.[44]

Although London had other 'standards' Lawrence Manley differentiates between 'cisterns' and standards, suggesting that the latter is more identified with a ritual place than simply a quotidian civic amenity.[45] Even in Munday's day its occasional use as a place of execution dated back some centuries. Indeed, Munday himself exploited this fact, for one of those executed at the Standard was John Lincoln, a disenchanted London 'broker' and the supposed ringleader of the 1517 Evil May Day riot which is dramatised in the co-authored play *Sir Thomas More*.[46] The first seven scenes of this play map its action on to the London streets and represent the City's civic government very fully: for instance, More's role in putting down the riot derives from his post as under-sheriff of London. Unusually for an early modern play, Lincoln's execution takes place on stage, so the Standard itself is represented physically as well as textually in Munday's text. In the play, a messenger reports

> the Councelles pleasure,
> for more example in so bad a case,
> a Jibbit be erected in Cheapside,
> hard by the Standerd,

> whether you must bring
> *Lincolne*, and those that were cheefe with him,
> to suffer death, and that immediatly.[47]

Perhaps because of the executions carried out at the site, the records show that the Cheapside standard has a special nature, as in most sources it is '*the* Standard', not 'a standard'. In the *Survay* Stow emphasises that it is 'of what antiquitie, the first foundation I have not read'.[48] He seems a little unsure of its history:

> whether the Standarde in West Cheape, so oft spoken of in former times [as a place of punishment], be the same and stoode just in this place ... may be some question: for it is manifest that in the raigne of Edwarde the thirde ... there was no such Standarde ... it is verie likelie therefore that the olde Crosse in Cheape (which was then [i.e. 1293, the date of Stow's first recorded punishment at the site] newlie builded) was also the Standarde.[49]

His conclusion is that the Standard is so named regardless of its use as a conduit, underlining its difference from London's other standards, such as the one at Cornhill. There is some confusion and/or elision in Stow's text between the 'old cross' at the west end of Cheap and an (or the same?) 'old crosse', again called 'the standart', located 'without the north doore of S. Pauls ... at the East ende of the parish Church called S. Michael in the corne by Paules gate'.[50] There had, in fact, been two standards on Cheapside: one, the oldest and furthest to the west, had been demolished in 1390, which means that the Standard at which Lincoln was executed in 1517 was the one nearer to St Paul's, which had from at least the fifteenth century acted also as a public conduit. Although Lincoln was executed at the newer Standard, the previous one also has a link to him, for at the west end of Cheapside, near the church of St Michael le Querne, stood the Little Conduit, built in 1442 at the site of an earlier cross, taken down in 1390, which was 'sometimes called the Brokers' Cross'.[51] John Lincoln calls himself 'a Broaker by profession' in Munday's play.[52] As far as Stow is concerned, his lack of certainty over this location might relate to the two conflicting interests he has in the Standard: it is an example of civic beneficence of the kind he often celebrates (the building of the conduit) but it is also a cross and place of execution with a long part to play in London's history.[53] Here, as with so many of these resonant London locations, there is both a synchronic and a diachronic dimension to Stow's interpretation. Places can have a history, but they often have a *use*, too.

As we see in the case of John Lincoln, as Stow says, 'diverse executions of the law before time had beene performed' there. Stow lists 'executions at the Standard in Cheape' from the thirteenth to the fifteenth centuries, including in '1381. *Wat Tiler* beheaded *Richard Lions* and other there ... in the yeare 1450. *Jacke Cade* captaine of the Kentish Rebels, beheaded the Lord *Say* there'.[54] One can note the parallels between Evil May Day and previous insurrections – in the earlier instances, however, the rebels exact punishment, rather than suffer it, at the Standard. However, it appears to have been as often the venue for punishment of those who had offended the City as of action by citizens *against* authority. Lincoln's case indicates that a temporary pillory was set up 'hard by' the Standard when required. William Hacket, another disturber of the civic peace, was executed on Cheapside; the venue was chosen on the basis that his punishment should be carried out where his offences took place, as had been the case for some of the 1517 May Day rioters.[55] As well as executions, other forms of punishment were sometimes carried out at the Standard. Mark Jenner remarks that 'conduits were symbolic and moral centres of the City'; their use as places of punishment was thus no coincidence but rather was intended to demonstrate civic disapproval of anti-social behaviour.[56]

As well as being a place of execution, as the nexus of four city wards – Cheap, Bread Street, Cordwainer Street and Cripplegate – the Standard also served as an important geographical marker of London's ward boundaries. It is used by Stow's (and Munday's) *Survay of London* to indicate the point of division of the City's 'partes' from Aldgate in the east, 'through Cheape to the Standarde ... then by the Standard to the great crosse' and thus to Ludgate in the west.[57] The Standard punctuates Stow's written perambulation across the centre of the City from east to west. In the *Survay* it is also one of the markers of the extent of Cripplegate ward itself: 'a part of west Cheape, to wit from the standarde to the [Eleanor] Crosse is all of Cripplegate warde'.[58] Cripplegate ward, Munday's home for most of his life, was therefore bounded at its southern end by the Standard, and at its northern end by the location of the Fortune, where Munday worked in the early years of the seventeenth century. On another north–south axis, the Standard lay at an almost exact equidistance from the Rose on Bankside to the south to the Fortune in the north of the city (see figure 5, p. 128, where the Standard is just to the right of 'Cheapside'). Munday's theatre career can therefore be mapped on to London with the Standard at its centre.

The Standard had another role to play in Munday's cultural productions, for it was one of the pageant stations on the route taken by the Lord Mayor's Show back from Westminster to the Guildhall.[59] Having been met with a water show at Baynard's Castle, the Mayor's procession passed up towards St Paul's and from thence along Cheapside to the Standard. Manley stresses that Cheapside itself was 'the City's most important ceremonial route'.[60] During the Lord Mayor's festivities, each consequent stage of the pageant was 'inserted into the procession' at these important points, performing, as Manley remarks, 'the traditional position of conquered victims in Roman triumphs'.[61] Cheapside was a crucial stage in this ritual journey through the City; as Manley puts it, 'the ceremonial temperature shot up exponentially ... between the Great Conduit, Cross and Standard in Cheapside and the Little Conduit at the gate into Paul's Churchyard'.[62] Theodore Leinwand reinforces the point by stressing that 'the real show was not at Westminster in the morning or at Paul's in the afternoon; its actual and symbolic locus was the streets of London'.[63] That stretch of Cheapside where the Standard lay (between the Great Conduit at its eastern end and Paul's Gate at the west) Manley calls 'the central core of the City's ceremonial space'.[64]

The 'fame', or fate, of John Lincoln once more reverberates through these later cultural moments: the October Mayors' pageants were effectively substituted for other more 'popular' and potentially unruly forms of entertainment, especially those occurring on May Day.[65] It is perhaps fitting (if poignant), then, to note that Lincoln's death, which was the result of a May Day over which the City authorities lost control, should have taken place at a location, so loaded with meaning, which later was to form part of the annual demonstration of civic power and cohesion that was the Lord Mayor's Show. For all these reasons the Standard can be seen to act as Munday's London compass, pointing the way towards those geographical and cultural areas with which he (and this book) is most concerned. In a chapter entitled 'the Citie divided into partes' *The Survay of London* establishes first a north–south and then an east–west axis of division for the city. The east–west line crosses the Standard.[66] As Lincoln himself was literally 'quartered' at the Standard, so the place itself, which functioned also a cross, follows Stow by dividing the city into quarters and marks out Munday's routes and locales with uncanny precision.[67]

NOTES

1. Stow, ed. Munday et al., *The Survey of London*, sig. A4v.
2. For instance, Kathleen McLuskie's otherwise valuable book on Heywood and Dekker (two of Munday's regular dramatic collaborators and both pageant-writers, as was he) makes no mention of Munday, nor does John Twyning's more recent study of Dekker and London.
3. *Dictionary of National Biography*, s.v. 'Anthony Munday'.
4. Ingram, *A London Life*, p. 7.
5. Munday, *John a Kent and John a Cumber*, p. 54.
6. Ingram, *A London Life*, p. 286.
7. I have discussed Munday's personal involvement in the suppression of Counter-Reformation Catholicism further elsewhere (see my '"This is as true as all the rest is"' and 'Marked down for omission').
8. Sullivan, *The Drama of Landscape*, p. 231. Twyning says of Dekker that he was 'the quintessential urban writer of his period', and suggests, as with Munday, that it is Dekker's versatility as a writer that has lead to his neglect by literary critics (*London Dispossessed*, p. 7).
9. As Laura Stevenson argues, the 'state of mind' of writers from this period can be characterised as 'so nearly familiar yet so utterly foreign to the post-industrial world' (*Praise and Paradox*, p. 8).
10. See Johnson, *Elizabethan Bibliographies*, Ward and Waller, *The Cambridge History of English Literature*, vol. V, and Haaker, 'Anthony Munday'. Leonard Ashley says, rather more generously, that Munday 'is the most fascinating of all the minor dramatists of his time' ('Munday, Anthony', p. 1005).
11. McLuskie, *Dekker and Heywood*, p. 3.
12. *Ibid.*, p. 67.
13. Heinemann, 'Rebel lords, popular playwrights, and political patronage', p. 70. Twyning has commented that the exclusion of 'popular' writers such as Dekker (and Munday) has prolonged the 'unwritten elitism' that pervades so much literary criticism and history. He points out that '"booke-trade" literature remains ... excluded from the canon which necessarily needs to expunge such works for its own definition' (*London Dispossessed*, p. 14).
14. McLuskie, *Dekker and Heywood*, p. 23.
15. Salgādo, *Four Jacobean City Comedies*, pp. 9–10.
16. See also Leinwand, *Theatre, Finance and Society*, p. 5 and *passim*.
17. Mann, 'Sir Oliver Owlet's Men', p. 309.
18. Freedman, 'Elizabethan protest', p. 22. Blair Worden has argued recently that 'the division of academic labour, which hands historiography to historians and plays to literary critics' is an 'obstacle' to scholars making necessary connections ('Which play was performed', p. 23).
19. Ingram, *The Business of Playing*, p. 224. See, for example, Greenblatt, *Shakespearean Negotiations*.
20. Ingram, *The Business of Playing*, p. 48.
21. Moretti, *Atlas of the European Novel*, p. 7.
22. Jonson, *The Devil Is an Ass*, I.i.102.
23. McRae, '"On the famous voyage"'.
24. Moretti, *Atlas of the European Novel*, pp. 3–4.
25. *Ibid.*, p. 3.

26 St Giles was the only one of Cripplegate's six parish churches that was outside of the City walls.
27 A large number of stationers and drapers (including Munday's father) were resident in this parish.
28 Like St Giles Cripplegate, St Stephen's had a reputation as a church with 'radical religious traditions'. In the early sixteenth century Coleman Street became 'a centre of incipient Lutheranism'. It was known as 'a loyal street to the Puritan party' in the 1640s, some of whom sheltered from Charles I in St Stephen's (Brigden, *London and the Reformation*, p. 608).
29 Freedman, 'Elizabethan protest', p. 45.
30 Cited in Manley, *Literature and Culture*, p. 2.
31 Marcus, *Puzzling Shakespeare*, p. 36. See also Twyning, *London Dispossessed*, p. 4.
32 Marcus, *Puzzling Shakespeare*, p. 37.
33 Dekker, *Troia Nova Triumphans*, cited in Leinwand, 'London triumphing', p. 143. These are Justice's words at the finale of Dekker's 1612 pageant for John Swynnerton.
34 'Cheap' or 'Chepe' means a market, or to sell or bargain.
35 Agnew, *Worlds Apart*, p. 18. See also Heywood, ed. Rowland, *Edward IV*, pp. ci–ii.
36 Holmes, *Elizabethan London*, p. 31. One book that 'suffered martyrdom by fire' at the Standard by order of the Star Chamber was William Prynne's 1633 *Histriomastix* (Sugden, *A Topographical Dictionary*, p. 112).
37 Sugden, *A Topographical Dictionary*, p. 485.
38 See Munday, *Zelauto*, p. 188.
39 Anthony Munday, *Sidero-Thriambos*, sig. B4r. *Sidero-Thriambos*, as we will see, is more concerned with contemporary social disorder than most of Munday's pageants. Throughout this book u/v and i/j have been modernised.
40 Ibid., sig. B3v–4r.
41 See also Leinwand, 'London triumphing', p. 143, Kipling, 'Triumphal drama', p. 50, and McLuskie, *Dekker and Heywood*, p. 79.
42 Withington, *English Pageantry*, vol. II, p. 35.
43 See Weinreb and Hibbert, *The London Encyclopaedia*, p. 139.
44 Munday, *Chruso-thriambos*, sig. Cv; see also Marcus, 'City metal and country mettle', p. 28.
45 Manley, *Literature and Culture*, p. 225.
46 Hall's 1548 *Chronicle* describes the execution of Lincoln thus: 'On Thursday the vii. day of May was Lyncoln, Shyrwyn, and two brethren called Bets, and diverse other adjudged to dye … Then all the sayd persons were layd on the hardels and drawen to the Standarde in Chepe' (*Sir Thomas More*, ed. Dyce, p. xvi).
47 *The Booke of Sir Thomas More*, scene vii, lines 571–6.
48 Stow, ed. Kingsford, *A Survey of London*, vol. I, pp. 264 and 17.
49 Ibid., vol. II, p. 251.
50 Ibid., vol. I, p. 267.
51 Sugden, *A Topographical Dictionary*, pp. 111–12.
52 *The Booke of Sir Thomas More*, scene i, line 61.
53 The description of the history and location of the Standard in the 1598 edition 'differs a good deal from the parallel passage in the 1603 edition' (Stow ed. Kingsford, *A Survey of London*, vol. II, p. 251). The earlier version is longer,

more discursive, and tries to explain the history of the Standard more fully; in contrast, the 1603 text emphasises the Standard's use as a place of execution rather than its antiquity.

54 *Ibid.*, vol. I, p. 265. See also Heywood, ed. Rowland, *Edward IV*, pp. lxxxix–xc.
55 Hall's further account of the aftermath of the 1517 riot is as follows: 'for execution ... were set up xi. Payre of galowes in diverse places where the offences were done, as at Algate, at Blanchechapelton, Gracious Strete, Leaden Hal, and before every counter one, and at Newgate, at S. Martens [St Martin's, north of St Paul's, was the only liberty within the city walls where a number of aliens had congregated], at Aldrisgate, [and] at Bishopsgate' (*Sir Thomas More*, ed. Dyce, p. xvi). In 1567 a porter was hanged (like Lincoln) in Cheapside for 'stirring up apprentices, "telling them that that night following would be like the stir against strangers as was at Evil May Day"' (Rappaport, *Worlds Within Worlds*, p. 54).
56 Jenner, 'From conduit community to commercial network?', pp. 254–5.
57 Stow, ed. Kingsford, *A Survey of London*, vol. 1, pp. 117–18.
58 *Ibid.*, vol. I, p. 290.
59 The Mayor took his oath of office at Westminster and then returned to the Guildhall for an inaugural banquet (see Dillon, *Theatre, Court and City*, pp. 29 and 52–3).
60 Manley, *Literature and Culture*, p. 229; see also Griffiths, 'Politics made visible', p. 176, and Dillon, *Theatre, Court and City*, p. 51. It was important not only in Lord Mayor's Pageants, for during Elizabeth I's 1559 coronation procession, 'at the Standard in Cheap, which was dressed fair against the time, was placed a noise of trumpets, with banners and other furniture' (Manley, *London in the Age of Shakespeare*, pp. 339–40).
61 Manley, *London in the Age of Shakespeare*, p. 337. See also Lobanov-Rostovsky, 'The Triumphes of Golde', p. 894 n.12, and Kipling, 'Triumphal drama', p. 49.
62 Manley, *Literature and Culture*, p. 225.
63 Leinwand, 'London triumphing', p. 140.
64 Manley, 'Of sites and rites', p. 46. The Midsummer Watch, the predecessor of the civic pageants, also followed an 'east–west route', taking the same 'St Pauls–Cheap–Leadenhall–back to Cheap' progress that the later shows replicated.
65 Berlin, 'Civic ceremony', p. 20; see also McLuskie, *Dekker and Heywood*, p. 78 and Dillon, *Theatre, Court and City*, p. 106.
66 Stow, ed. Kingsford, *A Survey of London*, vol. I, p. 117–19; see also Stow, ed. Munday, *The Survay of London*, sigs. P3v–4v.
67 Hall writes that thirteen of the rioters, including Lincoln, were 'found giltye of high treason, and adjudged to be hanged, drawen and quartered' (*Sir Thomas More* (ed. Dyce), p. xvi). I am indebted to Gordon Brotherston for this insight.

1

'Are ye a dweller in this citie, pray?'[1]

Munday's London milieu

MUNDAY'S 'London-ness' was pronounced and regularly reflected in his works for he was a lifelong inhabitant of the city who sought employment across its cultural range. His status as a Londoner, a freeman of the City and a resident of certain locales of London is not incidental – it permeates his texts. This chapter will establish that Munday's representation of his city often has biographical significance and will foreground significant aspects of his life history.

Munday's London-ness had some fixed points of reference. He was regularly self-declared and named by others, for instance in his will, his epitaph and the title pages of most of his pageants, as a 'citizen and draper of London'. A number of others associated with the theatre also had City affiliations: Philip Henslowe, for instance, was a man of the City, a Dyer, as well as a man of the theatre, and Francis Langley, the builder of the Swan, was a Draper, like Munday.[2] It is noticeable that, where literary critics do mention livery companies, it is almost always in connection with players (or businessmen such as Henslowe), not with writers, as if the status of player is already sufficiently compromised as a 'trade' to admit to such a context. Thus John Shank's membership of the Weavers' Company has been considered relevant to theatre history and criticism, but not Webster's equivalent status within the Merchant Taylors.[3] Ingram has stated that 'we typically pay insufficient attention to such connections between the craft of playing and other City crafts'.[4] As Dillon argues:

> the social backgrounds and professional activities of playwrights themselves may offer a window into the way affiliations to a variety of locales and social classes may come together and contest one

another in a range of complex ways ... closer attention to the status of individual playwrights shows up some of the tensions and anomalies around these categorisations.[5]

This book aims to restore these connections. It is important to keep in mind that Munday was a man of theatre companies such as Oxford's Company and the Admiral's Men as well as being free of the Drapers' Company. He was thus associated with *two* forms of livery: the Drapers' and his aristocratic patrons'. The first of these probably had greater consequences for him in civic circles and he certainly was a member of the Drapers for a longer period of his life. Generally, he had connections with several, perhaps competing metropolitan communities and institutions within the City, the theatre and, as a Messenger of her Majesty's Chamber, the court. During the latter two decades of the sixteenth century he moved in all three circles simultaneously. In this he was not entirely exceptional: Henslowe, as well as being a London citizen and theatre entrepreneur, also had court duties from 1592 as a Groom of the Chamber to Elizabeth.[6] It is traditional criticism's insistence on exploring these facets of the careers of men such as Munday and Henslowe in isolation from each other that can present a misleading picture. The Drapers' Company, ironically, had no problem with identifying Munday as a writer rather than a tradesman, for Munday's freedom record calls him 'a poet by Criplegate', as do the later quarterage records.[7] Similarly, a number of Henslowe's *Diary* entries refer to 'antony the poyet'.[8]

To make these disparate civic connections more explicit, it is revealing to analyse the ways in which Munday describes a place with which, from a variety of standpoints, he himself would have been familiar: the London street called the Poultry, which runs east from Cheapside, London's major thoroughfare. Three particular buildings on this street which stood in close proximity to each other can be seen to bring together apparently separate aspects of Munday's life and works: the 'Long Shoppe', John Allde's printing shop where Munday was apprenticed during the 1570s, St Mildred's church, and the Poultry Counter (or Compter), a City gaol used throughout the sixteenth century. The Long Shoppe was located 'at the stocks beside St Mildred's church'.[9] Munday's 1618 edition of the *Survay of London* states that St Mildred's church was 'some foure houses West from ... a Prison-House, pertaining to one of the Sheriffes of London ... called the Counter in the Poultrie [which] hath beene there kept and continued time out of minde'.[10] John Allde, Munday's master, was imprisoned in the Poultry Counter in 1568, and Munday's sometime collaborator Thomas Dekker was held there too in 1597.[11]

Munday's 1618 edition of Stow's *Survay* identifies this St Mildred's (London had two churches of this name) as 'the proper little church, that beareth the name of Saint Mildred in the Poultrie, the Virgin'. Munday explains, somewhat implausibly, that its suffix 'the Virgin' has no Catholic overtones but is merely an aid to identification with no religious (let alone superstitious, a code-word for Catholic) connotations. He claims that the name of the church

> was given surely for distinction, not for superstition: for so was the custome of the Kingdome (and yet is) in building these things for the Service of God, that the Founders called them by the name of some Apostle, Saint, Martyr, or Confessor, as best liked their owne conceit at the present time, to distinguish them from others.[12]

The name of this church is thus represented as uncontroversial, for it merely indicates long-standing *and* present practice, which is elided as that of 'the Kingdome', not any religious body. Munday is at pains to stress that it cannot therefore cause any offence in terms of religious politics, although by the use of the word 'surely' he himself has raised the possibility that the name of the church might be misconstrued. Even a specifically civic text such as the *Survay* has a bearing on Munday's disputed religious credentials and his high-profile role in the capture and execution of Catholic priests during the 1580s. As we will see further below, the church of St Giles Cripplegate was one with which Munday had even more extensive links. In 'The Remaines', an account of improvements and alterations to the City churches which formed the concluding section of his 1633 edition of the *Survay of London*, Munday gives St Giles an entry that differs to many of the others. 'How this church', he writes, 'hath from time to time beene kept, supplyed and maintained, *all men that know it know*, to the perpetuall credit and commends of those worthy Gentlemen, to whom ... the charge of it hath beene committed'.[13] This proud and enthusiastic tone that Munday takes on here is quite different to the more neutral descriptions of endowments to other churches, as is the way in which he alludes to his own close familiarity with St Giles.

Munday's personal history in his city informs his texts in various ways. London itself is represented as the orphan Munday's foster-mother or nurse many times in his works. Both of his parents had died by 1571, which is when Munday is first listed in the Corporation records as an orphan under the recognisance of four citizens until he reached his majority.[14] The City was responsible for orphans of freemen in a kind of *loco parentis* role: for instance, the orphans needed civic permission to marry before the age of twenty-one.[15] As an orphan Munday was entitled, in fact obliged, to claim his portion from the City once he reached his majority, the age of twenty-one. Thus he is recorded as 'one of the Children & orphans of Christofer Mundaye stacyoner' in the January 1580/1 City record that is entitled 'Orphan Mundaye satisfyed'.[16] This entry tells us that Munday did claim his right in due course, but his likely birthdate of October 1560 (he was baptised in that month) would not actually have made him twenty-one in January 1581 when he thus appears in the Corporation records. Mark Eccles suggests that Munday may have 'found witnesses to testify that he had been born earlier, so that he could receive his portion sooner', and comments that Munday 'was a young man of enterprise'.[17] Such youthful 'enterprise' would not have been uncharacteristic: in 1581 Munday also sought to exploit his recent familiarity with certain Catholic priests, and it was also only the year after he had written his opportunistic antitheatrical diatribe, *A second and third blast of retrait from plaies and Theaters.*

So when Munday writes of the City as a mother-figure in so many of his civic texts his usage is more than metaphorical, for London was indeed for him, as he says in the *Survay of London*, both a 'Birth-place and a breeder'. His praise of London in that same text for her longstanding tradition of having 'Honourable Sonnes of her owne bearing and breeding' has an especial and quite literal relevance to his own situation, as he had been brought up by that city's paternalistic (or in this case 'maternalistic') administration.[18] His sense of identification with the city of his birth gives a particularly personal note to otherwise general remarks about London, such as when in the *Survay* he calls the City a 'carefull Nurse ... to bring [city dignitaries] up'.[19] Certainly, it is worth noting in this regard that as at least a second-generation Londoner Munday had more in the way of City roots than a number of the civic dignitaries whom he was employed to praise.[20] As evidence for this, one has only to look at the chronology of mayors and aldermen which concludes Munday's 1618 *Survay*: in 1597, for instance, the mayor's father was from Yorkshire, in 1598, from Suffolk, in 1599, Lancashire, in 1600, Staffordshire, and so on.[21]

In the *Survay* Munday alludes to himself and John Stow, the text's progenitor, as 'Londons Offspring'. If he and Stow are the 'offspring' then London itself (or herself) is the mother. Indeed, Munday

2 The lemon tree and pelican device from *Chrysanaleia* (1616)

writes in the dedication to his 1633 edition of this work that London is 'the tender mother and Nurse to us both'; later in the same text London is celebrated more broadly as 'the Mother of authentike Memory'.[22] His dedication to the Fishmongers' Company in his 1616 Lord Mayor's Show *Chysanaleia*, a text which is particularly preoccupied by matters of birth and parentage, appeals to their patronage specifically on the grounds of his orphaned state. He suggests that this powerful body might stand in *loco parentis* towards him and begins the text with a rather poignant appeal: 'I doe but send you that, which in right and equity belongs unto you, the Patronage and protection of this Orphan childe, begotten in your service, bredde up hitherto by your favour and kinde cherishing, and not despayring to dye, through your want of regard'.[23] Here the Fishmongers' Company perform in a metonymic fashion the maternal role that London more generally often does for Munday. In contrast to the usual representation of the City 'Fathers', the Fishmongers are presented as a mother figure in relation to those who seek employment with them, whom Munday (utilising an image that derives from their trade) likens to 'Rivers' directing themselves naturally towards 'their nursing Mother the Sea'.[24] The master, warden and assistants of the Fishmongers, he claims here, had been entirely responsible for his birth and upbringing and even in adulthood he still places himself as dependent on their collective ability to nurture him.

As in the *Survay*, in *Chrysanaleia* Munday also employs the metaphor of the City as a nurse. In this instance he draws a parallel between London's government and that famed emblem of selfless motherhood, the pelican. 'A Magistrate', he asserts, 'at his meere entrance into his yeares Office, becommeth a nursing father of the Family: which, though hee bred not, yet, by his best endeavour, hee must labour to bring up'.[25] In this male-oriented account of parentage, London is implied as the mother, she who actually 'bred' the family (albeit very much in the background) whilst the Mayor, her temporary spouse, is the active foster-father of the citizenry 'labouring' to meet his responsibilities. The gender reversal of the image is somewhat strained, however, as Munday calls the magistrate that impossible creature, 'a nursing father', and there is an ambiguity too in his use of the word 'labour'. Later in the text the connection between city governance and familial relations becomes even more overt and sustained, to rather peculiar effect. John Leman, the Mayor honoured by *Chrysanaleia*, is noted to be exceptional for being the first unmarried Mayor since the fifteenth century. This is a point which Munday chooses to highlight, partly because this means he can cleverly suggest that Leman 'marries' London by becoming her Mayor and also because he might be trading on the alternative meaning of 'leman' as 'lover or sweetheart'.[26] Indeed, Leman's bachelor status means that through the pseudo-marriage ceremony of becoming mayor he can devote himself to the care of his 'wife', London, in the absence of any competitor. Munday takes the idea further, emphasising that there was 'never any L. Maior a Batcheler before M. Iohn Leman but one', and he goes so far as to link bachelordom with virginity. Leman's famed predecessor, William Walworth, calls the new mayor, somewhat embarrassingly for Leman, 'a Mayden-man, a Batchelor'.[27] Even Munday's magisterial *Survay* does not spare Leman's blushes, annotating his entry in its list of mayors with the comment 'This Maior was the 2. Batchelor'.[28]

In a microcosm, or perhaps a domestication, of the common trope in Jacobean writing (especially in those texts written by the monarch himself) of King James as the husband of his realm, London is figured by Munday as the mayor's 'chaste wife' and Leman as 'Londons Lord'; the Mayoral installation which the Show itself celebrates is thus 'Londons and Lemans wedding day'.[29] To preserve the usual assumptions of early modern gender politics London has to be represented as a 'chaste' wife for a 'chaste' husband, although once the union has been legitimated at the conclusion of the pageant and the 'mariage Rites [have been] solemnized', Leman is encouraged by Walworth to take his new wife to 'the Bridall bed' and there to 'love' and 'delight' his 'Bride'.[30] The emphasis on the blushing bride's chastity, however, is rather undercut by Walworth, the Show's main and authoritative narrator, who attempts to relate Leman to a succession of mayors (or husbands) of whom he himself was once one:

> shee's a Bride,
> Nere slept by such a Husbands side
> But once before. She hath had many,
> And you may prove as good as any
> Have gone before you in this place.

The number of Leman's predecessors seems rather uncertain – is it 'one' or 'many'? Walworth's words also insinuate that Leman's performance in that bridal bed may be compared (positively, one hopes) to these auspicious predecessors, although when he says 'you *may* prove as good as any' he leaves room for doubt. To compound Leman's potential mortification, it is *he*, not his bride, who is a 'Virgin Husband'.[31] Twyning has commented that 'mayoral inaugurations were a celebration of ... [a] pure City Father': this is an idea which Munday's pageant perhaps took rather too literally.[32]

'MASTER MONDAY', CITIZEN AND DRAPER OF LONDON

If the Lord Mayor was at the pinnacle of the civic hierarchy then Munday inhabited a more lowly region. I now turn to Munday's own social 'place' in his city. Social status in early modern London was fine-grained and of great importance to its inhabitants. Lawrence Manley discusses the convergence of merchant and gentleman in the City's hierarchy, which did provoke hostility in some quarters: 'civic leaders often demanded to be addressed as gentlemen, while London aldermen styled themselves esquires and the Lord Mayor was knighted'.[33] Even the Lord Mayor was by definition one who had once been an apprentice, knighthood or not. Something of this tension between citizens, gentlemen and the educated elite can be seen in Munday's works, and also in the way in which he is regarded by a number of his contemporaries such as Nashe and Jonson.

Munday's own social status is rather indeterminate since little is known about his family background for more than one previous generation. The available evidence is not altogether consistent but it does suggest that Munday, appropriately enough, held some liminal status between artisan and gentry of the kind dramatised on many a London stage.[34] He sought patronage as their self-confessed inferior from wealthy city merchants but at the same time was 'Master Munday' to his peers. A number of contemporary records of Munday identify him specifically as a gentleman. All five of his children's baptism records call him 'gent' or 'gentleman'. For example, his daughter Elizabeth's baptism at St Giles on 28 June 1584 is recorded as 'Elizabeth Mundaye daughter of Antonye Mundaye gent'.[35] In 1584 Munday was not yet a freeman of the City so his nomination as a 'gent' at the time of his daughter's baptism suggests that this status was one he inherited rather than gained in adulthood.[36] When he was examined in 1598 by the Consistory Court regarding a will he scribed for a friend (which was during the time when he was regularly writing for the Admiral's Men), he was formally declared 'Civitatis'. This translates literally as 'citizen' or 'of the city', but with a fitting ambiguity as far as Munday is concerned it is glossed by Leslie Hotson as 'gentleman'.[37] This civic acknowledgement of Munday's social status was very significant, for his claims to be a gentleman 'had to be validated by gestures of gentility and supported by the readings of the local community'. In such 'local estimations of standing', Neal and Holmes explain, 'there were always ambiguities at the margin'.[38]

Despite an inevitable ambiguity Munday was also regularly identified as a gentleman by his contemporaries. In the prefatory material by 'H.C.' (probably Henry Chettle) to part two of *Primaleon* (1596), Munday is called 'M.' and also 'Ma:' Anthony Munday, both of which are abbreviations for 'Master'.[39] The honorific 'Master' generally confers upon its recipient the social status of a member of the gentry or esquire. Thomas Middleton calls Munday a 'Gentleman' in his pageant *The Triumphs of Truth* whereas John Grinkin, the artificer, has no honorific although Middleton praises his contribution more fulsomely than he does Munday's.[40] Even the satirical depiction of Munday in the play *Histrio-Mastix* as Posthaste, the ballad-maker and playwright, highlights his social status amongst his peers. Posthaste is called 'Maister Post-hast' and 'a Gentleman scholler [who] writes for us' by his company of players (although the company emphasise that they are 'townesmen all'). He says of himself that 'a Gentleman's a Gentleman, that hath a cleane shirt on, with some learning, and so have I'.[41] He alone of all the players is called 'Maister', and he takes pleasure in 'translating' the supposedly 'learned' words used by the scrivener such as 'appellations' and 'nomenclature' for the benefit of his less well-educated colleagues. His social aspirations and his desire to differentiate himself from the hoi polloi are exemplified when the character Bougle asks 'what fancy knaves are these?', Posthaste tells his colleagues that in calling them 'knaves' 'A speakes to you *players*; I am the poett'.[42] Other evidence for players with the status of gentlemen exists in the form of the 'plott' in Munday's handwriting for *The Seven Deadlie Sinns*. This play was probably written for Strange's Men at the Rose in the early 1590s; its 'plott' is often cited because, unusually, it includes the names of those who would have performed the roles in the play. It lists three of its actors (Thomas Pope, George Brian or Bryane and Augustine Phillips) as 'Mr'; the others, including Richard Burbage ('R. Burbadg', as Munday calls him) do not have the honorific associated with the status of gentleman.[43] That some of these players were given the honorific and some were not indicates that this was a distinction worth making. Civic records do the same: for instance, the Court of Goldsmiths' minutes refer to Munday as 'Mr Mundy the poet' but to John Lowin, the player, simply as 'John Lowen' (the Goldsmiths' Wardens, of course, are '*Mr* Wardeins').[44]

If Munday was a gentleman born (his ancestry beyond his parents is unclear, although Seccombe speculates that he might have been connected with two other Mundys 'who were attached to the royal household'), this would have made his eventual career path quite unusual.[45] The Stationers' records indicate that only fourteen sons of gentlemen, one of whom might well have been Munday himself, were apprenticed to the Company between 1576 (the initial date of his apprenticeship) and 1585 (the year he gained the freedom of the Drapers).[46] Gentry recruitment to the livery companies was to increase during the seventeenth century but was still fairly rare in the period of Munday's youth.[47] In the 1620s Edward Coke declared that 'if a Gentleman by birth ... be bound prentice to arts and trades in London ... he ought to be named by the degree of a Gentleman'.[48] However, attempts to establish clear-cut boundaries between gentlemen and tradesmen indicate that these boundaries were as much porous as distinct. William Harrison declared in his *Description of England* (1587) that the demarcation between citizen and gentleman was becoming increasingly indistinct 'by a mutuall conversion of the one into the other'.[49] A 1586 text, *The blazon of gentrie*, stated provocatively that 'merchaundizinge, is no competent, or seemelye trade of lyfe, for a gentleman'.[50] The writer of these words was Sir John Ferne – one can imagine that Munday might have seen things differently.

Given his background Munday had little option but to regard writing as a trade. Both Munday and his close associate Henry Chettle began their careers as printers, the most 'literary' of trades, and one can imagine that working with books would have prompted literary ambitions in young men such as these. Christopher Munday, Anthony's father, was free of the Drapers but worked as a stationer (which is how he appears in civic records); hence Munday's apprenticeship to John Allde in 1576. Munday's turn to pageant production at the beginning of the seventeenth century may have been motivated by a typically opportunistic desire to exploit his roots in both printing and drapery. One of his best-known Lord Mayors' Shows, *The Triumphes of re-united Britania* (1605), bears this out, for he did not only write the entertainment. The Merchant Taylors' records list a payment to him of twenty shillings for providing drapery services: he was reimbursed for 'xij yarde of leven taffita white and watchett ... at xx^d the yard'.[51] In the (anonymous) 1602 mayoral pageant for the Merchant Taylors where Munday's name first appears in livery company records for such an activity he is mentioned explicitly in relation to both of the city trades with which he was associated, as according to the Merchant Taylors' records he was paid 'for prynting the booke of speeches in the pageant' and 'for provyding apparell for all the Children in the pageant'.[52] In later civic productions he was to combine these two trades with another which he had practised – the stage – by employing actors, children and otherwise, to perform in the shows. The Goldsmiths' accounts from 1611 show Munday 'demanding' payment of eighty pounds for 'apparell ... for all the persons and children in the Orpherie', 'to make fit and apt speeches for expressing of the Shew', and also for '500 books thereof to be made and printed'.[53] David Bergeron suggests that Munday may have actually worked as a draper 'if the frequent references to his providing apparel for the pageant actors can be taken as a measure of his understanding of the cloth business'.[54] That his burial record calls him a 'haberdasher' does seem to indicate that in his latter days at least Munday was engaged in the cloth trade.

Gaining freedom of the Drapers by patrimony, as Munday did in 1585, was a difficult process (agreement of all parties concerned had to be gained and the individual's certificate had to be amended); it was not encouraged by the City and was thus uncommon compared to freedom by 'servitude' (i.e. completed apprenticeship).[55] Jonson, similarly, was made free of the Tylers' and Bricklayers' Company by patrimony in 1599.[56] This date, 1585, is more than seven years after 1576, the likely date for the commencement of Munday's apprenticeship with Allde, but Munday did not complete his term and furthermore had got married in the interim, which made him doubly unfit for gaining freedom of the Stationers' Company. Indeed, in the absence of a completed term of apprenticeship, Allde (according to Munday, 'unrequested') provided the latter with a 'certificate' in his anti-Catholic text *A breefe Aunswer made unto two Seditious Pamphlets*. This was intended to rebut Thomas Alfield's accusation, in the pamphlet that prompted Munday's rejoinder, that Munday had deceived his master. Allde's 'certificate' reads 'This is to let all men understand, that Anthony Munday, for the tyme he was my Servaunt, dyd his duetie in all respects, as much as I could desire, without fraude, covin or deceyte: if otherwise I should report of him, I should but say untrueth. By me John Allde.'[57] Allde's statement echoes Munday's frequent attempts in this and other texts to affirm his personal integrity, not least in the ambiguity of all the double negatives of 'if otherwise I should report of him, I should but say untrueth'. That this assertion appears in the context of a propagandist pamphlet where Munday is seeking to restore his reputation in the face of doubts about it makes Allde's own certainty (or lack of it) all the more significant.

The 'custom of London' meant that any freeman who had served his time could become a member of another company by 'translation'. Owing to this custom and the prevalence of gaining freedom to one of the Great Companies by patrimony (another form of 'translation'), there were especially blurred lines in the Drapers' Company between company membership and actual trade: from a total number of 528 yeomen in 1624 (which probably included Munday's own son Richard) only twenty-five were practising Drapers.[58] Despite this freedom of movement between trades it is apparent that one's livery company affiliation bore some meaningful social identification as there is ample evidence of men 'translating' from a minor to a major company.

Munday would no doubt have gained some kudos in civic circles for being able to claim membership of the Drapers, one of the wealthiest and most powerful of the twelve Great Companies, and he certainly celebrated his entitlement regularly. His own son Richard, although employed as a painter-stainer, was made free of the Drapers in 1613 by patrimony, as his father had been.[59] Richard Munday further continued in family traditions by aiding his father in painting banners for one of his later civic pageants, *Sidero-Thriambos*, in 1618: indeed, Munday's son was involved in pageant-making from 1613, the year of his freedom, right through to the year of his death in 1639.[60] Drawing on his background in pageantry, and continuing his father's interest in history (specifically, the lineage of important people) Richard Munday also produced a text on 'the Descents and Armes of the Gentry of Middlesex'. The two livery companies with which Munday was associated, the Drapers and the Stationers, had strong if sometimes fractious links.[61] John Charlewood, one of Munday's printers and originally a Grocer, was apparently 'coerced' into joining the Stationers; between 1581 and 1583 Charlewood assisted John Wolfe (of whom more below) in his campaign against the Stationers' monopoly by deliberately printing texts for which the letters patent had been issued to others.[62] A number of Munday's printers (Charlewood, Roberts, Danter and Creede) helped drapers to publish books by disguising this illicit if tolerated practice under their own approved names.[63]

As well as being a member of the Drapers' Company Munday was also a Cripplegate parishioner for most of his adult life. He clearly had a strong and lifelong affiliation to this northern edge of the City, for, unlike many of his contemporaries involved with the Admiral's Men (such as Edward Alleyn) who are recorded as residents of the parish of St Saviours in Southwark, he stayed put in Cripplegate and did not move across the river even while writing for the Rose in the 1590s.[64] Local residence was a meaningful matter in the early modern period, as each ward and parish made various demands of its residents. In the absence of a complete set of the relevant records from the parish of St Giles, Cripplegate (some of which were destroyed during the Blitz when the church was badly damaged), one can only speculate about the likelihood of Munday having been employed in parochial business but as he was a freeman of the City, a householder and a man who claimed acquaintance with his well-known parish priest, Robert Crowley, it is certainly possible that he did undertake some local responsibility.[65] His associates Philip Henslowe and Edward Alleyn both held a number of these posts in their localities.⁶⁶ Citizens might also have had roles to play as officers in their respective livery companies or in other civic bodies if they rose sufficiently high in the hierarchy.⁶⁷

Munday was occasionally associated with the Cripplegate area by his contemporaries. For instance, Robert Greene claimed in *Farewell to Follie* (1591) that the author of *Fair Em* 'cannot write true Englishe without the helpe of Clearkes of parish Churches'. This might be a reference to Munday's acquaintanceship with his parish priest, Robert Crowley, especially since Greene goes on to state more specifically that 'the sexten of Saint Giles without Creeplegate, would have beene ashamed of such blasphemous Rhetorique' as this unnamed writer had produced.⁶⁸ There are documentary as well as polemical traces of Munday's residence in Cripplegate. The City Corporation holds records of leases to Munday for tenement property in the ward of Cripplegate Without in 1602 (the year of his first recorded involvement in pageantry), 1604/5 and 1622. The last such entry has Munday 'surrendering' his extant lease of a twenty-one-year term, which I presume would have been the termination of the original 1602 agreement.⁶⁹ Charles Forker has suggested that Munday owned as well as leased property in London, which would have made him a more substantial citizen than he appears to have been, with his pleas of poverty in his literary works and in his will, his willingness to take on any commission and so on.⁷⁰ He certainly had tenants in Cripplegate around 1620, when one William Webb left legacies in his will to Munday, his 'landlord', his wife and his daughter Priscilla.⁷¹ In addition, despite Munday's statement in his will that he had little to leave his family, at the time of his death the value of his movable property was estimated at the quite substantial sum of £135 7s 10d. His will, however, bequeaths only twelve pence to each of his children. Munday's explanation for this parsimonious bequest reveals an aspect of his personality, for the will states that 'they may take [the twelve pence] as a love token rather than in any respect of neede they have', on the grounds that '[their] expectation from me can be nothing because they live in as good (if not better estate) than I did'.⁷²

Munday's preferred localities had an impact on his life and work in many ways. He would have had men of similar interests as neighbours, for the Cripplegate area where he lived for many years was home to a large number of printers, stationers and other men with literary associations. Indeed, Grub Street itself was in Cripplegate, adjacent to the Barbican where Munday lived.⁷³ Since one of the

London playhouses, the Fortune, was located within the parish of St Giles on Golden Lane (also adjacent to the Barbican) there were other residents alongside Munday who worked for the theatre.[74] Robert Wilson, one of Munday's collaborators during his days at the Rose, and a writer who has been put forward as a possible author of *Fair Em*, may have been buried at St Giles in November 1600.[75] Munday probably lived in the area from early adulthood. When examined by the Consistory Court in 1598 he testified that he had been living in the parish of St Giles Without Cripplegate for 'twenty years and more', which would date his residence there back to the late 1570s.[76] He signed the Reader's preface of *A breefe Aunswer made unto two Seditious Pamphlets*, his response to Thomas Alfield's 'Caveat to the reader touching A,M his discovery', from 'Barbican this 22. of March 1582'; the second edition of this text was printed by Charlewood, another Cripplegate resident 'dwelling in Barbican, at the signe of the halfe Eagle and Key'.[77] Alfield himself had commented on Munday's 'behavior in Barbican with his good mistres, and mother'.[78] The epistle to the 'courteous Reader' in Munday's 1589 translation *Palmendos* (also published by Charlewood) is signed off 'from my house at Cripplegate' and the readers' preface of *Palladine of England* (1588) ends likewise with Munday writing 'from my house without Cripplegate this 23 of Aprill'.[79] Munday's regular printers also illustrate his strong sense of locality. The title page of *A Briefe Chronicle, of the Successe of Time* (1611), for instance, states that the text, dedicated to the Mayor and his company, the Merchant Taylors, and printed by William Jaggard, the official printer to the City from around 1608, was 'to be sold at [Jaggard's] house in Barbican'. Munday evidently preferred to use a local printer, for his texts were printed from the same Cripplegate location by Charlewood, Roberts and Jaggard consecutively. Munday's 1603 pamphlet *A True and admirable Historie, of a mayden of Consolens* had been printed by James Roberts, who was then based at what was to become Jaggard's premises in Barbican.[80] Edward Allde, who was the son of John Allde, Munday's master back in the 1570s and then an apprentice alongside Munday, printed from c.1589 at the sign of the Gilded Cup in Fore Street, next to Barbican; amongst a number of other works by his ex-contemporary, Allde printed *Londons Love*.[81] Two of Munday's 1590s printers, Thomas Creede and John Danter, had also been St Giles parishioners during the 1580s and between 1598 and 1603 respectively.[82]

The date at which Munday moved from Cripplegate to his final parish, St Stephen Coleman Street, is uncertain. The Drapers' Quarterage Book entries for Munday from 1615 onwards are somewhat ambiguous in respect of Munday's domicile, for he is initially listed as 'Monday Anthony fils Monday Christopher. A poet by Criplegate'; 'Criplegate' is then crossed out in a different hand and replaced with 'Moregate', which suggests that Munday moved from Cripplegate to Moorgate at some indefinite point between 1615 and 1626, the period covered by this volume of records.[83] In addition, the Drapers' records indicate that Munday faithfully paid his quarterage from 1605 to 1615, but did not do so consistently after 1616; he does not appear at all in the volume covering the period from 1627 onwards (unlike his son Richard, who features regularly in entries from 1617 to 1639). Munday was, however, definitely living in the parish of St Stephen Coleman Street from the mid-1620s, for there are consecutive entries in the St Stephen's churchwarden's accounts for tithe payments of one shilling and five pence by Munday for every year between 1625/6 and 1632/3, the year of his death; the entries then continue for the same sum in the name of 'widow Munday' until 1634/5.[84] My view is that it is most likely that Munday was still based in Cripplegate until around the early 1620s, about the time of the expiry of his lease, when he moved east to the nearby parish of St Stephen Coleman Street until his death; he may have leased his Cripplegate residence to tenants including William Webb after his removal to Moorgate.[85]

As well as consistently using a local printer, Munday moved in some influential circles within his Cripplegate locality and attempted to trade on these connections for personal advancement. Two men in particular recur as patrons and/or associates of Munday – Robert Crowley, the parish priest, and John Swynnerton, a wealthy and influential alderman (of whom more below) later to become Lord Mayor. Owing to their roles both of these men would have held some sway over the parish and the wider civic environment. Munday seems to have been well acquainted with Robert Crowley, who was the widely known vicar at St Giles Cripplegate from 1566 to 1588, with a two-year tenure at St Lawrence Jewry, Middleton's family church, between 1576 and 1578.[86] Crowley's time at St Giles exemplifies the church's nonconformist traditions.[87] Despite his pronounced opinions he also played a part in the Marprelate crisis, as did his parishioner Munday. By 1588 Crowley was sufficiently part of the religious establishment to be included as a senior member, along with 'certen [other] Preachers', on a 'panel of correctors' set up by Whitgift to license printing.[88]

Munday did not come into proximity with Crowley solely in his parish. The latter acted as the clerical gaol visitor when Edmund Campion, Ralph Sherwin and other Catholic priests were imprisoned and interrogated in the early 1580s. Crowley's role entailed gaining confidences and then passing on information to the authorities as well as ministering to the captives' spiritual needs from a properly Protestant position. Munday himself testified against some of the priests whom he had met during his sojourn in Rome. It is clear from Munday's early 1580s anti-Catholic pamphlets that he was prepared to exploit his links with Crowley, such as when he disputed with Luke Kirbie and cited Crowley as a Protestant authority.[89] On this occasion Munday referred both to Crowley's role vis-à-vis the Catholic captives and to his own acquaintanceship with the cleric, stating that Kirbie was wrong about a point of theology because 'Maister Crowley *him selfe* gave *me* to understand [of his answer] … at such time as hee conferred with the sayde Kirbie in the Tower'.[90] Munday's youthful anti-Catholicism persisted. He is on record for reporting the recusant poet Hugh Holland to the authorities as late as 1612: back in 1579, however, he had written censoriously of those who 'to the utter undooing of their Neighbours [labour] by all meanes possible to deprive him of his honest name, hoping therby to get great commendation'.[91]

'Great commendation' was often Munday's aspiration, and as a means of gaining it he had developed an eye for an advantageous patron from early in his career. He had a particular orientation towards powerful intermediary figures and on at least three occasions he presented works to men who acted as commissioners for torture. In 1587 he dedicated a translated religious treatise entitled *The True Image of Christian Love* to the influential magistrate and fervent anti-Catholic Richard Young, whom he perhaps optimistically describes as his 'very good Friend'.[92] Munday's dedication implies that Young had previously been the recipient of another text, now lost, called *A Godly exercise for Christian Families*. Young, here identified in all his various roles as 'one of the Collectors of her Maiesties Custome in the Porte of London, and one of her Highnesse Justices of Peace and Quorum in the Countie of Middlesex', is highly praised by Munday, who expresses extreme gratitude for the 'great and undeserved favour' that he has already received from Young and makes it plain that he wishes such favour to continue. He writes in the Epistle:

> let this small argument of a farre greater good will excuse my insufficiencie, and win acceptance in your woonted affable nature:

perswading your selfe, that I live, in hart and unfained affection, next under God and the Queene my gracious Mistres, to do you the utmost devoire and service I can ... I remain devoted to you and yours in all hartie and humble affection.⁹³

This lavish grovelling may have been prompted by Munday's awareness that this particular text would have been regarded as rather controversial when addressed in the midst of the 1580s anti-Catholic panic to a man of known anti-Catholic sympathies. It was translated from an original work written by those whom Munday – somewhat recklessly – describes as 'Friers, men of no smal reckoning among the Papists'. The translator, however, explains to his putative patron that these Catholic clerics were none the less worth the hearing because 'they write against their own idolatry, superstition and trumperie, & inveigh at the great follies and disorders among themselves'; indeed, Munday claims, their denunciation of their faith is precisely why he chose to publish this particular text in these 'dangerous days' when 'men of that coat and cognisance, grow to so many wicked and rebellious attempts'.⁹⁴

A few years beforehand, when Munday's involvement with Counter-Reformation Catholicism was even more of a live issue, he had dedicated his vicious 1582 anti-Catholic pamphlet about the executions of Kirbie, Ford *et al.*, *A breefe and true reporte, of the Execution of certain Traytours at Tiborne*, to Richard Martin, a wealthy civic dignitary who participated in the trial and execution of these Catholic martyrs.⁹⁵ Like Young, Martin was known to have strong anti-Catholic sympathies.⁹⁶ By dedicating to Martin, Munday implicitly linked local to national politics. He addresses Martin in his London roles as 'the godly and woorshipfull Maister Richard Martin, Sherife, and one of the woorshipfull Aldermen of this Cittie of London'.⁹⁷ In an echo of Thomas More's part in the 'Evil May Day' unrest, Martin's part in these trials derived from his municipal post of sheriff. Munday states specifically that the reason for his dedication was Martin's actual presence at the execution of the Catholic prisoners where Munday's own account of his dealings with the latter had been attacked. In the context of a high-profile execution of famous 'traitors', who said and did what to whom constituted a matter of not only personal but also national import. However, what is evident is that Munday's main concern in this dedication is to restore his personal reputation in the eyes of one who had influence in the diverse areas where he sought employment. He writes:

> I thought it good to present [this pamphlet] to your woorship, for that your selfe hath beene an eye witnesse, how I was there challenged ... to avoyde therefore the speeches of people, who now a dayes will judge lightly, and condemne quickly, because I was there called foorth, somewhat in woordes touched ... I present to your woorships perusing, as my defence against slaunderous tongues, in that I have reported nothing therein, but the meere truthe.[98]

It is worth noting by way of additional context that both Richard Martin and Richard Young were named on a Court of Aldermen minute from 1587 (the year in which Munday dedicated to the latter) as part of a delegation to be sent to the Privy Council 'to move theyre honours for the suppressinge of playes and interludes within this Cittye and the libertyes of the same'.[99] A few years later Young was one of the Middlesex justices requested by the Privy Council in June 1592 to ensure that no plays took place 'in any place neere theraboutes, as the Theator, Curtayne, nor any other usuall places where the same are comonly used'.[100]

Munday had other acquaintances who were equally close to the centre of late sixteenth-century governmental and municipal power, and who illustrate the range of his activities and the way they connected. During his early theatre days in the 1580s he was simultaneously employed as a pursuivant tracking down Catholic priests and sympathisers, working for Richard Topcliffe, an even more notorious torturer than Young.[101] Topcliffe, like Richard Martin and Richard Young, performed a variety of roles across London. For instance, as a Middlesex magistrate he was one of the officers charged by the Privy Council with taking action over Jonson and Nashe's now-lost Swan play, *The Isle of Dogs*, in 1597. On that occasion Topcliffe arrested Jonson, Gabriel Spenser and Robert Shaa (Nashe left town for Yarmouth before the same fate could happen to him).[102] This took place shortly after what had become the annual ritual of a letter from the Mayor and Aldermen in July of that year, asking the Privy Council to help them enforce the closure of all places of theatrical performance inside and outside of the City.[103] The Council instructed Topcliffe and the others 'to examine those of the plaiers that are comytted [to gaol in the Marshalsea], whose names are knowne to you, Mr. Topclyfe ... wee praie you also to peruse soch papers as were fownde in Nash his lodgings'.[104] Munday's acquaintance with Topcliffe was luckily much more benign for him than that of his unfortunate contemporaries. In 1588, the year he was appointed a Messenger of her Majesty's Chamber (but also, it would appear, suffering from some personal misfortune, for he talks of 'the world ... frown[ing] upon me, that I cannot as I woulde'), Munday dedicated the singularly inappropriate work *A Banquet of Dainty Conceits* – a collection of 'sweete Ditties' – to Topcliffe in the most fulsome terms. He praised his erstwhile colleague's 'manifold good turnes, and favourable deedes of freendship' towards him and reminded Topcliffe that he 'will remaine ready in any thing I may' although at the same time he did not presume that 'your worshippe hath any neede of mee or mine'.[105]

Munday's apparent unscrupulousness when it came to selecting patrons and dedicatees can, at least in part, be explained by the 'marketplace of print', in Alexandra Halasz's phrase, within which he was attempting to thrive. The following chapter explores Munday's status as a writer in that civic marketplace.

NOTES

1. Munday, ed. Meagher, *The Downfall of Robert, Earle of Huntington*, line 581.
2. Roslyn Knutson details the livery company affiliations of a number of writers and players to demonstrate 'both the variety of guilds represented by players and the ubiquity of freemen in the men's [theatre] companies' (*Playing Companies and Commerce*, p. 22).
3. See Jones and Stallybrass, *Renaissance Clothing and the Materials of Memory*, p. 179. See also Bentley, 'Records of players', pp. 819–20, and Baldwin, *The Organization and Personnel*, p. 151.
4. Ingram, *The Business of Playing*, p. 28.
5. Dillon, *Theatre, Court and City*, p. 15.
6. See Baldwin, *The Organization and Personnel*, p. 83 n. 169. Cerasano points out that both Henslowe and Alleyn 'were implicated with the nobility' via their diverse patronage networks ('The patronage network of Philip Henslowe and Edward Alleyn', p. 89).
7. Drapers' Freedom List, 1567–1656, fol. 53.
8. See Foakes, *Henslowe's Diary*, pp. 203–5.
9. See Sugden, *A Topographical Dictionary*, p. 133, and Duff, *A Century of the English Book Trade*, p. 2. Munday's 1582 anti-Catholic pamphlet *A breefe and true reporte, of the Execution of certaine Traytours at Tiborne* stated that it was 'to be sold from the Long Shoppe'; *Palmerin d'Oliva* was 'to bee solde at [Charlewood's] Shoppe, adjoyning to S. Mildreds Church in the Poultrie' (title page).
10. Stow, ed. Munday, *The Survay of London*, sig. Hh6r.
11. In the 1604 triumphal entry *The Magnificent Entertainment* the St Mildred's site stood for the royal presence chamber in the King's progress through the City.
12. Stow, ed. Munday, *The Survay of London*, sig. Hh4r. Stow's original text refers to the church only as 'the proper Parish Church of S. Mildred' (Stow, ed. Kingsford, *A Survey of London*, vol. I, p. 262).

13 Stow, ed. Munday et al., *The Survey of London*, sig. Ffff2r; my emphasis.
14 The Mayor in the year of Munday's majority was Sir John Branche, who, coincidentally, was a Draper and had first been a Cripplegate Alderman in 1571, the year Munday was orphaned.
15 See Foster, *The Politics of Stability*, pp. 87–8.
16 CLRO Rep. 20, fol. 161v. As far as I know, no trace of any of Munday's siblings has survived.
17 Eccles, 'Anthony Munday', pp. 96–7.
18 Stow, ed. Munday, *The Survay of London*, sig. 4r. Munday had previously named John Swynnerton 'the foster-father of [his] meane desarts' (Munday, *The Third and last part of Palmerin of England*, sig. A2r).
19 Stow, ed. Munday, *The Survay of London*, sig. 4r.
20 In Munday's *Briefe Chronicle*, 'out of about 130 Lord Mayors mentioned … from 1485 to 1611, only 17 appear to be Londoners': hence Munday's emphasis, perhaps (Cockayne, *The Lord Mayors and Sheriffs of London*, p. 45 note c). London's overall population, and ultimately its throughput of civic dignatories, was fuelled to a large extent by immigration from outside the city (see Seaver, 'The artisanal world', p. 95).
21 Stow, ed. Munday, *The Survay of London*, sig. Ppp6r.
22 *Ibid.*, sigs A3r and A4r. There is another mother figure, 'the breeding and teeming Mother of all Gold, Silver, Minerall, and other Mettals' in Munday's Show *Chruso-thriambos* (sig. A4v). In *The Seven Deadly Sins of London* Dekker calls London 'Mother of my Life' (cited in Twyning, *London Dispossessed*, p. 64).
23 Munday, *Chrysanaleia*, sig. A3v.
24 *Ibid.*, sig. A3r–v.
25 *Ibid.*, sig. B2r. In respect of Munday's own history it is interesting to note that the seal that Munday used when writing a will in 1598 featured 'the pelican in her piety' (see Hotson, 'Anthony Munday's birth-date', p. 4).
26 In this period 'leman' could also mean 'unlawful lover or mistress' (see *OED*). I am indebted to Ian Gadd for bringing this point to my attention.
27 Munday, *Chrysanaleia*, sig. Cr. Here he also might be alluding to 'batchelordom' as a rank in the livery companies. Leman died in 1632 at the age of eighty-eight, still unmarried (see Nichols (ed.), *Chrysanaleia*, p. 14).
28 Stow, ed. Munday, *The Survay of London*, sig. Ppp7r.
29 Munday, *Chrysanaleia*, sig. Cv. Twyning argues that 'for the vigorously patriarchal James I', a feminised London 'flattered and soothed his sense of royal authority' (*London Dispossessed*, p. 64). See also Clegg, *Press Censorship*, pp. 10–13 and Corns, 'Literature and London', p. 547.
30 Munday, *Chrysanaleia*, sig. C4r. See also Paster, 'The idea of London', p. 59. In *The Triumphes of Truth* Middleton, in contrast, presents London as the Mayor's mother, which as Lobanov-Rostovsky has observed, 'suggest[s] a vastly different relation of power and duty' ('*The Triumphes of Golde*', p. 895 n. 15). See also Twyning, *London Dispossessed*, p. 64.
31 Munday, *Chrysanaleia*, sig. C4r.
32 Twyning, *London Dispossessed*, p. 67.
33 Manley, *London in the Age of Shakespeare*, p. 77.
34 Martin Butler has remarked that city comedy in particular 'trains attention on the age's most hotly contested category – the problematic but intensely desired label of "gentleman"' ('Literature and the theatre to 1660', p. 577).

35 Corporation of London Record Office MS 6418 vol. 1.
36 His son Richard was called a 'yeoman' by the Middlesex Sessions in 1609 when he was twenty-one; the term 'yeoman' probably indicated his status within the livery company with whom he worked, the Painter Stainers, since four years were to elapse before Richard Munday gained the freedom of his father's company by patrimony (see Eccles, 'Anthony Munday', p. 102).
37 See Hotson, 'Anthony Munday's birth-date', p. 3.
38 Heal and Holmes, *The Gentry in England and Wales*, p. 7.
39 Munday, *The second Booke of Primaleon of Greece*, sig. A5r.
40 Humphrey Nichols, who produced the firework, is 'Master' Nichols (see Dutton, *Jacobean Civic Pageants*, pp. 163–4). Both Munday and Middleton are named 'Gent' by the Grocers' Company (see Munday, ed. Pafford, *Chrusothriambos*, p. 47).
41 ?Marston, *Histrio-Mastix*, sig. C3r.
42 *Ibid.*, sig. Br.
43 For a facsimile reproduction of the 'plott' see Greg, *Dramatic Documents*. Greg then assumed that 'Mr' attached to an individual's name indicated that this person was a sharer in the company rather than a mere actor, a view which has recently been disputed (see Foakes, *Henslowe's Diary*, pp. xlii–xliii).
44 See Bergeron, 'Actors in English civic pageants', p. 24, and Munday, ed. Pafford, *Chruso-thriambos*, p. 13.
45 Munday may have been related to the composer William Mundy, who was 'sworn a gentleman at Chapel Royal in 1563', and whose family 'bore the arms and crest of Mundy of London' (*Dictionary of National Biography*, s.v. 'William Mundy').
46 See McKenzie, 'Apprenticeship in the Stationers' Company'.
47 See Ferdinand, 'Towards a demography', p. 58, and Burnett, *Masters and Servants*, pp. 41–2.
48 Burnett, *Masters and Servants*, p. 44.
49 Cited in Manley, *Literature and Culture*, p. 7.
50 Cited in Burnett, *Masters and Servants*, p. 40.
51 Sayle, *Lord Mayors' Pageants*, p. 79.
52 *Ibid.*, p. 65. From this evidence, Bergeron is prepared to 'credit Anthony Munday with the authorship of the show' ('Actors in English civic pageants', p. 19).
53 Munday, ed. Pafford, *Chruso-thriambos*, p. 13.
54 Bergeron, *Pageants and Entertainments*, p. xii. Turner speculates (without offering any evidence) that Munday's status as Draper became more tangible after 1602 when he may have 'opened a small shop after leaving the employ of Henslowe' (*Anthony Mundy*, p. 143).
55 See The Corporation of London, *The Corporation of London*, p. 220. It was possible, if unorthodox, for a citizen to gain associate membership of a second company; thus Charles Forker claims that Munday may also have been conferred the honorary freedom of the Merchant Taylors at some point before 1615 in recognition of his three Shows and other services to the company ('Two notes on John Webster and Anthony Munday', pp. 30–3).
56 See Seaver, 'The artisanal world', p. 96. Given their relative literary statuses it is ironic that the socially aspirant Jonson had to gain his freedom via the lowly Tylers and Bricklayers (his stepfather's company) whereas Munday could claim membership of one of London's most powerful companies by

benefit of his parentage. When Henslowe wrote to Alleyn in 1598 to inform him that Jonson had killed Gabriel Spencer, one of the Admiral's Men's actors, he referred to Jonson as 'Benjamin Jonson bricklayer' (Wickham et al., *English Professional Theatre*, p. 281).

57 Munday, *A breefe Aunswer*, sig. Diiir. Without such a testimony from Allde Munday may have been in danger of imprisonment under the terms of the 1563 Statute of Artificers, which punished those apprentices who absented themselves without their master's permission (although non-completion of a term of apprenticeship was by no means unusual).

58 Ashton, *The City and the Court*, p. 49.

59 See Eccles, 'Anthony Munday', p. 103. See also Robertson and Gordon, *A Calendar of Dramatic Records*, p. 177.

60 Bergeron, *Pageants and Entertainments*, p. 133. See also Bergeron, 'Anthony Munday's son', and Robertson and Gordon, *A Calendar of Dramatic Records*, p. 97 and *passim*. Despite being in trouble with the London authorities over the suspicion of having fathered an illegitimate child in 1609, Richard Munday eventually become a respectable citizen and parishioner, acting as churchwarden at St Botolph's Aldgate (as such he witnessed a land indenture in 1638 (Guildhall Add. MS 112)). See also Eccles, 'Anthony Munday', pp. 103–4.

61 See Johnson, 'The Stationers versus the Drapers', p. 5, and Jones and Stallybrass, *Renaissance Clothing and the Materials of Memory*, p. 180.

62 See Turner Wright, 'Young Anthony Mundy again', p. 153; Aldis et al., *A Dictionary of Printers and Booksellers*, p. 297. Although he had been apprenticed to a Stationer (John Day) Wolfe, like Munday, did not complete his term of apprenticeship (Clegg, *Press Censorship*, p. 234 n.15).

63 See Johnson, 'The Stationers versus the Drapers', pp. 8–9.

64 Like St Stephen Coleman Street, Cripplegate and its parish church had strong nonconformist traditions from the sixteenth century onwards (John Milton was originally buried in St Giles). Cripplegate Ward was a strong supporter of the Parliamentarian side in the 1640s.

65 If a householder was free of the City, he was eligible for parish appointments. The Churchwardens' accounts for 1570–80 and 1597–1607 have survived; from them it appears that Munday did not perform that particular role, although he may have acted as a scavenger or had some other more lowly parish function.

66 See Rutter, ed., *Documents of the Rose Playhouse*, pp. 5–6, and Carson, *A Companion to Henslowe's Diary*, p. 2. Despite the intermittent friction over the theatres between the City, the Privy Council and the county JPs, Alleyn was made a Surrey magistrate in 1610 (Cerasano, 'Edward Alleyn', p. 23).

67 In addition, freemen of the City such as Munday were entitled to vote in elections for 'wise and discreet citizens' to assist the Aldermen (see Gordon and Dewhirst, *The Ward of Cripplegate*, p. 50).

68 Cited in Henning, ed., *Fair Em*, pp. 65–6. Munday could also be associated with this play in relation to Greene's text on the basis that the former often used ballads as his dramatic sources. The ascription of the play to Munday on the evidence of Greene's words is not definitive, however, since the St Giles reference might apply to Robert Wilson.

69 Corporation of London Grant Book 1, fols 59r, 75r, and Book 2, fol. 26v.

70 Forker, 'Two notes on John Webster and Anthony Munday', p. 33. The absence of Munday's name in the lay subsidy records for both the Cripplegate and Coleman Street wards might indicate that Forker is wrong about this, but

since these assessments are notoriously incomplete it is difficult to prove either way. A 'Mr Mondaye' was assessed for the sum of £5 on land in the Ward of Cripplegate in 1577, but as Munday himself would only have been seventeen years old and still an apprentice at the time and his father had by then been dead for some years, this is most likely to be another person of the same name (see Mundy, 'Anthony Munday, dramatist', p. 181, and Turner, *Anthony Mundy*, pp. 5–6).

71 See Hotson, 'Anthony Munday's birth-date', p. 4.
72 Guildhall MS 9171/26, fol. 516. See also Hotson, 'Anthony Munday's birth-date', p. 4.
73 Stow says of Grub Street, somewhat censoriously (he was not keen on pastimes), that it had 'a number of bowling Allies, and Dicing houses, which in al places are increased, and too much frequented' (Stow, ed. Kingsford, *A Survey of London*, vol. II, p. 79). John Foxe lived on Grub Street. One hundred years after Munday's birth, that other consumate 'hack' Daniel Defoe was probably born on Grub Street.
74 Both Jonson and Dekker may have lived for a while in the Cripplegate area (Baldwin, *The Organization and Personnel*, p. 153). See also Denkinger, 'Actors' names', pp. 100–1, and Knutson, *Playing Companies and Commerce*, pp. 34–5.
75 See Baldwin, *On the Literary Genetics of Shakspere's Plays*, pp. 515 and 518. There are however two burial records for men called 'Robert Wilson', the other being in 1610 at St Bartholomew the Less. I return to Munday's putative authorship of *Fair Em* below.
76 Eccles, 'Anthony Munday', p. 100. See also Hotson, 'Anthony Munday's birth-date', p. 3.
77 Charlewood had been working from Barbican since 1567 (see Aldis *et al.*, *A Dictionary of Printers and Booksellers*, p. 229, and Miller, 'Printers and Stationers', p. 23). As a Redcross Street resident he was assessed for three shillings (the minimum sum payable) in the 1582 lay subsidy roll (Lang, *Two Tudor Subsidy Assessment Rolls*, p. 215).
78 Alfield, *A true reporte of the death*, sig. Er.
79 Munday, *The famous, pleasant, and variable Historie, of Palladine of England*, sig. ivv.
80 In 1593 Roberts married the widow of John Charlewood, Munday's printer in the 1580s, and then sold his business c.1608 to William Jaggard (Aldis *et al.*, *A Dictionary of Printers and Booksellers*, p. 229). He was assessed as 'James Roberts Printer' in the 1597 lay subsidy (see Public Record Office E179/146/390, rot. 33 and E179/146/409, rot. 4).
81 Edward Allde, like his father and Charlewood before him, was in trouble with the Stationers' Company for printing Catholic works during the 1590s (see Miller, 'Printers and stationers', p. 18). John Danter too, who printed the 1595 edition of Munday's *The First Book of Primaleon of Greece*, had his press impounded the following year for printing a Catholic devotional text (Aldis *et al.*, *A Dictionary of Printers and Booksellers*, pp. 5–6 and 84). Henry Chettle, Munday's sometime dramatic collaborator, entered into a partnership with Danter between 1591 and 1592 (see Henning, ed., *Fair Em*, p. 3); Chettle called himself 'Printer' in Munday's *Primaleon* and relates how he 'met' that text 'in the Printing-house' where he helped to bring it to publication (*The second Booke of Primaleon of Greece*, sigs. A3r–v). Danter probably printed

Fair Em (see Henning, ed., Fair Em, pp. 1–4 and 75–80).
82 Miller, 'Printers and stationers', p. 24.
83 Drapers Quarterage Book, 1617[actually 1615]–1626, fols 168v–169r. See also Eccles, 'Anthony Munday', p. 100.
84 See Guildhall MS 4457/2, fol. 242r (1625/6) and *passim*. This is a fairly low figure compared to most and appears to have been the minimum amount levied in the parish.
85 There is no burial payment record for Munday at St Stephen's, which may suggest that his funeral was cheap, with no ringing of bells and so on.
86 St Lawrence Jewry was another parish with a 'Puritan' reputation in Cripplegate ward; here Middleton was baptised (see Heinemann, *Puritanism and Theatre*, p. 49). Crowley's successor at St Giles was the equally renowned Launcelot Andrewes, who held the post between 1589 and 1605. Crowley christened at least four of Munday's children at St Giles during the 1580s.
87 Crowley was apparently the first cleric to be called a 'Puritan' and had a high profile in London, preaching before the Lord Mayor in 1574 (see Gordon and Dewhirst, *The Ward of Cripplegate*, pp. 115 and 118, and Foster, *The Politics of Stability*, p. 12). If one includes Munday in this category, it appears that historians, or pseudo-historians, favoured Cripplegate as a place to live, for Crowley himself wrote chronicles, and John Foxe, John Speed and Henry Spelman, the antiquary, were also Cripplegate residents (see Gordon and Dewhirst, *The Ward of Cripplegate*, p. 46).
88 Clegg, *Press Censorship*, pp. 29 and 235 n.24. See also Henning, ed., *Fair Em*, p. 76.
89 Munday, it seems, liked to associate with clerics: as well as Crowley, he was claimed to be 'very well and familiarly acquaynted' with Francis Roberts, the rector of St George's church in Botolph Lane, Eastcheap, whose will he wrote out in 1598 (see Hotson, 'Anthony Munday's birth-date', pp. 2–3, and Eccles, 'Anthony Munday', pp. 100–2). As far as Crowley is concerned, however, one ought to be cautious about believing Munday's version of their acquaintance, for Crowley has been ascribed the authorship of a pamphlet *attacking* Munday's inaccurate reporting of the capture and execution of Everard Haunse in 1581 (see Hill, '"This is as true as all the rest is"', pp. 53–5).
90 Munday, *A breefe and true reporte*, Cir; my emphases.
91 Munday, *The Mirrour of Mutabilitie*, p. 65. For Munday's testimony against Holland and another recusant, Thomas Bell, see Eccles, 'Anthony Munday', p. 103.
92 Young, a Grocer, was according to Archer, one of the three men who 'ran' the Middlesex magistracy in the mid-1580s (*The Pursuit of Stability*, p. 227). He is mentioned on more torture warrants than any other individual and has been called 'an expert torturer' (Langbein, *Torture and the Law of Proof*, p. 86). He was also one of the Queen's 'high Collectors' for the 1582 subsidy (see Lang, *Two Tudor Subsidy Assessment Rolls*, p. 114).
93 Munday, *The True Image of Christian Love*, sig. [unsigned] 1v–2r.
94 Munday, *The True Image of Christian Love*, sig. [unsigned] 2r–v. The year, 1587, incidentally, was the year in which Munday gained the reversion of certain properties from the Queen, and the year before his role as Messenger of her Majesty's Chamber was made official, although he does claim the latter post on the title page of this translation (see Hamilton, 'Anthony Munday and *The Merchant of Venice*', p. 95).

95 After becoming an alderman Martin also took on the post of Master of the Mint in the Tower, a Crown position, from 1581 to his death (Foster, *The Politics of Stability*, p. 142; see also p. 84). There were some tensions between those Goldsmiths who, like Martin and his son, worked for the Crown at the Mint and those based in the City (see Jenstad, 'Institutional uses of pageantry', p. 9).
96 Archer states that Martin was 'very probably a puritan' (*The Pursuit of Stability*, p. 257).
97 Munday, *A breefe Aunswer*, sig. Aiir.
98 Ibid., sigs Aiir–v. Later in this pamphlet Munday cites in dialogue form what he represents as Martin's own words such as when he has Martin ('Maister Sheriff' in the text) reprove the prisoners for contradicting Munday's own version of events (see, for example, sig. Ciir–v).
99 Chambers, *The Elizabethan Stage*, vol. IV, p. 305.
100 Ibid., p. 310.
101 Topcliffe also officiated at the 1595 execution of the Catholic Robert Southwell (see Archer, 'Popular politics', p. 36).
102 See Dutton, *Mastering the Revels*, pp. 107 and 261 n. 36.
103 See Ingram, *A London Life*, pp. 168–88. Munday's association with Topcliffe may explain Nashe's dislike of the former, further discussed below.
104 Chambers, *The Elizabethan Stage*, vol. IV, p. 323. Richard Rowland suggests that *The Isle of Dogs* may have received such severe treatment because, like *Sir Thomas More* only a few years previously, it 'ventured into similarly evocative and provocative [London] territory' (Heywood, ed. Rowland, *Edward IV*, p. xcv n. 41).
105 Munday, *A Banquet of Daintie Conceits*, sigs Aiiv–A3r. Hamilton, in contrast, is of the view that this text 'does not praise ... [but] libels' Topcliffe ('Anthony Munday and *The Merchant of Venice*', p. 95).

2

'I purposed nothing, but found it to my profit'[1]

The writer in the marketplace

LONDON was the cultural centre of early modern England and as such offered many prospects to a writer who was prepared to turn his hand to any available cultural form. Munday, once again, is an epitome: he made 'himself' in all his forms – his texts, his opinions, his multifarious literary modes, his wide range of acquaintance – into a commodity available in both the cultural and the political marketplaces.[2] As such, he was both vulnerable to and taking advantage of the social flux that characterised early modern London, where individual initiative might conflict with as much as benefit from institutional needs such as those of the City and the court.

As his diverse sources of patronage indicate, Munday worked hard at developing his connections across a wide range of forms of civic authority. This is one of the reasons for his nomination as a hack writer. He did not do so naively, however, for he was a highly self-conscious writer in the most literal sense. He foregrounds his own subjectivity to a remarkable degree in a range of texts from political polemics through to his editions of Stow. As we will see below, Munday's work is frequently evasive and ambiguous, even cryptic.[3] All these qualities bring into question the validity of the traditional critical dismissal of his work as mere hack-writing. He wrote to make a decent living, that much is true, but this in itself does not entail that his literary productions are without interest. It is possible that Munday's exclusion from critical scrutiny because of his versatility is grounded less in the supposed aesthetic demerits of his work than in a Jonsonian-style reaction to his offensive presumptuousness, to the new freedoms offered a man of his status by London's growing literary scene and its voracious audiences and readerships. As Twyning has argued of Dekker, he was 'a particularly porous, plastic and receptive writer of a kind which embarrasses more modern conceptions of authorship'.[4]

One can regard Munday as a kind of salesman exploiting his versatile talents in as many fora as possible and thus as symptomatic of his moment and milieu. Manley has written about professional writers in terms that describe Munday only too well: 'linked to the practices and dynamism of the marketplace by the publishing trade and the new public theater industry ... the pioneering professional writers ... were "liminary-luminaries", whose uncertain, marginal status was inseparable from their development of highly mobile forms and styles'.[5] Munday's undoubted versatility is testimony to his desire to provide whatever the literary or political market most valued at a given time, and Manley's use of the word 'mobile' serves as a reminder to what extent Munday literally moved around London in order to exploit that very versatility. As Dekker neatly put it in *The Gull's Hornbook*, 'the Theatre is your poets' Royal Exchange upon which Muses ... are now turned to merchants'.[6] At the same time in the livery companies too, which offered Munday regular employment for over twenty years, there were tensions between 'craftsmen', i.e. those who *made* the artefact or commodity, and the merchants, those who (often more lucratively) *sold* such products.

Munday himself was quite prepared to act as a salesman for his books. 'Therefore you should buy it the sooner' is one of his typical self-advertisements, on this occasion for the second part of *Zelauto*.[7] Similarly, witness the two-part form of *Palmerin d'Oliva*, which was split, in Gerald Hayes's words, 'for purely commercial reasons, about which [Munday] is engagingly frank'.[8] Indeed he is: the preface 'to the courteous Readers' begins by reminding its consumers that they had been promised the current text in the second part of *Palmerin of England*. Rather than passing over the fact, Munday then – without embarrassment, it would appear – discusses at some length his tactic of publishing *Palmerin d'Oliva* in two parts when the original was only one volume. Ever with an eye to others' opinions, he writes that 'some (perhaps) may make exceptions against me, that being but one Booke in other languages, I now divide it twaine'. He reassures his readers, however, that the division of the work is actually done in their own best interests: 'my aunswer is, that to glut men with delight, may make them surfeit', especially, as he helpfully points out, since 'a Booke growing too bigge in quantitie, is profitable either to the minde nor to the pursse'.⁹ Munday claims further that by publishing part one separately from its sequel he is guaranteeing that 'the other part will be new at the comming forth, where now it wold be stale'. His own sole 'profitte' in the matter, he would have us believe, is some respite from writing, for 'a little pause dooth well in so long a labour'.¹⁰ He makes no pretence that his aim is not to offer his readers one text for the price of two, as it were. Indeed, he positively celebrates that fact by trying to flatter his bourgeois readers' financial acumen by putting forward the case that to buy part one followed by part two would be a prudent investment rather than an extravagance. He explains that 'I am of the minde that a man grutcheth not so much at a little mony, payd at severall times, as he doth at once, for this advauntage he hath, in meane time he may imploy halfe his mony on more needful occasions, and raise some benefit toward buying the second parte'.¹¹ On that note, he concludes the preface with a shameless hint to his readers about the forthcoming sequel: 'the second parte goes forward on the Printers presse, and I hope shalbe with you sooner then you expect'.¹² Munday's skill at mobilising or even constructing his readership is evident here. Even at the youthful age of nineteen he had an eye to the main chance when it came to marketing his texts: for instance, he subtitled his *Mirrour of Mutabilitie* a 'principall part of the Mirrour for Magistrates' and also dared to claim that it was 'rightly named' as such, a ruse clearly intended to trade on the extensive popularity of that earlier text, which had been republished only the year before.¹³ Almost concurrently, however, but in a quite different context, that of his antitheatrical pamphlet *A second and third blast of retrait from plaies and Theaters*, Munday perversely decries his audience's appetite for new cultural products, especially plays: the London public are, he complains, 'alwaies eating, & never satisfied; ever seeing, and never contented; continualie hearing, & never wearied'.¹⁴

Whatever the pretext, Munday's habitually pragmatic attitude to his works eschews the Aristotelian bias that David Hawkes discerns in antitheatrical writing. In such polemics the theatre is criticised, according to Hawkes, because 'it is art designed with the primary end of making money, but making money is not the natural telos of art'.¹⁵ However, literary art and the art of making money may have an uneasy relationship in Munday's *oeuvre* but they can never be separated. Indeed, Hawkes reproduces Munday's own words in *A second and third blast* as an unwittingly (on the part of Hawkes, at least) well-informed delineation of the life of a 'hack' writer, dependent on the whims of a variety of patrons, audiences and readerships, repeatedly 'negotiat[ing] the price of [his] services in a market economy'.[16] Hawkes appears to assume that those writers whom we do not now consider to be 'hacks' never sullied their minds with thoughts of patrons and markets, which strikes me as somewhat unlikely. Unless they had private means, writers, like printers, were prepared to produce texts for anyone who would offer them work. Indeed, in his antitheatrical text Munday claims that since the inception of the aristocratically sponsored playing company (such as Oxford's Men, one supposes, with which he himself had been associated in the early 1580s), 'the credite of Noble men hath decaied' and their erstwhile servants are reduced to living hand-to-mouth. They live, he writes, 'at the devotion or almes of other men, passing ... from one Gentlemans house to another, offering their service, which is a kind of beggarie'.[17] Munday's polemical intentions notwithstanding, one is irresistibly reminded here of the way in which he himself hawked his service around various noble and civic patrons for so many decades. Mutual interdependence characterised the economic relations between the various sectors of urban society and were represented as such in its culture. Munday and his stage collaborators would have been fully aware of the role of venture activities in London's culture in the person of their own patron, the Lord Admiral, who was involved, for example, in the taking of the Spanish ship the *Madre de Dios* in 1592.[18] The small world of early modern London produced many cross-overs and blurring of boundaries: as Leinwand has persuasively argued, be it in the fields of trade or culture (or both, in the case of the theatre), 'venturing typically depends upon partnerships'.[19] Here, once again, Munday can be seen as a point of intersection.

Such opportunism is understandable for a writer who relied on maximising his potential readerships and audiences. Even during his most prolific play-writing days at the Rose and the Fortune Munday's income would have been unpredictable, for the Admiral's Men, unlike some of their rival companies, did not retain a consistent body of in-house dramatists who also acted as sharers in the company, but rather bought plays through a system of more or less open competition between a range of writers, a number of whom (including Munday) formed consortia and thus shared the payment.[20] Munday was quite evidently prepared to write to order: the consequence of this is that it is unwise for us simply to 'read off' religious and/or political allegiances from his texts. Clearly, there were instances when he positioned himself quite overtly towards one side or another (in his anti-Catholic pamphlets of the early 1580s, for instance) but that is not to say that he necessarily signed up to the views his texts expressed. Similarly, a printer's religious affiliation would not have prevented him from taking on a commission for a text with which he may not have been in sympathy: it would have been a foolish self-indulgence not to have done so. A contemporary account suggests as much: George Wither denounced the fickleness of a Stationer who was willing to 'furnish [his customer] with Bookes tending to his opinions. To a Papist hee rayles upon Protestants; to Protestants he speakes ill of Papists.'[21] Wither's denunciation brings to mind Giles Wigginton's description of Munday's unclear loyalties (see below) and also goes some way towards explaining how Munday could produce numerous vicious anti-Catholic diatribes in 1582 and then engage in baiting ultra-Protestant Martinists only six years later. Equally, just because John Charlewood and John Allde were suspected Catholics, it does not necessarily follow that they printed only pro-Catholic texts; they would probably have gone out of business (or ended up in gaol, as happened to Allde anyway) had they tried to do so.[22] As Ian Gadd points out, John Wolfe (who notoriously compared himself to Martin Luther although the former is thought to have been a covert Catholic) was capable of printing both Munday's anti-Catholic translations and Robert Southwell's *St Peters Complaint*.[23]

A writer in the literary marketplace of early modern London often had to act as a salesperson as much as a creator of literary works. As I have already suggested, Munday was not coy about doing so. In 1592 he translated *Archaioplutos. Or the Riches of Elder ages*, a quasi-historical French work which he dedicated to the Earl of Shrewsbury. Although the dedication to his patron is nothing out of the ordinary (the latter is praised fulsomely; the text, 'unskilful' though it is, is 'humbly' offered for his delectation), the preface to 'the courteous Reader' takes a somewhat different tack. 'If thys harshe and unpleasant translation', it unpromisingly begins, 'may passe with your wonted kind acceptance: expect a worke from the Presse very shortly, more answerable to your humours, namely, the sweet conceited Historie of *Orlando Amareso*'. As with the *Mirrour of Mutabilitie*, Munday once again tries to trade on a better-known work than his own and steal some of its fame to reflect on his own creation, for, he claims, his forthcoming text, although 'farre inferiour to [the] already extant ... *Orlando Furioso* [will] complete *Orlandos* whole Historie'.[24]

As this example suggests, Munday was an adept self-fashioner. Like a proto-advertising slogan, one way in which an author could represent his or her own literary qualities was by the use of a motto. Munday, needless to say, had two. As Cicero was Munday's favoured classical writer, he took the motto he used most often, the proverbial 'Honos alit Artes' (which translates as 'honour comes from art') from Cicero's *Tusculan Disputations*.[25] Jack Stillinger comments that in Cicero's work it functions as a '"lawful excuse" for lack of skill'.[26] This motto appears six times in *Zelauto* alone and generally features on Munday's self-authored works, including his political pamphlets, rather than his translations. It can be regarded as appropriate for Munday in more ways than one, as in the context of his life and work 'art' might be considered to denote 'artifice' as much as it does literary creation.[27] Feigned authorial humility was a rhetorical commonplace much recommended by Cicero. In respect of an (apparent) reluctance to go into print and a consequent modesty about his literary ability Munday regularly followed Cicero's advice throughout his writing career. In *A second and third blast*, for instance, Munday exemplifies both of Cicero's admonitions. Writing in the third person (as he tends to do in his prose works), he explains: 'loth was the Autor ... to have his worke published ... through a too too base conceipt of his owne worke'.[28] As well as 'Honos alit artes' Munday at times used another motto, 'Patere aut abstine', which can be translated as 'suffer or desist', or more colloquially as 'put up or shut up'. This motto appears most often on his translations rather than self-authored texts: for example, the romances *Palmerin d'Oliva*, *Palladine of England*, *Palmerin of England* and *Gerileon of England*, as well as at least three rather more disparate texts: *A Womans Woorth* (of which more below), *Archaioplutos*, and *The Masque of the League and the Spanyard discovered* (another French translation printed in 1592 by Charlewood). In the absence of any other evidence it is sometimes, as we will see, the sole authorial identifier.

'SAYING AND DOING ARE TWO MENS LABOURS'[29]
THE ELUSIVE AUTHOR

As even his choice of motto indicates, Munday presented himself as an author in complex ways. His prose works in particular belie his reputation as an unsophisticated hack and challenge the critical neglect they have received. He rarely dealt with matters of authorship in a straightforward fashion. In the antitheatrical polemic *A second and third blast*, for instance, the writer of the 'Preface to the Reader' refuses to disclose the identity of the actual author, but cannot resist hinting at it: 'touching the Autor of the latter blast, thou [the reader] maist conjecture who he was, but I maie not name him at this time for my promise sake: yet this do I saie of him, that he hath bine ... a great affecter of that vaine Art of plaie making'.[30] In his more directly fictional works Munday tries to confuse the reader to an even greater extent. The author's preface to the reader in part two of *Zelauto* makes the bizarre claim that 'you can have no more of a Catte but her skyn: nor of me more then I am able to doo'.[31] Here Munday, speaking in in an apparently frank way in what *might* be his own direct voice as 'the author', addresses his audience with a statement that becomes more obscure the more one tries to pin it down. His cryptic remark implies that there might be a difference between the 'skyn' or the outside, i.e. the readable text, that which Munday 'does', and the 'inside', i.e. the person himself, the enigmatic 'Catte' who remains unknowable. Such elusiveness is not only a feature of *Zelauto*, for, as we will see further below, in a number of his works Munday presents a character called 'the Author', who may or may not be Munday himself, and who intervenes to mediate (and complicate) the relationship between the reader and author(s).

In *Zelauto* itself there is a great deal of both narrative and narrator/ author complexity: there are, for example, authorial interjections between each discrete part of the text which point up its deliberately erratic narrative form. Stillinger, the text's editor, regards Munday, in terms of his convoluted narrative, as a forerunner to Nashe, which is ironic when one recalls Nashe's treatment of Munday's literary 'inferiority' (further discussed in the next chapter).[32] Paul Scanlon, one of the few critics who have discussed this text at any length, puts the shifts in *Zelauto*'s narrative down to the haste with which it was composed by Munday, which might certainly account for some of the work's disjointedness. However, he also suggests that Munday's inadequacies as a writer have a role to play here too: he claims that the 'more sophisticated' parts of *Zelauto* are 'much more derivative' and not as 'loosely knit, wordy, and quite simple' as those sections undoubtedly invented by Munday.[33] He credits Munday with barely any literary sophistication, stating simply that the text demonstrates 'curious narrative manipulations', and also says of Zelauto that he is 'a less than credible character'.[34] As well as replicating the debate about

Munday's apparent plainness of style and purpose to which I will return, Scanlon's reading implicitly rules out the possibility that Munday might at times have consciously been playing with varieties of narrative and authorial voice. Indeed, if Donna Hamilton is right to argue that *Zelauto* actually offers a coded defence of Catholicism then Munday's cryptic position is all the more deliberate.[35]

In a similar fashion, his early work *The Mirrour of Mutabilitie*, which on the surface is an uncomplicated work of moral exemplars rather than a proto-novel like *Zelauto*, can be seen to articulate multiple levels of authorship.[36] There is the 'Anthony Munday', celebrated in seven separate verses at the beginning of the text, who expresses grand sentiments of praise and gratitude to Oxford, his patron, but as in *Zelauto* there is also 'the *Author*', never fully identified and always referred to in the third person, who has conversations with biblical figures in the text. This second 'Author' has Munday-like features – he disclaims his writing skill as 'but base and simple', for instance – but he is also provided with a range of authorial options in a series of prose sections, all of which are headed 'The Author', implying some kind of marginal status between actual author and contributing character. 'The Author' is at times enjoined by those he encounters to publish their sorry history (as with 'Nabuchodonozor'), or he is given the opportunity to comment piously on the failings and just deserts of figures such as Herod and Judas. As a figure very much on the margins of the text he even at one point surreptitiously takes down Pharao's story for future publication. The latter instance is particularly interesting: the Author describes his underhand note-taking as 'his pretended purpose' and it is unclear whether or not Pharao notices 'the Author' on his arrival on the scene (unlike most of the other figures, who address him directly). When 'King David', the next character, materialises, the Author shifts his position once again and participates directly in the narrative, almost as if he himself is one of its characters. He reacts to King David's appearance and words to an even greater degree than before, being 'so amazed … that he stood in a great quandary, not knowing what were best to doo'.[37] The Author oscillates between the role of passive narrative device and fully integrated fictional character in part one of this text, to such an extent that his continual interventions serve extensively to complicate the work's use of both historical chronology and narrative voice (he disappears completely from part two, to be replaced by much more flatly descriptive sections entitled, in theatrical style, 'The Induction'). Were it not for the fact that this is a sixteenth-century text, Munday's subversion of the author function here might even be regarded as postmodern.

His authorial versatility is further illustrated in the ostensibly anonymous French translation *A Womans Woorth*, printed by John Wolfe in 1599. This hitherto obscure piece repays prolonged scrutiny. It can be ascribed to Munday for a variety of reasons, including the fact that the motto he commonly used on translations, 'Patere aut abstine', appears on the title page; it is also the case that he worked as one of Wolfe's 'in-house' translators in this period.[38] In addition, it bears the hallmarks of his generally consistent spelling, such as his preference for double vowels, e.g. 'woorth', and its sententiousness has a look of Munday about it. The title page is self-conscious about the text's very anonymity. It intriguingly announces that the work has been 'written by one that hath heard much, seene much, but knowes a great deale more'. Teasingly, it does not supply a name nor does it indicate if this omniscient individual is the author or the translator. However, the reader is immediately presented with a dedication (to Elizabeth, Countess of Southampton) which is signed by 'Anthony Gibson'.[39] The presence of Anthony Gibson in this work constitutes further evidence of Munday's hand, for Gibson is quite probably the 'An. Gybson' who wrote a commendatory verse for the third part of Munday's *Palmerin of England*, published only three years later. The plot thickens, for Gibson, it then transpires, is neither author nor translator but performs some other intermediary role, the chief function of which, it would seem, is to bring this text to a wider audience. Gibson explains that this self-described 'apologie of womens faire vertues' had originally been 'written in French by a Lord of great reckoning' and was then 'given by him to a very honorable Duchesse'; in the meantime, the text had been 'since translated by a fellow and friend of mine [i.e. Gibson's] now *absent*, who gave me trust to see it should not wander in the world unregarded'.[40] As if this complicated provenance were not enough, Gibson's absent 'friend', the translator, is only henceforth referred to in passing by the current narrator. Gibson ends the dedication thus: 'if eyther then for the subject, my selfe, or my friends sake, it may seeme any way pleasing to you: the French Lord never thought his labour halfe so graced, as I will continually confesse our fortunes honored'.[41] The use of personal pronouns is so indeterminate that the nameless translator effectively disappears from view part way through the sentence. Finally, by his use of the pronoun 'our' Gibson makes himself and his friend indistinguishable.

Gibson goes on to present additional prefatory material in the form of dedicatory epistles and verses addressed to a variety of noble ladies (maids of honour to the Queen), in which it is clear that he acts as a go-between. Once more and at greater length he alludes to another shadowy person, again representing his intentions in absentia. In the process he concedes the information that both he and his friend are employed by the Court. Gibson writes 'a friend and fellow servant with me to her Maiesty [had] left in trust with me this litle treatise, being a Paradoxe Apologicall of womens vertues, written in French by an honorable person ... knowing my friendes intent to sute with mine, that on you ... the same should be bestowed'. 'In his absence', Gibson continues, '(though yet in his harts meaning I know) I offer both his good will and mine thus joyntly together'.[42] As with the first dedication, Gibson and his 'friend' are so intimately allied that their needs and motives are as one; the phrase 'harts meaning' amplifies this sense of almost bodily unity between the two. Gibson expresses the hope (speaking for both, one presumes) that '*his* labour and *my* love' will be amply rewarded by their (joint) patroness.[43] One begins to wonder who this 'other' Anthony might be (if Munday is indeed the translator) who appears to be so closely identified with his friend, and what interest does he really have in the fate of a text to which he appears so committed? It is unclear.

Before the text proper begins, however, this remarkably convoluted authorial and translatorial trail has further twists for the reader. Yet another epistle is supplied, this time more broadly aimed at 'all the Honorable Ladies, and Gentlewomen of England'.[44] This epistle, which invokes an English audience for this hitherto French text, and thus, one might expect, would have been put forward by the translator, the man responsible for 'English-ing' the work, expresses the opinions of womankind held by its writer, citing classical authorities along the way. The views and feelings of the writer of the epistle are given at length: apart from brief extracts from Sappho and Mercurius Trismegistus, there is not a single sentence in the epistle that does not feature the word 'I' prominently. Unlike the previous sections written by Gibson, however, and despite its high incidence of the first-person pronoun, it is coyly signed 'Anonimus'.[45] For a writer so fond of talking about himself, Munday can be surprisingly elusive.

Munday's authorial obscurity could also manifest itself as versatility; he can therefore be regarded as a 'Proteus' (in Agnew's sense) of the literary marketplace.[46] As his predilection for translation indicates, he was prepared to ventriloquise a variety of literary voices and modes. A translator is also a kind of literary intermediary whose own authorial agency is complicated. Indeed, Gybson's commendatory verse in the third part of *Palmerin* (1602) reveals the ways in which Munday wrote in disguise by stating that in his translations Munday's 'voyce [is] under other mens'.[47] Munday's career certainly demonstrates that he could switch from one genre to another with relative ease. On the whole, pastoral, courtly and 'romance' elements appear more in his work in the late 1570s and 1580s than in those texts he produced in the seventeenth century: for instance, in *Zelauto* and in some of his poetry written in the 'Shepherd Tonie' mode, including 'The Woodman's Walk'. These earlier works tend to be dedicated to courtiers such as the Earl of Oxford rather than aldermen or even members of the Privy Council.

Here Munday may have been trading on the current aristocratic taste for literary pastoral. Pastoral has a complicated relationship with court culture in this period. In *Zelauto*, a work dedicated to the Earl of Oxford, we find elements of Munday's dual allegiance. The hero himself is happy to celebrate the worthiness of his lordly patron, whereas his alter-ego Astroepho has tasted court life to little satisfaction, saying of it 'in Court I served, to my small avayles'. The latter prides himself on the independence of both court and civic patronage that his pastoral lifestyle brings, now that his 'preter delightes [and] wanton conceyts' are in the past: 'heere I lyve as a Prince within my selfe, not foe to any, nor none to me'.[48] In a similar vein, in *The Downfall of Robert, Earle of Huntington*, Munday draws on the pastoral tradition when his hero – now simple 'Robin Hood' since he has spurned the 'name of Earle, Lord, Baron, Knight, or Squire' – praises the natural joys of 'country sport, in Sherewodde', which exceed those 'courtly pleasures' he and Marian have left behind. Sherwood Forest has replaced 'Arras hangings, and rich Tapestrie' with 'sweete natures best imbrothery'.[49]

Munday was even prepared to express a negative view of the city he elsewhere celebrated so ostentatiously. In *The paine of pleasure* (1580) he affects a fashionable disenchantment with the decline of contemporary society. The work concludes with 'The Authors Dreame', a lengthy verse written entirely in rather laboured rhyming couplets, which presents itself as a sidelight on the various dangerous 'pleasures' that have been previously described. Here, like a sixteenth-century

William Morris, Munday briefly evokes in the civic domain a near Utopia of plenitude and neighbourliness in which 'money lay about the street, [so] none needed to purloyne'. As a result Londoners had no need to exploit each other as was the case in 'real life': 'The Merchants sold their wares good cheape, they made no count of gaine, / Why? Cittizens were never found, in such a goodly vaine.'[50] Such ideal conditions – 'this heavenly sight', as Munday calls it – did not last, however: 'some froward fate began to frowne', the sky darkened, and 'the streetes that erst were fayre and dry, grew full of mire and dust'. The poem then presents a lively if disorderly picture of citizens drinking, swearing, fighting and resorting to lawyers in the aftermath of this torrential rain storm that washed away 'the money that ... did lye in heapes in every streete', leaving 'a secrete envie' in those left needy.[51] For the youthful Munday, it would appear, *lack* of money is the root of all evil.

As a dramatist, of course, Munday exploited his ability to extemporise on a variety of themes. He himself noted in *A second and third blast* that 'plaiers can not better be compared than to the Camelion'.[52] William Rankins, a recanted player like Munday, declared with equal unselfconsciousness that 'Pamphleters' were 'detracting and deluding Alchemyists', who were writing, like playwrights, in order to entice their readers to 'live idlely'.[53] Hackwriting in its purest (or perhaps most degraded) form then becomes a counterfeit practice in both cultural and economic senses of the word: it deludes its audience like players habitually do, and engages in a literary marketplace like some kind of merchant. Indeed, in 1615 John Stephens claimed that 'a common player ... for his chief essence is, *A dayly Counterfeite*'.[54] As Manley argues in relation to Robert Greene, another writer stigmatised as a 'hack', 'the scandal of the scribbling profession ... [lies in] its immersion in the fraudulence of theater, marketplace and "common haunted places"'.[55] McLuskie has remarked that, when players such as Rankins and Munday commented on the place of the theatre, 'the voices in their polemic were always in disguise'.[56] Feigning is held to be endemic not only in theatrical practices but in writing *per se* as well as in buying and selling; it becomes more than a metaphor when manifested by an individual such as Munday, switching between personae as he did so regularly, with tangible consequences both for himself and for others.

Even in the apparently uncompromised environment of the Lord Mayor's Show theatricality lies close to the surface. As Sergei Lobanov-

Rostovsky has written, 'a magistrate who is an actor offers to deceive; one who must learn his good governance ... might learn, as well, the advantage to be gained by enactment'.[57] Or, as Munday himself put it, pragmatic as ever: 'a man in such affayres, dealeth the best he can, for the savegarde of him selfe, is his cheefest desire'.[58] Wearing another of his many hats, in *A second and third blast* Munday sternly rebukes those who write for profit (as he himself surely was in this very text): 'who writeth for reward, neither regardeth virtue nor truth; but runs into falsehood, because he flattereth for commoditie'.[59] It is interesting to note in this regard that Pennell has argued that with *John a Kent and John a Cumber* in the early 1590s Munday 'began a trend' for 'disguise plays' which 'doubtless gave a versatile actor some fine opportunities for improvisation'.[60] Improvisation, coincidentally, was one of the theatre skills that Munday was sarcastically applauded for by his Catholic adversary in the 'Caveat': 'this scholler ... did play extempore, those gentlemen and others whiche were present, can best give witnes of his dexterity, who being wery of his folly, hissed him from the stage'.[61] In *Histrio-Mastix*, another hostile depiction of Munday probably written c.1589 when Munday's own career as a player was probably not yet all that distant, the character of Posthaste does not miss an opportunity to show off his skills at extemporisation.[62] Incle, one of the players, tells Posthaste that 'our action [could] answer your extempore'.[63] When another player asks 'how shall we doe for a Prologue for lords?', Posthaste is quick to offer his services: 'I'le doo't extempore'.[64] In another guise Munday condemns extemporisation, however: he writes in *A second and third blast* that 'usual jesting, and riming extempore ... are in a Christian-weale ... not sufferable'.[65] Munday's ability to ventriloquise brings to mind *Kind-Harts Dreame*, a 1592 text written by one of his closest associates, Henry Chettle, in which Chettle presents a highly plausible mimicry of antitheatrical rhetoric which could easily be taken for unambiguous belief as Munday's pamphlet has so often been.[66]

Improvisation of this kind can elsewhere be regarded as hypocrisy. Munday's life and work frequently raises the problem that if his position can be ventriloquised so easily, who can say where the authentic self lies. For this reason it is unwise to associate Munday too closely with his creations. Thus Mann's claim that a passing reference to a playwright called 'Mr Poet' in *Sir Thomas More* might be 'a self-reference by Munday' is based on very little evidence and also underplays Munday's evasive authorship and his tendency to set traps for the reader: he can, as we have seen, be quite equivocal about his status as a writer.[67] From *A second and third blast* onwards, it is easy to find instances where Munday condemns in highly moralistic terms what is otherwise exactly his own type of conduct. In *Zelauto*, for instance, Munday's quasi-*alter ego* protagonist proclaims that 'to dissemble were no part of freendly familiaritie, to lye, would impayre my name and credite, to tell trueth also, may heere perhappes to returne to myne owne endamagement'.[68] As is often the case with Munday's prose, a number of levels of ambiguity can be found in this apparently commonplace statement. Thanks in part to his overly conscientious use of punctuation, the 'to tell trueth' sub-clause can be read in at least two different ways. On the one hand, Munday might be admitting that if he is genuinely (as opposed to merely rhetorically) honest, lying would not only 'impayre [his] name and creditte' but might in addition be personally damaging. On the other hand, he may be saying that to tell the truth itself can also sometimes rebound to his disadvantage. A third possibility exists, however: Munday may well imply both of these possibilities at the same time. He is often as cryptic – or as cynical – as this, and not only in his writing.

When in 1588 the preacher Giles Wigginton was apprehended by Munday (then a pursuivant in the employ of Archbishop Whitgift) under suspicion of involvement in the Marprelate texts, the captive gave a perplexed account of Munday's relationship to the truth. Munday, Wigginton recounted, had inveigled the latter into offering incriminating evidence by covertly requesting that he should elucidate for him certain aspects of 'Puritan' doctrine; this Wigginton obligingly if naively did by making reference to a recently printed Martinist pamphlet. Munday then reported this exchange to Whitgift as evidence of his prisoner's 'treason'. Wigginton later remarked that Munday 'seemeth to favour the Pope *and* to be a great dissembler'.[69]

This incident bears out what Munday says in *Zelauto*, writing at this point in his own persona (or at least in the persona of 'The Author' – it would be reckless to assume that they are the same): 'the wise man of his verie enemies (contrarie to expectation) shall obtaine some profite'.[70] Drama, of course, has ambiguous identity built into its very essence; even so, Munday often produces further twists. In his *Huntington* plays, as John Meagher has observed, even supposedly 'good' characters are not necessarily averse to falsehood but rather lie 'with surprising freedom'.[71] After his interventions, literary and otherwise, in the prosecution of Counter-Reformation Catholicism in the early 1580s and then in the Marprelate crisis at the end of that decade Munday may have been something of a byword for mendacity in London literary circles. This is certainly the case if Sir John Davies's 1594 epigram 'In Mundayum' is anything to go by: 'Munday I sweare shallbee a holidaye, / If hee forsweare himselfe but once a daye'.[72]

William Scott's often-cited 'An Essay of Drapery, or the Complete Citizen' (1635) describes its protagonist in terms that reflect interestingly on the particular citizen draper that this book addresses. Scott writes:

> my citizen may mingle profit with honesty and enter into a composition [compromise] with both. He must never turn his back on honesty, yet sometimes go about and coast it, using an extraordinary skill, which may be better practis'd than exprest ... Some things, which may be done openly, must be done secretly ... of just ways, take those that are most plausible.[73]

Here we see a similar negotiation of the conflict between honesty and pragmatism as in so many of Munday's works, and indeed in much of his personal history too. Moral behaviour, by Scott's account, is always subject to exigencies that at times might require one to employ secretive and compromised tactics, here glossed as 'skill'. So much for the merits of honest plain virtue celebrated in many of Munday's pseudo-religious prose works, such as the accusation in *A second and third blast* that 'the notablest lier is become the best Poet; he that can make the most notorious lie, and disguise falshood in such sort, that he may passe unperceaved, is held the best writer'.[74] As in his life, so in his works: Munday used his ability to feign to good effect in his plays, where, however, as we will see, such a technique might be praised rather than condemned.

'SUCH BASE COUNTERFAITING': MUNDAY'S HUNTINGTON PLAYS

Munday's 1598 Rose play *The Downfall of Robert, Earle of Huntington* demonstrates a very complex metatheatrical dimension alongside the more overt concern for assumed identities and disguises in the main plot. As Jeffrey Singman has argued, the play is 'full of disjunctures'.[75] For instance, the characters of John Eltham, alias Little John, and John Skelton, alias Friar Tuck, move back and forth in the induction (and elsewhere in the text) between their multiple theatrical roles and their 'real' identities as players, also confusing in the process the boundaries between invented and historical figures, since one of them is fictional and the other based on a real person. William Simeone claims that the induction and the use of the dual characterisation of Skelton and Eltham is a way of 'managing' the play, which somewhat underestimates the twists Munday brings to bear on the dramatic convention of the induction.[76] William Wolf, in contrast, argues that Munday's twist on the induction convention 'produces some interesting effects' and describes the play, rather as I do, as 'self-conscious'.[77] Although the play attempts to impose a kind of biographical framework on the Robin Hood story, in practice its historical chronology is not at all straightforward. The play begins with Skelton and Eltham, figures from the late fifteenth and early sixteenth centuries, then moves some centuries further back to the troubled reign of Richard I, whilst simultaneously alluding to its own very contemporary moment in places, such as where 'the King' is mentioned; this is ostensibly Henry VIII rather than Richard I, but is also surely a veiled reference to the play's performance before yet another monarch, Elizabeth I. 'Here', as one editor of the play has commented, 'Munday is having fun with "history".'[78] A further contemporary context, as Liz Oakley-Brown points out, is suggested at the beginning of the play when Skelton tells John Eltham that he has been employed 'in survaying Mappes, / Sent over from the good King Ferdinand, / That to the Indies at Sebastians sute, / Hath lately sent a Spanish Colonie'.[79] This gestures towards the ongoing conflict between England, the Netherlands and their mutual enemy, Spain.[80] Munday himself had a personal familiarity with this area of contemporary international relations, since he had visited the Low Countries on governmental business only three years before the play was written. As well as adding yet another historical framework to the play, the reference to King Sebastian of Portugal also constitutes further evidence of intertextuality, for Munday wrote a history of this monarch only a few years later (further discussed below). Layered historicity is juxtaposed to nuanced metadrama in this play. Shortly before his exile, Robin, still the Earl of Huntington at this point, plans with Marian to expose the deceit of Queen Elinor (à la Hamlet) through the use of some visiting players, 'quaint Comedians', as Robin calls them.[81] Robin talks of his and Marian's plight as a 'Scene tragick' in which they both have roles to play; the scene ends with the arrival of their enemies, at which point Robin says to Marian 'but now our audience comes, wee must looke sad'.[82]

As a consequence of the two plays' various sources and antecedents, or perhaps mistakes in the editing process, or even a deliberate wish to confuse the audience, Munday provides a number of the characters in the *Huntington* plays with two names and often two separate identities, not least the Earl of Huntington himself, of course, who is transformed into 'Robin' upon exile. Both Marian/Matilda and her father also have two names, a fact which the first play deals with somewhat awkwardly. To Marian's father's query 'Why did she chaunge her name?', 'Robin' responds with the abrupt 'What's that to thee?'[83] More bizarrely still, at one point in *The Death* she is called 'Marilda', a 'composite' of her two names.[84] Marian/Matilda's father himself is called Lord Lacy until line 781 of the play, after which he becomes Fitzwater ('Lacy' is in fact also the name of one of those aristocrats who conspired against Huntington at the beginning of *The Downfall*). It is, however, the four fold characters of Skelton/Tuck and Eltham/Little John who demonstrate the play's metatheatricality most fully. 'Friar Tuck', for instance, falls at his first entrance into a long speech in the persona of 'Master Skelton' with which he began the play's induction. The speech echoes (or perhaps mimics) antitheatrical attitudes, attacking base writers' 'foolerie, paltry, and foppry, dissembling knavery' and it ends with the lines 'God give no blessing, / To such base counterfaiting'. The Friar is then immediately reminded by the equally doubled 'John Eltam, little John' that he interrupts the action of the play: 'stoppe master Skelton: whither will you runne?'[85] As far as the narrative of the play is concerned, however, the Friar's function at this point is negligible and he really serves only to remind the audience of the stereotypically lustful venality of friars by leering at Matilda/Marian and later at Jinny (in this respect he is like Sir John of Wrotham in Munday's co-authored *Sir John Oldcastle*).[86] The dramatic purpose of his initial speech itself remains obscure.

As well as alluding to antitheatrical writing, these plays have a connection with yet another form of Munday's early writing, propagandist pamphlets. In *The Death* the Prior, Robin's uncle, is subtly associated with the supposed deceits of Catholicism when he offers Robin poison in the form of 'a pretious drinke … from Rome' which is allegedly an elixir.[87] The play's casual anti-Catholicism resembles that in *Oldcastle*: later in the same scene of the former play Doncaster, the inveterate villain, swears 'by the Masse' that he does not know why he hates Robin.[88] That the character of Warman is referred to as 'Judas' in *The Downfall* might also serve as a reminder of Munday's role in betraying Catholic priests in the early 1580s, especially as his sometime colleague, George Ellyot, was called Judas too by those he captured.[89] The anonymous anti-Marprelate tract *An Almond for a Parrat* indicates in the same fashion that Munday had been regarded as a turncoat. 'Beware Anthony Munday be not even with you for calling him Judas', it warns 'Martin' and his allies, in response to a pretended Archbishop Whitgift figure in the Martinist text *The Just Censure and Reproofe of Martin Junior* saying to Munday that he is a 'Judas ... that hast alreadie betrayed the Papistes'.[90]

Towards the end of the play, 'Little John' and 'Tuck' are again left alone on the stage and fall back into their Induction roles of John Eltham and Skelton. This digression, like the earlier one, deals explicitly with matters theatrical, for Munday has 'John Eltam' complain about the play's lack of 'jeasts' and 'merry morices'. The genre and intended audience of the play seems a matter of debate: Eltham was expecting a comedy full of 'pleasant skippings up and downe the wodde', and Skelton has written 'Robins Tragedie', or perhaps a 'historie' – no one seems sure. Such hybridity is endemic to this play. The real Skelton was a famed writer of a few generations back, a fact that Munday's audience might have been expected to recall, especially since Skelton's own characteristic literary style is imitated during the play, sometimes by Friar Tuck, otherwise by Skelton himself when he is not performing the role of Tuck but being 'himself'.[91] In one example of the former kind of intertextuality, the Friar's 'Skeltonicall' speech prompts the comment from Robin 'Why then it seemes that thou art Frier Tucke': here the two roles seem to be indistinguishable, since a speech that explicitly alludes to Skelton is actually cited as a clear marker of *Tuck*'s identity.[92] As Oakley-Brown comments, other aspects of dramatic performance, such as cross-dressing, are brought to the fore in the quasi-theatrical space of the induction. 'Little Tracy', a boy player, is reminded that he is also required to play the role of 'our maid Marian' and thus should now cease 'leaping like a lad'.[93] The 1598 performance at court is also implied when, in response to Eltham's concern that 'the kings majestie' might 'mislike' the play, Skelton reassures him that 'his Majestie himselfe survaid the plat'. Furthermore, he reminds him that 'merry jeasts ... have bene showne before' and that 'our play expresses noble Roberts wrong', hence its mixture of comedy and tragedy.[94] Skelton, it appears, gets too involved in his role of author when he admits 'I doe forget oft times my Friers part' and asks that John Eltham 'pull mee by the sleeve when I exceed'.[95]

When these two have the stage to themselves for the final time they appear, as they did at the very beginning, in the guises of John

Eltham and Skelton. In a typically Munday fashion, their concluding exchange is employed chiefly to whet the audience's appetite for 'other matters tragicall, / That followe in the processe of the storie' by giving enticing snippets of the action of the follow-up play, *The Death of Robert, Earle of Huntington*.[96] Skelton purports to be at a loss as how to encompass in one play all the events of Huntingdon's latter days until he has the idea that Eltham can assist. In another fine example of the plays' extensive metatheatricality, he requests of Eltham that he should 'crave the king / To see two parts'.[97] The current audience, 'all these beholders', as John Eltham calls them, will then have to be asked to be patient as they wait for Part Two. Munday here subtly fuses the theatrical commonplace of including the audience's hoped-for approbation at the end of the play with a much more complex interplay between disparate forms of 'audience' and, implicitly, of temporality: 'the King' (i.e. the shadowy Henry VIII), the real monarch at the time, Elizabeth, who actually saw the play at court, and the other, Southwark audience of the play.[98] Munday also continues the note of historical and generic complexity with the role of John Skelton, a character in the play who is also ostensibly its author as well as being a well-known writer himself. In the induction scene of *The Downfall*, Skelton – here in his role of author – asserts that while others have represented Robin Hood from a historical distance, with his theatrical time machine he alone 'writes of Robin Hood what he [Skelton] doth truly knowe'.[99] Finally, with an plug for the forthcoming sequel – 'the second part shall presently be pend' – we also experience Munday's and the Admiral's Company's immediate desire to exploit the play's popularity by producing a successor to it.[100] The successor itself begins with Skeltonicall verses which would have served to remind the audience of *The Downfall*, within which there is a backward glance to 'where wee left' the preceding play's characters.[101] As far as the division of the plays is concerned, Henslowe's *Diary* indicates that the original intention was to have a one-part play, so Skelton's remark in the text that there is too much material for a single production echoes the experience of the 'real' playwright, Munday himself.

In his interesting and sustained reading of the *Huntington* plays Singman discusses their 'mixing of genres'. His interpretation of their sometimes baffling complexity is that Munday was drawing upon more heterogeneous material than he could comfortably accommodate in a coherent playtext, which indeed might explain the way in which the plays combine various literary and historical traditions (as an instance of the latter, the fact that the Earldom of Huntington was first created, coincidentally for Munday's version, by Henry VIII).[102] Simeone concurs that the *Huntington* plays draw upon both historical and pastoral traditions of the Robin Hood story.[103] Singman's overall view is that Munday was attempting, not entirely successfully, to enforce both dramatic and ideological consistency on to the wide-ranging Robin Hood legend, although I do think he overstates the case somewhat by claiming (despite critiquing Stephen Knight's account of the plays for precisely the same reason) that Munday had an 'officializing agenda'.[104]

The second part of the story, *The Death of Robert, Earle of Huntington*, commences with extensive references back to the first *Huntington* play which establish an almost seamless link between the two. Traces of the original one-part form of the play might be visible here: it is possible that Tuck's Skeltonic Induction might mark the eventual point of severance between the two parts and the rewriting by Chettle, for Meagher has claimed that this scene might have been intended to conclude part one of the *Huntington* plays rather than begin part two.[105] As before, Friar Tuck begins the play with the now-familiar Skeltonic form of speech, in which he reminds the present audience of the conclusion of the earlier drama, 'our last play', as he calls it. His frequent use of the pronoun 'wee' further accentuates the fiction that he is speaking to exactly the same viewers. What is more, the Friar is once again not fully in character, even admitting that he 'like a sot / [has] ... wholly forgot / the course of our plot'.[106] Such is his disassociation from the main body of the play in this induction scene that he is not even yet fully costumed and actually narrates his process of getting into character for the benefit of the audience in a way guaranteed to destroy any theatrical illusion from the outset: 'cross-bowe lye downe, / Come on friers gowne, / Hoode cover my crowne'.[107] Dieter Mehl comments of this framing device that its 'chief function ... is to introduce the actors and to create the atmosphere of a theatrical entertainment'.[108] However, it might equally be said to *prevent* the 'atmosphere' of theatre, such is its defamiliarising effect. As the previous play ended with hints of the action to come in the follow-up, so the latter play begins with a brief summary of the final events of its predecessor together with the introduction of new characters, such as 'Sir Doncaster', about 'whose villainies and theft', the audience is told, 'You never heard of, but too soone yee shall'.[109]

Friar Tuck regularly takes on this kind of disruptive role, switching in and out of character at crucial moments. Further on, immediately after Robin's death, which takes place only eight hundred lines or so into the play, he tries to end the entire action with the end of Robin's life, despite admitting in the process that to do so would result in a 'short play'.[110] It is only with the intervention of the Earl of Chester that the play resumes after this untimely hiatus, and even he is required to don another costume, this time of 'Kendall greene', in order for the drama to continue. Russell Peck suggests that Chester might still be wearing the green outfit from *The Downfall*, which would constitute another visual reminder of the link between the two plays.[111] Chester asks 'let not thy Play so soone be at an end', reminding Tuck that 'Mathildaes Tragedie' is still to be enacted, despite the latter's belief that he 'thinkst there now remaines not one, / To act an other Sceane or two for thee'.[112] Although the connection to Tuck's double role as Skelton in the first play remains implicit here, his function in part two is equally as much author as actor. Nevertheless, despite Friar Tuck's reluctance to extend 'his' play the show must go on, even if to do so necessitates the audience accepting an immediate chronological leap from the reign of Richard I to that of King John. Finally, the epilogue to the second part of the *Huntington* plays, appropriately enough, points up rather than disguises the haphazard nature of the sequel's structure and takes the conventional authorial modesty of the epilogue to extremes. It reveals rather more about the writing process and the level of skill of its author than it might generally be considered wise to share with an audience: 'This is Matildaes story showne in act', it reads, 'And rough heawen out by an uncunning hand, / Being of the most material points compackt, / That with the certainst state of truth doe stand'. As Mehl has remarked of this play, it 'does not pretend to any "realism" but is frankly presented as a piece of make-believe that can be shortened or drawn out at the audience's pleasure'.[113] Offering the audience so much apparent autonomy was evidently a productive strategy, for such was the currency of this story that the Robin Hood/Richard I/King John sequence was exploited by Munday, Chettle and their other collaborators even further with the lost sequel from 1598, *The Funeral of Richard Coeur de Lion*.[114]

The *Huntington* plays show Munday collaborating successfully on well-received texts. He and his works were not uniformly praised however, and the next chapter explores the attitudes towards Munday of a number of his contemporaries.

NOTES

1. Munday, *Zelauto*, p. 56.
2. Dillon writes that early modern London, especially in the theatre, featured 'conscious performers, inhabiting multiple identities without embodying any one of them' (*Theatre, Court and City*, p. 64).
3. Byrne remarks that Munday has an 'inconvenient Jack-in-the-box habit of appearing suddenly in the midst of some respectable academic controversy, as if maliciously determined to introduce as many complications and uncertainties as possible' ('Anthony Munday and his books', p. 225).
4. Twyning, *London Dispossessed*, pp. 7–8. Peter Lake says that 'Munday and [George] Whetstone ... epitomise the socio-cultural milieu of literary production ... Here was a place where writing was for the market' (*The Antichrist's Lewd Hat*, p. xxviii).
5. Manley, *Literature and Culture*, pp. 300–1. Twyning argues that compared to Jonson, for instance, Dekker's work too was 'more ambiguously placed, more pressured by the complex insecurities of his own position as a professional writer' (*London Dispossessed*, p. 97).
6. Cited in White, 'Shakespeare, the Cobhams, and the dynamics of theatrical patronage', p. 75.
7. Munday, *Zelauto*, p. 61.
8. Hayes, 'Anthony Munday's romances of chivalry', p. 57.
9. Munday, *Palmerin d'Oliva*, sig. iiir.
10. Ibid., sig. iiiv.
11. Ibid., sigs iiir–v.
12. Ibid., sig. iiiv. See also Hayes, 'Anthony Munday's romances of chivalry', p. 60.
13. Munday, *The Mirrour of Mutabilitie*, pp. xviii, 2 and 24. See also Parry, 'Literary patronage', p. 120.
14. Munday, *A second and third blast*, sigs Fir–v.
15. Hawkes, 'Idolatry and commodity fetishism', p. 261.
16. Ibid., p. 266.
17. Munday, *A second and third blast*, sigs Fivr–v.
18. See Leinwand, *Theatre, Finance and Society*, pp. 120–8.
19. Ibid., p. 128.
20. See Carson, 'Literary management', p. 194.
21. Cited in Gadd, 'Hunting down John Wolfe', p. 196.
22. To underline the point (and to reiterate the Cripplegate connection), in 1588 Charlewood printed an anti-Catholic text by Robert Crowley (see Turner Wright, 'Young Anthony Mundy again', p. 158).
23. Gadd, 'Hunting down John Wolfe', p. 196. See also Unwin, *The Gilds and Companies of London*, p. 260, Bennett, *English Books and Readers*, p. 69, and Aldis *et al.*, *A Dictionary of Printers and Booksellers*, pp. 296–8.
24. Telin, trans. Munday, *Archaioplutos*, sig. A2r–v. Munday's *Orlando* text is not extant.
25. Heinrich comments that Munday's citation of Cicero in the preface to *The Mirrour of Mutabilitie* is based chiefly on his desire to 'show off' his use of this then most 'fashionable' of classical authorities (Munday, *The Mirrour of Mutabilitie*, p. xvii). Munday also quotes Cicero extensively in the preface to *A discoverie of Edmund Campion* (1582).

26 Munday, *Zelauto*, p. 189. See also Munday, *The Mirrour of Mutabilitie*, p. 4.
27 In a typically self-depreciating dedication to Essex, Munday describes *Palladine of England* as 'not handled with arte, because I want it' (sig. iiir).
28 Munday, *A second and third blast*, sig. Avr.
29 Munday, *Zelauto*, p. 141.
30 Munday, *A second and third blast*, sig. Aivr.
31 Munday, *Zelauto*, p. 62.
32 See *ibid.*, p. xii.
33 Scanlon, 'Munday's *Zelauto*', p. 13.
34 *Ibid.*, p. 14.
35 See Hamilton, 'Anthony Munday and *The Merchant of Venice*', p. 92.
36 See Turner, *Anthony Mundy*, pp. 26–8. Hamilton comments that the 'authorless position' of many of Munday's texts can be related to 'issues of nonconformist rhetorical positioning' ('Anthony Munday and *The Merchant of Venice*', p. 96).
37 Munday, *A Mirrour of Mutabilitie*, p. 41.
38 The number of published translations from French and other continental languages rather than Latin increased during the 1580s and 1590s when Munday was particularly active in this regard (see Barnard and McKenzie, *The Cambridge History of the Book*, p. 789).
39 Munday, *A Womans Woorth*, sig. A2v.
40 *Ibid.*, sigs A2r–v; my emphasis.
41 *Ibid.*, sig. A2v.
42 *Ibid.*, sigs A4v–A5r.
43 *Ibid.*, sig. A5v; my emphases.
44 *Ibid.*, sig. A9r.
45 *Ibid.*, sig. A10v.
46 See Agnew, *Worlds Apart*, p. 14.
47 Munday, *The Third and last part of Palmerin of England*, sig. A4v.
48 Munday, *Zelauto*, p. 63.
49 Munday, *The Downfall*, lines 330–75.
50 A poem by Robert Crowley expresses the same sentiment in a similar form of verse: 'And this is a city / In name, but in deed / It is a pack of people / That seek after meed; / For officers and all / Do seek their own gain' (Manley, *London in the Age of Shakespeare*, p. 161).
51 Munday, *The paine of pleasure*, sigs Fiiiiv–Fir.
52 Munday, *A second and third blast*, sig. Hviv. 'Camelion' was a common term for players during this period (see Mann, 'Sir Oliver Owlet's Men', pp. 306–7).
53 Cited in Manley, *Literature and Culture*, p. 312.
54 Cited in Jones and Stallybrass, *Renaissance Clothing and the Materials of Memory*, p. 187.
55 Manley, *Literature and Culture*, p. 343.
56 McLuskie, *Dekker and Heywood*, p. 3.
57 Lobanov-Rostovsky, 'The Triumphes of Golde', p. 892.
58 Munday, *Zelauto*, p. 97.
59 Munday, *A second and third blast*, sig. Hvr.
60 Munday, *John a Kent and John a Cumber*, p. 197.
61 Alfield, *A true reporte of the death*, sig. Er. As others have noted, Munday fails to rebut this accusation in his response to Alfield.

62 See also Mann, 'Sir Oliver Owlet's Men', p. 305, and Bednarz, 'Representing Jonson', pp. 12–14.
63 ?Marston, *Histrio-Mastix*, sig. Br.
64 Ibid., sig. Cv; see also sig. C4r.
65 Munday, *A second and third blast*, p. 43.
66 See my 'He hath changed his coppy'. Munday himself might have featured in Chettle's text as the ballad-seller 'Old Anthony Now-Now'.
67 Mann, 'Sir Oliver Owlet's Men', p. 309.
68 Munday, *Zelauto*, p. 67.
69 Cited in Turner, *Anthony Mundy*, pp. 84; my emphasis. This incident brings to mind what Manley says of Dick Tarleton, who was 'an ambiguous creature who ingratiated himself with his victims by alternately posing as their servant and preceptor ... and sometimes betrayed them to the authorities' (*Literature and Culture*, p. 326).
70 Munday, *Zelauto*, p. 111.
71 Cited in Knight and Ohlgren, *Robin Hood*, pp. 389–90.
72 Cited in Ayres, 'Anthony Munday', p. 14.
73 Cited in Manley, *London in the Age of Shakespeare*, p. 204; see also Agnew, *Worlds Apart*, pp. 79–84.
74 Munday, *A second and third blast*, sig. Hiiv.
75 Singman, 'Munday's unruly Earl', p. 71.
76 Simeone, 'Renaissance Robin Hood plays', pp. 193–4.
77 Wolf, 'Anthony Munday as popular artist', p. 660.
78 Knight and Ohlgren, *Robin Hood*, p. 390. Liz Oakley-Brown says that these plays 'manufacture a version of reality that hinges on a *mise-en-abîme* of temporal frames' (Oakley-Brown, 'Framing Robin Hood', p. 4).
79 Munday, ed. Meagher, *The Downfall*, lines 10–13.
80 Oakley-Brown, 'Framing Robin Hood', p. 6.
81 Munday, ed. Meagher, *The Downfall*, line 238.
82 Ibid., line 301.
83 Ibid., lines 1536–7.
84 Ibid., line 762. Peck comments of this that 'the spelling seems intentional. Here we find the two titles blended as Maid Marian, assuming the role of Countess of Huntington, resumes her noble name. Henceforth ... she is Matilda' (Knight and Ohlgren, *Robin Hood*, p. 438). See also Oakley-Brown, 'Framing Robin Hood', pp. 13–14.
85 Munday, ed. Meagher, *The Downfall*, lines 846–92.
86 See also Barton. 'The king disguised', pp. 112–14. 'Sir John' was 'the conventional name of a parson' (Henning, ed., *Fair Em*, p. 127n).
87 Munday, ed. Meagher, *The Death*, lines 250–1.
88 Ibid., line 306. See also Levin, *Propaganda in the English Reformation*, p. 221.
89 See my '"This is as true as all the rest is"', p. 52.
90 Nashe, ed. McKerrow, *The Works of Thomas Nashe*, vol. III, p. 374.
91 There are also 'Skeltonicall'-style verses in *Fair Em*: see, for example, lines 26–44.
92 Munday, ed. Meagher, *The Downfall*, lines 1601–8.
93 Ibid., lines 29–30. See Oakley-Brown, 'Framing Robin Hood', p. 12.
94 Munday, ed. Meagher, *The Downfall*, lines 2221–6
95 Ibid., lines 2239–40.
96 Ibid., lines 2788–9.

97 *Ibid.*, line 2810.
98 Peck points out that the King might equally be Henry VII, as the Bishop of Ely's name in the play is Morton, Henry VII's Chancellor (Munday, ed. Peck, *The Downfall*, note to line 2741). See also Levin, *Propaganda in the English Reformation*, p. 216.
99 Munday, ed. Meagher, *The Downfall*, lines 117–18.
100 *Ibid.*, line 2821.
101 *Ibid.*, line 18.
102 See Simeone, 'Renaissance Robin Hood plays', p. 198 n. 12.
103 See *ibid.*, p. 185.
104 See Singman, 'Munday's unruly Earl', pp. 66–8, 69–70, 76 n. 17 and *passim*.
105 See Munday, ed. Peck, 'Excerpts from *The Death*', p. 22n. Henslowe's *Diary* indicates that the licences for both plays were paid for at the same time, March 1598. Carson concludes that one of Henslowe's inventories 'drawn up sometime during Lent, 1598', which lists clothing for 'Maryan' and 'Roben', denotes an investment in costumes specifically for these plays ('Production finance at the Rose theatre', p. 181). Perhaps it is no wonder, then, that *The Death* itself highlights these costly properties at the expense of dramatic verisimilitude.
106 Munday, *The Death*, lines 12–13.
107 *Ibid.*, lines 13–15.
108 Mehl, 'Forms and functions of the play within a play', p. 56.
109 Munday, *The Death*, lines 26–7.
110 *Ibid.*, line 864. See also Levin, *Propaganda in the English Reformation*, pp. 216–18.
111 Munday, ed. Peck, 'Excerpts from *The Death*', p. 26n.
112 Munday, *The Death*, lines 866–71.
113 Mehl, 'Forms and functions of the play within a play', p. 56.
114 See Carson, *A Companion to Henslowe's Diary*, p. 62, and Rutter, ed., *Documents of the Rose Playhouse*, p. 144. There is a large number of payments during May–June 1598 from Henslowe to Munday, Chettle and Wilson for this play, which suggests the urgency with which a sequel was sought. There is an echo of this lost play in Munday's 1611 Show *Chruso-thriambos*, where 'King Richard the first, surnamed *Cordelion*' is invoked by the figure of Time (see Munday, *Chruso-thriambos*, sig. A3v).

3

'I must needes be derided'

Munday and his contemporaries

GRAHAM PARRY has recently shown how prone late sixteenth-century writers were to receive criticism: 'publication exposed an author to a good deal of bitter griping and condemnation ... though authors were few, critics were many'.[1] Munday often appears to be acutely aware of how his contemporaries might have regarded him and is willing to defend the literary aspirations of non-elite writers such as himself. In *Zelauto* he disclaims any especial literary skill, but in the face of potential criticism he still reserves some merit for himself on the basis of his unshowy good intentions: 'neyther dooth the bluntness of my Booke, altogether condempne me: nor the meane methode of the matter, diminish any jot of the good wyll of the Author'.[2] Again, one can note that Munday differentiates between 'my' book and 'the Author', suggesting that they are not necessarily the same person. Those of Munday's friends and associates who wrote verses to accompany his works echoed Munday's position in *Zelauto* by stressing the 'pains' he took over his text and the worthiness of his purposes rather than the literary merit. Thus, for example, Thomas Spigurnel's verse in praise of Munday's *Mirrour* compares its author positively to Chaucer, whose 'pratling pen' he calls a self-regarding 'abuse' of 'his muse [and] his minde' intended only to bestow 'fame' upon the writer.[3] Munday's work, in contrast, is characterised in more self-effacing terms as 'playne' and 'woorthy'.[4] In the same vein, 'M. D.' (probably Michael Drayton) applauds Munday's style in *Primaleon* for its 'home-borne' qualities, calling it a 'true method' of writing.[5] In the later work *Palmerin of England* John Webster's commendatory verse reiterates this attitude: 'nor for the fiction is the worke lesse fine', he tells the translator and his readers, for 'fables have pith and morall discipline'.⁶ In *The Defence of Poetry* even the patrician Sir Philip Sidney compliments the story of *Amadis de Gaule*, which Munday was to translate, for its ability to foster virtue in the reader by a process of mimesis. Sidney writes: 'I have known men that, even with reading *Amadis de Gaule* ... have found their hearts moved to the exercise of courtesy, liberality, and especially courage'. However, as is implied by his use of the word 'even', Sidney does comment in parenthesis that the text fails aesthetically, for 'God knoweth [it] wanteth much of a perfect poesy'.⁷

In some respects *Zelauto* itself bears out its author's modesty about its style. Despite its euphuistic pretensions – in 1580 Munday was working alongside Lyly under the patronage of the Earl of Oxford – it is written in a sturdy vernacular full of proverbial tags and it habitually uses everyday images, comically so at times.⁸ Signor Truculento for example, 'an extorting Usurer', is depicted as a mincing idiot: 'having pounced [i.e. 'ponced'] him selfe up in his perfumes, and walking so nice on the ground, that he would scant bruse an Onion', he then prepares himself to make a speech by 'bustl[ing] up his braynes lyke a bunch of Radishe'.⁹ The bathetic humour is not always deliberate (Munday's work is hardly notable for its jokes), as its portentious proverbial wisdom sometimes betrays its ostensible purpose. Thus the lovelorn Strabino is represented in a down-to-earth rather than a high-flown romantic fashion: for instance, he is asked by his mistress why he has his 'heart in [his] hose', and a friend exclaims, when enquiring why he looks so depressed, 'Oh Strabino, in fayth the blacke Oxe never trode on your foote yet'.¹⁰ Munday was unabashedly pragmatic as a writer: he was more than willing to use others' insights or research (sometimes, as we will see, leading him into embarrassing errors), he avoided systematic or sustained philosophies, and rarely passed up any opportunity to trade on other writers' currency.¹¹ As a consequence he did sometimes make mistakes over Greek and Roman mythology that would have provoked the scorn of better-educated contemporaries such as Nashe or Jonson.¹²

Nevertheless, Munday defended his limited ambitions stoutly on occasion. Although, as I have shown, his contemporaries were careful to insist on his status as a 'gentleman', he himself more often than not identified with the middle-ranking citizenry. In his 1602 translation *The True knowledge of a mans owne selfe* he is in philosophical vein. He tries to establish as a religious principle that a modest social status is a desirable condition, for, he argues, it inhibits undue social pretensions: 'the ambitious man pretends to know what honour & height of dignity is; yet findes his knowledge to be meere ignorance, when the miserable downfall from his expectation, teacheth him (too late) that a meane estate hath beene much better'.[13] In *Zelauto* Munday puts forward a similar defence of the value of a 'meane estate', in which he represents the lowly citizen as being poor but worthy. In the course of an extended simile likening his offering of the text to the Earl of Oxford to 'a poore Cittizen''s present of a 'handfull of Flowers' to his Emperor, one of the 'Gentlemen' present questions the Citizen's right to present something so insignificant to their lord. The Citizen, standing in for Munday in this fictionalised version of the writer/patron relationship, defends himself in the following terms:

> I am poore (quoth the Cittizen) and therefore I give such a meane gift, yet hath it beene gratefully accepted: And although they descend of such noble Linages ... poore as I am, I beare him as true a heart as the best: Even so my poore gift hath beene as faithfully delivered: as the richest Jewell that was by them presented.[14]

Later in the text, the 'Lady' (a thinly disguised portrait of Elizabeth I) reminds an over-proud knight that aristocratic breeding does not necessarily entail virtue – indeed, it requires those so privileged to take pains to demonstrate their moral qualities: 'a meane person adorned with vertue: is a precious Jewell aboove such a Gentleman' and 'vertulesse Gentillyitie', Munday has her claim, 'is wurse then Beggarie'.[15] In the same way, Munday addresses the mediocrity of his background (and thus, by inference, his literary productions), raising and then rejecting arguments that both are necessarily inferior: 'the homelyest house, may be hansome within: the simplest Garden, may have Flowers woorth the smelling ... and many an honest man, may walke simply arrayed ... [thus] the meane array of the Citizen [does not] impayre any of his honesty'.[16] The epistle to the Reader reiterates Munday's defence of 'good will' and 'honest intent' over 'wit'; in the process he alludes to another of Oxford's current 'servants' (albeit one with a greater literary reputation), John Lyly, as 'that Lilly whose sent [sic] is so sweete'.[17]

If Munday's works did espouse 'citizen values' it is only to be expected, then, that his prose romances found a keen readership amongst the citizenry, especially, one presumes, with apprentices such as the fictional Rafe in *The Knight of the Burning Pestle*, who is shown 'like a grocer in's shop' with his fellow apprentices reading from one of

Munday's *Palmerin* translations.[18] Mark Thornton Burnett cites an apparently typical apprentice preference for 'vain and corrupt books as *Palmerin de Oliva* ... and others like'.[19] Not all of *Palmerin*'s readers, however, were from the apprentice class, for some of the later editions of his *Palmerin* texts were dedicated with Munday's fervent assurances that he would be 'alwayes yours with my uttermost endevours' to his sometime patrons Francis and Susan Young of Brent Pelham, Hertfordshire.[20] Munday's *Palladine of England* (published in 1588) was evidently considered in some quarters to be 'vain and corrupt', for it appeared in the Index Expurgatorius in Francis Mere's 1598 *Palladis Tamia*, a work which otherwise praised Munday's dramatic work.[21] In the romance itself Munday appears conscious of potential criticism, for he highlights the harmlessness of this work on its title page: 'Heerein is no offence offered to the wise by wanten speeches, or encouragement to the loose by lascivious matter'.[22]

Other writers of the period were scornful of Munday's lowly aspirations and achievement. As with Robert Greene's attack on the unnamed author of *Fair Em* (further discussed below), Thomas Nashe wrote a coded condemnation of another writer of the period. In *Pierce Penilesse* (the title page of which, one should note, calls its author 'Gent.') Nashe demonstrates a snobbish attitude towards the background of an unnamed contemporary believed by some to have been Munday. He also laments at length the decline of learned and well-bred writers such as himself in favour of inferior tradesmen such as Munday. In a section entitled 'The Nature of an Upstart' Nashe writes of how 'all malcontent sits the greasie son of a Cloathier, & complaines (like a decaied Earle) of the ruine of ancient houses'.[23] This 'Squier of low degree', as Nashe calls him, demonstrates impertinence both in his attempt to undertake a variety of literary genres and also in his relentless search for patronage. Heinemann, for one, identifies Munday as the 'son of a Cloathier' from his membership of the Drapers by patrimony, but, even if he is not the particular target here, he is exactly the kind of writer whom Nashe maligns. *Pierce Penilesse* is also in part a defence of the stage in the face of antitheatrical tracts and 'Citizens objections against Players'; in it Nashe celebrates 'famous Ned Allen' (and by implication Strange's Men, Alleyn's then company).[24]

There are contradictions here (for instance, insomuch as Munday was most probably actually working for Alleyn's company, Strange's Men, in 1592) that can be in part ascribed to Munday's intermediary position. He was a writer for the theatres, of which Nashe is in favour, and a writer of pamphlets, ballads and 'popular' romances, about which Nashe is scathing. Nashe himself of course was as prone as Munday to write across genres, and Manley has ascribed the former writer's venom towards 'hack' writers and unlearned historians to his own 'anxiety with his marginal status'.[25] Martin Butler has also made the point that 'quarrels between playwrights were as symptomatic of likeness as of difference, indicating the felt necessity to stake out a place in a literary market that had suddenly started to seem congested'.[26] Nashe's attack is undeniably vituperative. 'Every grossbrained idiot is suffered to come into print', he exclaims, citing a ballad about 'the exploits of Untruss' that has been attributed to Munday as an example of the kind of talentless workaday publication that was allegedly dominating the literary profession. Nashe also claims that the prevalence of hack writers (those he calls 'drones') denies work to the better-bred and better-educated such as himself.[27] In a part of *Pierce Penilesse* entitled 'The dispraise of lay chronigraphers' he also attacks chroniclers such as 'Master Stow' who 'write of nothing but of Mayors and Sheriefs, and the deere yeere, and the great frost, that can endow [citizens'] names with never dated glory: for they want the wings of choise words to fly to heaven'.[28] Similarly, in *Nashes Lenten Stuffe* he rejects conventional dedications such as Munday's in favour of one to a fellow hack-writer, for 'neither to rich, noble, right worshipfull, or worshipfull, of spirituall or temporall, will I consecrate this woorke'.[29]

Nashe's 1589 epistle *To the Gentlemen Students of Both Universities* takes issue with unnamed writers from the tradesmen class, particularly those who engage in translation, as Munday did extensively in the 1580s. Nashe's critique has a number of resonances for Munday and is worth citing at length. He castigates 'a few of our triviall translators' who are symptomatic of the decline of literary worth, going on to comment that such debased hacks are willing to try their hand at any literary form:

> It is a common practise now a dayes amongst a sort of shifting companions, that runne through every Art and thrive by none, to leave the trade of Noverint, whereunto they were borne, and busie themselves with the indevours of Art, that could scarcely Latinize their neck verse if they should have neede ... these men, renouncing all possibilities of credite or estimation, ... intermeddle with Italian Translations: Wherein how poorely they have plodded ... let all

indifferent Gentlemen that have travailed in that tongue discerne by their two-pennie Pamphlets: & no marvell though their home borne mediocritie bee such in this matter.[30]

The phrase 'indifferent Gentlemen' might well apply to Munday and he had of course been notorious for his travels in Italy some years before. A commendatory verse by Drayton in Munday's second book of *Primaleon* uses the same words as Nashe, but rather to praise the translator's 'true method of his home-borne stile'; at the same time he stresses that Munday 'follow[s] the fashion of a French conceate'.[31] This verse epitomises positive accounts of Munday's works, for where the original French text takes the form of a 'conceate', Munday's translation is 'true'. T. W. Baldwin is confident that Nashe's epistle is attacking Munday, and his reworked translation of *Fedele and Fortunio* specifically. One of the former's criticisms of tradesmen translators such as Munday is that they are unable 'to distinguish of Articles': Baldwin points out that Munday had recently 'translated [Luigi Pasqualigo's] *Il Fedele*, "the" faithful one, simply as Fedele'.[32] Such inferior men, Nashe also argues, have 'no more Art in their braine then was nourished in a serving mans idlenesse'.[33] This comment could be read as a dig at Munday's literary pretensions honed in his early service to the Earl of Oxford.

Munday himself deflects such criticism by arguing that the work of translation inherently inhibits that literary excellence that a writer might elsewhere display: 'to translate, allowes little occasion of fine pen worke', as he puts it in the 1588 edition of *Palmerin d'Oliva*.[34] 'In translating', he further explains in *Palladine of England*, 'men are bound to their Writers words.'[35] By this token, faithfulness to the original source takes priority over the translator's own literary ambitions. Indeed, Chettle insists on the faithfulness of Munday's translation of *Primaleon*: 'the same forme [as the original] is observ'd by the Translater, / *Primeleon* (sweet in French) keeps here like grace'.[36] Dekker, however, keen to defend his 'deere' friend's literary reputation, writes in his commendatory verse to Munday's 1602 *Palmerin of England* that 'pure translation [might] reach as high a glory / As best invention'.[37] As Helen Moore has shown, although Munday states that translation might be secondary to original creation, there are other, less purely aesthetic merits in rendering a foreign text into English and hence making it available to a domestic readership.[38] The same nationalistic ideal informs Drayton's verse in part two of *Primaleon*, where Munday is lauded for having 'brought [Primaleon] heere into this famous Ile'.³⁹ In *Zelauto's* characteristically egocentric, if simultaneously self-depreciating, dedication to the Earl of Oxford, Munday presciently predicts that men of more formal learning than himself might find him easy to despise: 'how dare so rude a writer as I, seeme to set foorth so meane a matter, so weake a woorke, and so skillesse a stile? ... I must needes be mocked, and when the skilfullest are scorned: I must needes be derided'.⁴⁰ In *The Mirrour of Mutabilitie* Munday also forsees that 'some ... might find more fault then needeth, some will carp on no occasion, & some will condemn before they have read'.⁴¹ Indeed, Chettle's commendatory verse (cited above) to part two of *Primaleon*, 'Of the Translation, against a Carper', is directed at some potential critic.

Jonson, never one to disguise his animosities, has long been known to be one such critic. Despite their years working alongside one another at the Rose, Munday is wheeled on to be mocked by Jonson, in an early scene of *The Case Is Altered*, in the guise of Antonio Balladino, whom the play calls the 'pageant poet to the City of Milan'. As such he is resorted to only, as he himself admits, 'when a worse cannot be had'.⁴² The attack on Munday was added by Jonson to this 1590s play for its publication in 1609, clearly indicating that Munday's work for the City had sufficient currency by that date for the jibe to work, as well as suggesting that by that date Jonson regarded Munday as a rival for civic patronage.⁴³ There are also allusions to Munday's work other than pageants in this play: Balladino's name in itself makes the association with ballad-writing, and the cobbler Juniper requests him to produce 'some pretty paradox or some allegory', alluding perhaps to Munday's paradoxical works such as *The Defence of Contraries* or *The paine of pleasure*.⁴⁴ To compound the satire, Jonson makes Balladino condemn himself. He expresses a preference for 'stale stuff', of which he states 'I do use as much ... though I say it myself, as any man does', reminding the audience of Munday's preference for familiar proverbs and borrowed truisms.⁴⁵ Via Balladino Munday is also identified as a popular playwright writing for 'the common sort', in contrast (implicitly) to Jonson, who, as the kind of writer who produces 'new tricks ... [and] nothing but humours', aims to 'please the gentlemen'.⁴⁶ Pointing explicitly to Francis Meres's notorious characterisation of Munday, Jonson has Balladino say that he 'cares not for the gentlemen ... no matter for the pen, the plot shall carry it', prompting the rejoinder from Peter Onion that 'you are in print already for the best plotter'.⁴⁷ Moore neatly summarises Jonson's objections to Munday in this play;

the former targets, she says, '[Balladino's] motivation (to please the masses), his system of patronage (indiscriminate), his subject matter and style (hackneyed) and his popularity (considerable)'.[48]

Marston too may have attacked Munday if the former was indeed the author of *Histrio-Mastix*.[49] Although the date and authorship of *Histrio-Mastix* is uncertain, if, as a number of scholars have speculated, the play in the printed version as we now have it (which does not necessarily represent the form in which it was performed) was revived if not written in 1599, this too suggests that Munday's work as a pageant-maker can be traced back to the late Elizabethan period. Posthaste, the parodied Munday figure, is called a 'peaking Pagenter' as well as being represented as a talentless if prolific playwright.[50] In this respect he is contrasted to the character Chrisoganus (probably intended to be Jonson), for when the latter fears a 'dearth of rich invention', Clout responds that this will never happen 'while goose-quillian *Posthast* holds his pen'.[51] Posthaste's productiveness is demonstrated when he is asked by his company how the 'new plot' is proceeding. He reassures them with the statement that 'my wit's grown no lesse plentiful then the time, / There's two sheets done in follio, will cost two shillings in rime'; the verse that he recites is, unfortunately, rhyming doggerel.[52] Such is his lack of skill that even one of his own company warns that 'It is as dangerous to read [Posthaste's] name at a playe-dore / As a printed bill on a plague dore'.[53] As this suggests, Posthaste bears a number of resemblances to Jonson's Balladino: Gulch remarks of Posthaste's writing that 'heer's no new luxurie of blandishment, / But plenty of old Englands mothers words', and Clout refers to Munday's 'other life' as a pursuivant, perhaps, when he replies to Gulch that 'I'st not pitty this fellow's not imploid in matters of State'.[54] Posthaste also declares that to make ends meet 'Ile een past all my ballads together, / And make a coate'; later in the play, when the players have been thrown out of town, he envisages that he must 'boldy fall to ballading againe'.[55] Although the identification of Munday with Posthaste is not definitive, it is certainly suggestive, for Munday had worked as a government agent, was certainly known to have published ballads, was famously celebrated by Meres in *Palladis Tamia* as 'our best plotter', and as we have seen was both praised and criticised for his assiduousness at writing in a prosaic and unadorned style.

If Munday was the author of the anonymous and much disputed Rose play *Fair Em* as some have speculated, then there is further evidence of animosity towards him from Robert Greene. Greene attacked a person who has been identified as the writer of *Fair Em* in his 1591 work *Farewell to Follie*, in which, as well as linking his antagonist to Munday's parish of St Giles Without Cripplegate (as discussed above), he suggests that the latter is a talentless individual who has been associated with the ever-despised practice of balladwriting and with works 'borrowed of Theologicall poets' (such as Munday's *The Mirrour of Mutabilitie*, perhaps) – two kinds of text that Munday busied himself with in the 1580s. There is also a passing reference in another text by Greene, *A Looking Glasse*, to a ballad written by 'an English Roman', whom Baldwin claims was likely to be Munday.[56] In *Farewell to Follie* Greene's antagonist is accused of hypocrisy and dissembling, whereas Greene himself, he emphasises, 'cannot Martinize ... or protest an open resolution of good, when I intend to be privately ill'.[57] Munday, as was well known, had had a role to play in the recent Marprelate controversy, one which brought him renewed notoriety. Greene's onslaught has been much trawled for topical referents, but, like the authorship of *Fair Em*, his target here is uncertain; nevertheless, this work adds to the sense of the 'carping' literary environment about which Munday complains. Even John Webster, whose literary standing today puts him firmly outside of the 'citizen dramatist' category inhabited by the likes of Munday, was famously called 'the playwright, cartwright' by one of his contemporaries because of his father's trade of coachmaker.[58] Unlike those other writers I have just discussed, however, Webster's own sense of literary equivalence with his much-maligned contemporary was such that he wrote a commendatory verse to Munday, his 'kinde friend', in *Palmerin of England* (1602).

Thomas Middleton is another of the pageanters-cum-playwrights who was not averse to pointing out what he regarded as others' deficiencies. It is widely believed that Middleton's pageants contained jibes directed at Munday, although, as the former was a Draper himself, naturally not on the grounds of Munday's 'trade'.[59] Middleton himself was criticised by George Chapman in much the same terms as Nashe censured Munday, as a 'true ignorant' and 'a poor chronicler'.[60] In his 1613 Lord Mayor's Show for the Grocers, *The Triumphs of Truth*, Middleton (demonstrating little gratitude for the assistance of his sometime collaborator despite the fact that he himself was then a novice at pageant writing) claims on the title page that he had had to improve on the original text and that his own version had 'directed, written, and redeem'd into form' the flaws in its predecessor.[61] This was at least the second time in his literary career that Middleton had cause to collaborate with Munday, the older and more experienced of the two, for their paths had crossed at the Fortune over a decade previously when they co-wrote *Caesar's Fall*. Later in his 1613 Show Middleton refers to another pageant-maker as an 'impudent common writer' for whom he feels 'much pity and sorrow', and he goes on to compare the magnificence of the mayoralty, 'so glorious a fire in bounty and goodnesse', to 'freezing art, sitting in darkness with the candle out, looking like the picture of Blacke Monday'. The phrase 'Blacke Monday' has lead many commentators (including Richard Dutton and, initially, Bergeron) to believe that Munday is the target of Middleton's abuse.[62] More recently, however, Bergeron has revisited this critical convention and is now not so certain that Munday was indeed Middleton's antagonist. There is evidence both for and against a mutual antipathy between the two pageanters. Towards the end of *The Triumphs of Truth*, as many have noted, the first acknowledgement of the role of Middleton's collaborators appears: these are Humphrey Nichols, 'a man excellent in his art' (fireworks), John Grinkin, the artificer, the 'beauties of [whose] workmanship [were] most artfully and faithfully performed', and Anthony Munday, who 'furnished [the show] with apparel and porters'. Middleton's account of Munday's contribution is devoid of the praiseworthy adjectives that the former confers on Nichols and Grinkin. The sole concession to his erstwhile rival's dignity that Middleton makes is to call him 'Gentleman'.[63]

Middleton's criticism of Munday in *The Triumphs of Truth* (if such it is) focuses on two aspects of his rival's productions – their artistic deficiencies and a stinginess in their execution (*The Triumphs of Truth* cost around £1,300, a great deal more than the £700 that was the average). As far as the second accusation is concerned, Munday was indeed castigated on occasion for cutting corners in expenditure (such as re-using 'old and borrowed' clothing in *Camp-bell*, his 1609 pageant), with the risk of endangering the prestige of the Mayor and his company, although Munday's later Show *Chruso-thriambos* was a particularly lavish affair.[64] It should also be borne in mind, as Janelle Jenstad has shown, that even the wealthiest livery companies experienced difficulties in getting their members to contribute towards the expenses of a civic triumph.[65] Middleton revived his attack on his contemporaries in the same kind of terms in his 1619 Show *The Triumphes of Love and Antiquity*, where he launches a critique of other shows 'wherein Art hath been but weakly imitated and most beggarly worded'.⁶⁶ For the 1617 Lord Mayor's Show, Munday and Dekker, old collaborators, both competed unsuccessfully with Middleton for the contract to write the pageant. Munday received five pounds for his thwarted 'project', and Dekker likewise four pounds.⁶⁷ In the dedication to the 1618 pageant *Sidero-Thriambos*, Munday does refer cryptically to his production being presented 'in the despight of envy, and calumnious imputations', indicating that he had once again received some criticism, which might have emanated from Middleton.⁶⁸

Whether these incidents reveal an extensive history of hostility between the pair or merely rhetorical denunciations resulting from their professional rivalry, all this had to be put aside in 1621, when Munday's name appears alongside Middleton's in the Drapers' records in respect of *The Sun in Aries* (although the relative roles of the collaborators are uncertain), and then again in 1623, when they collaborated once again on behalf of the Drapers on what was to be Munday's final pageant. For the latter event Munday wrote the water-borne show, contributing his by-now ubiquitous 'argoe', and Middleton was responsible for the part that took place in the streets.⁶⁹ Middleton's pamphlet version of his part of the show, *The Triumphs of Integrity*, is very terse about Munday's contribution and refers only in passing to 'some service upon the water', not mentioning the Argo or its mythical argonauts at all; indeed, Robert Withington suggests that the intention might have been to replace Munday's Argo with Middleton's 'Imperial Canopy'.⁷⁰ However, it is a little unclear whether the 'canopy' that Middleton mentions is the same property as Munday's 'argoe'. Bergeron appears to think so, in contrast to Withington, and he thus interprets Middleton's description of 'a proper and significant masterpiece of triumph called the Imperial Canopy' rather as praise for the achievements of Munday's water pageant.⁷¹ The evidence is ambiguous, for Middleton does write specifically of a triumph '*called* the Imperial Canopy' (my emphasis), indicating its formal title, whereas Munday calls his creation 'a beautifull and curious Argoe', using the motif of the argonauts' search for the golden fleece throughout the work.⁷² In an echo of Middleton's reluctance to compliment his role in *The Triumphes of Truth*, Munday does not acknowledge Middleton's contribution of the land-based show, crediting only Richard Simpson and Nicholas Sotherne.⁷³ Nevertheless, despite his apparent disparagement of Munday, Middleton did collaborate with him again over the next decade; indeed, since Munday was 'keeper of the properties' Middleton and the other pageant-makers would have been compelled to have dealings with him whether they liked it or not.⁷⁴ Munday's output in respect of civic entertainments was unparalleled and on a different scale to most of his contemporaries. Bergeron has commented of Munday's role in the Lord Mayors' Shows that 'the pageant writer [was] ... much more than just the deviser of the entertainment, certainly in Munday's case ... [as he] in many ways resembles a theatrical producer'.⁷⁵

Modern critics sometimes seek to construct differences between Munday and the other pageant-makers of the Jacobean City on the basis of their work rather than supposed personal animosities. Sergei Lobanov-Rostovsky identifies the 'formal innovations' that Middleton and Dekker brought to the conventional pageants as emanating from 'the dramatic structure and thematic unity of the private theatres'.⁷⁶ By stipulating private theatres such as the Blackfriars and the Cockpit, however, he excludes from consideration the work that both writers undertook at the so-called 'public' playhouse, the Fortune, alongside Munday.⁷⁷ His intention, it seems, is to create a division between Munday and these more highly regarded playwrights even where no such clear-cut distinction existed at the time. In particular, he describes Munday's characteristic approach to pageant-making as creating 'emblematic tableaux' rather than proto-theatrical, character- and dialogue-driven entertainments, which I think does a disservice to the quite complex dramatic structure in *Chrysanaleia*, for example, where Munday uses the role of Walworth to present a historical perspective that is not simply linear and static but which also involves the mayor himself in a metadramatic fashion. It is also somewhat counter-intuitive to believe that Munday would have discarded all he had learnt in his many years of playwrighting when he came to produce civic shows.⁷⁸ 'Emblematic tableaux' perhaps offer a faithful account of most of the spectators' experience of the entertainment, since only those who followed the procession from start to finish (the Lord Mayor himself and other chief dignitaries) were able to see the Show in its entirety; for most onlookers, the Show was witnessed in a fragmented form.⁷⁹ Working from within an argument misinformed by the assumption that the City livery companies were implacably opposed to all that the commercial theatre stood for (an assumption I will explore further in the next chapter), Lobanov-Rostovsky suggests that Middleton and Dekker's overly theatrical 'reforms' to the pageants were received with 'unease' by the companies because they implicitly turned the Lord Mayor into 'an actor'.⁸⁰ As Jenstad has shown in respect of the Goldsmiths' Company, the livery companies' rituals all had a theatrical dimension.[81] Civic pageantry can therefore be seen as part of a continuum of London life rather than an anomaly needing to be apologised for. The civic attitude of disapproval towards the theatre that Lobanov-Rostovsky presumes to exist might be exemplified by Munday's antitheatrical voice in *A second and third blast*, where he claims that 'none delight in those spectacles, but such as would be made spectacles'.[82] However, Munday's text cannot entirely be trusted and the Lord Mayors' Shows in themselves demonstrate that the City was not disinclined to use theatrical modes on occasion.

Regardless of the negative views of some other writers, Munday's labours were consistently appreciated by the civic bodies with which he came into contact during his career. He was rewarded by the City generously on occasion. On the recommendation of Lord Viscount Mandeville, the Lord President of the Privy Council, in 1623 Munday received the apparently extremely profitable right from the Corporation to nominate one freeman of the City by redemption per annum (i.e. by purchasing the freedom).[83] The Drapers' historian A. H. Johnson claims that Munday earned 'as much as £600 per year from the fees he charged', which is a vast and unlikely sum.[84] It is more likely that Munday gained a regular income from this benefit which served him as a kind of pension, although it certainly did not inhibit him from soliciting various livery companies for further sums in his later years. He himself dated his work for the City back as early as 1592. In the dedication to John King, the Bishop of London, in his 1618 edition of the *Survay* Munday claimed that he had spent 'sixe and twenty yeeres, in sundrie imployment for the Cities service'.[85] In fact, if one includes the Corporation's sponsorship of *A second and third blast* of 1580, Munday can be seen to have served the City for even longer.

The City Companies in turn repaid Munday's attentions. He received 'a gratuitie of vj^{li} xiij^s iiij^d ... in respect of his paynes taken about the compileing of a booke intituled a breife chronicle of the successons of tymes' from the Court of Goldsmiths after the publication of *A Briefe Chronicle of the Successe of Time* in 1611.[86] The Goldsmiths, it would appear, especially appreciated his efforts on their behalf, for 'it is conceaved', the entry continues, 'he hathe remembred the Worshipp and antiquity of the Companye'. Their gratitude was such that the Goldsmiths presented Munday with an even more lavish gratuity than the Merchant Taylors, who offered him a 'reward' of 'fyve pounds ... towarde his paines, and travell'.[87] Given that the text subjugates the whole history of time, 'from the creation of the world', as its title has it, to its final culmination in London's civic administration, one can understand why Munday might receive such generous recompense from the City. Indeed, Munday's chronicle is expressly intended to redress the omissions in previous historical works where, he writes, important matters of London history 'have not ... heeretofore bin remembered, or at the least, not plainly revealed'.[88] It may not, then, be a coincidence that Munday was employed the following autumn to write *Chruso-thriambos*, the mayoral pageant for a Goldsmith, James Pemberton, which might be regarded as a further demonstration of that company's gratitude for his 'paynes'. Equally, his gift of a copy of this historical work may well have been not entirely disinterested but rather an attempt to secure the commission for that year's Lord Mayor's Show. Jenstad has commented that, by writing epistles in the *Briefe Chronicle* to both the Merchant Taylors and the Goldsmiths, Munday was at that point rightly 'guessing that employment [for the Lord Mayor's Show] in 1611 could come from either company'.[89]

Munday himself, as one might expect, denies that his motives for the *Briefe Chronicle*'s dual dedication were in any way self-interested: 'I have done nothing heerein either for flatterie or vaineglorie, or in expectation of mercinarie recompence', he protests.[90] Alluding to the fact that he addresses two companies at the same time, he stresses that the second dedication to the Goldsmiths is presented 'without prejudice to any other Misterie whatsoever'.[91] Regardless of these disclaimers, however, he does remind the Merchant Taylors, the recipients of the first epistle, that the text stands as 'a promise of my uttermost imployment, in these, or any other endevours'.[92] If he was hedging his bets, the strategy paid off, for that year's Lord Mayor's Show was his commission. Unfortunately for Munday, as we will see, his knowledge of the 'antiquity' of the Goldsmiths as displayed in both the *Briefe Chronicle* and the Goldsmiths' pageant was to cause him major embarrassment in 1614. In 1617 his efforts in the *Briefe Chronicle* were once again recognised, this time by the less important Skinners' Company, whose gratuity was a more modest twenty-two shillings.[93] Munday was to haunt Goldsmiths' Hall again in late 1617 and early 1618 in search of 'further recompense', this time for his first edition of the *Survay*: he appeared before the Company Court three times to plead his case before finally receiving 'in gratuitye ... for his Booke of the Survey of London, a 22^s peice'.[94] The Fishmongers' Court records from 1616 indicate too that Munday was prepared to haggle over his fee for a pageant:

> Monday, did exhibitt his petition, to have some gratification gyven him or CC books of the late shewes and speeches at the presentment of the Lord Maior ... for which he seith he doth deserve to have x^{li} in recompence. And upon consideration had of the particulers of his bill, it is agreed that he shall have v^{li} xv^{s} gyven unto him, which he is content thankfully to accept in full satisfaction of all his demaunds.[95]

Even after Munday's death his widow Gillian and her daughter Susan were still receiving 'charitie' from various civic companies in respect of the 1633 edition of the *Survey*. Here, as elsewhere, Munday's history parallels that of Middleton, whose wife also petitioned the Corporation for money after his death.[96]

'A SORT OF FAWNING SYCOPHANT': MUNDAY AND HIS PATRONS

Munday was to hawk his texts around in search of patronage and reward throughout his career.[97] Unsurprisingly, his lifelong concern manifests itself in a number of his works. There is, for instance, a comment on the neediness of those who seek patronage in *The Downfall of Robert, Earle of Huntington*. Lord Fitzwater says to Prince John:

> I beseech you sir accept my love;
> Commaund mee, use mee, O you are too blame,
> That doe neglect my everlasting zeale ...
> A shame upon this peevish Apish age,
> These crouching hypocrite dissembling times.
> Well, well, God rid the Patrones of these crimes.[98]

The others present in this scene sound baffled by Fitzwater's *cri de coeur*: 'My Lord Fitzwater is inspir'd I thinke', comments Salisbury, prompting the would-be patron's harsh response 'I [ay], with some divell: let the olde foole dote'.[99] Prince John's traditionally bad character is in fact exemplified in the play by his rejection of honest Lord Fitzwater's offer of service. This passing moment recalls Munday's hyperbolic plea to the Fishmongers' Company at the beginning of *Chrysanaleia* where he asks them for 'the Patronage and protection of this Orphan childe, begotten in your service, bredde up hitherto by your favour and kinde cherishing, and not despayring to dye, through your want of regard'.[100]

'Mathew Wighthand', one of the writers of the commendatory verses to Munday in *The Mirrour of Mutabilitie*, openly exposes

Munday's need for regular patronage, although he disguises it as the desire for 'good report':

> Then let my friend obtaine your good report,
> Since for his paynes he craves no other hire:
> His hope is good, that of the friendly sort,
> He shall receive that which he dooth require.
> I leave you heere to judge and say the best:
> So Munday shall obtayne his due behest.[101]

Munday himself, however, in one of the commendatory verses actually addressed to his patron, raises the possibility that his motives might be more self-interested than honourable. He claims that the truth of his writing reflects the selflessness of his praise of his master, who should know 'no fables I expresse, as though I should encroache for private gayne'.[102] Despite this denial he goes on to suggest that some may not credit his motives with such sanctity, and leaves it to his patron to determine his real 'intent': 'Or once can say, he deales with flatterye: / Forging his tales to please the fantasye. / Of mine intent your Honnor judge I crave'.[103] In another text dedicated to Oxford Munday undercuts the patron/writer relationship in a similar fashion: 'I play the Parasite with mine owne mouth to extoll my selfe', one of the characters in *Zelauto* concedes.[104]

Munday's own patrons were of necessity diverse. Like many of his contemporaries, in his early days he often resorted to aristocratic circles for support. Edward de Vere, the Earl of Oxford, the dedicatee of the verse I have just cited, was Munday's patron from c.1577 to the early 1580s: Munday dedicated the now lost *Galien of Fraunce* to him, as well as the *Mirrour of Mutabilitie* and *Zelauto*, published the following year. The title page of *Zelauto* calls its author 'A. M. Servaunt to the Right Honourable the Earle of Oxenford' and reproduces Oxford's motto and coat of arms opposite the title page. The relationship was made explicit, for in the dedication de Vere is described as Munday's 'singuler good Lord and Maister' and Munday as his 'moste dutifull servaunt'. Munday was probably attached to Oxford's household in some secretarial kind of role as was John Lyly at the same time, and he also dedicated another 1580 text, *A View of Sundry Examples*, to some members of Oxford's household.[105] After a break of a few years, following the lifting of Oxford's temporary disgrace brought about in 1581 by suspicion of Catholicism, Munday dedicated part one of *Palmerin d'Oliva* as a new year gift to Oxford in 1588.[106] Munday actually alludes to this hiatus by addressing his patron as 'right noble

Lord, and sometime my honorable Maister', writing that he himself had 'once [been] so happy as to serve a Maister so noble' but was now Oxford's 'late servaunt'.[107] Given Munday's own personal problems over accusations of Catholic sympathies and the very public debate about his religious standing in a number of pamphlets published in the early 1580s, his decision to cease dedicating to Oxford for some years is entirely understandable. Even in 1579 Munday addressed his patron with caution, for the dedication to *A Mirrour*, his patron's probable Catholic sympathies notwithstanding, negotiates Munday's recent trip to Rome with an eye to highlighting the author's own religious orthodoxy. Here Munday represents the Catholics he encountered on the continent as being 'Idolaters [and] Woorshipers of stocks and stones'; he, of course, protected by both Protestantism and patriotism, saw through their 'Sathanicall illusions' and 'politique devises'.[108] He also reiterates the claim made in other texts produced at around the same time, such as *The English Romayne lyfe*, that his motives for travelling via France to Rome were quite innocent: 'I had enterprised this journey for my pleasure', he states, 'and in hope to attaine to some knowledge in the French tung.'[109]

Despite Munday's protestations, Turner Wright speculates (quite plausibly, given the context) that in *Zelauto*'s dedication he alludes in coded form to his predicament as a 'servant' of a disgraced master and points to his on-going service to the Crown to redeem his reputation. Munday writes that 'the puissantest Prince [i.e. the Queen] is not voyde of enemies, the gallantest Champion [i.e. Oxford] free from foes, and the most honest liver [i.e Munday himself] without some back-biters'.[110] In the body of the work too there is a fictional reiteration of Munday's attitude towards his actual patron in a reference to an unnamed 'noble Lord in the English Court', whose 'magnaminitie of minde, and valure of courage' impressed Zelauto to such an extent that he 'wrote a few [verses] ... in prayse of that noble Lord, to whome [he was] bound for his singuler bounty'.[111] Hamilton takes this reading of *Zelauto* further to claim that this text 'stands out as the work where Munday's projection of a Catholic identity is both most obvious and most dangerously present'.[112] There certainly was some dubiety about Munday's religion in the 1580s, but Hamilton's view that a number of Munday's texts contained coded expressions of sympathy for the old faith does not account for the full range of his works, nor for the provenance of many of them. She neglects to mention, for instance, that Munday's translation of two of Calvin's 'godly and learned' sermons was dedicated in 1584 to the Earl of Leicester, hardly a crypto-Catholic; indeed, Parry has stated that 'support of Calvinistical Protestantism was a high priority for Leicester'.[113] There are also other religious translations that belie such a view, such as *A breefe Treatise of the vertue of the Crosse* (of which more below), which was in fact a French *refutation* of a work by Francis de Sales.

Munday's interest in matters Italian in the early to mid 1580s might have been fuelled by his controversial visit to Rome in 1578/9. As we have seen, he discusses the journey in the dedication of *The Mirrour*, and it recurs in other texts of the same period. Stillinger states that it is 'highly relevant' to *Zelauto*, at least, and it is certainly possible to see an analogue for some of the episodes in *The English Romayne lyfe* in this near-contemporary fictional work.[114] For instance, Zelauto is asked by his disputant, Astroepho, towards the beginning of the book 'have you ben a Traveiler syr?', and then is requested to tell the story of his 'adventures' overseas.[115] Zelauto consequently discloses that he set off from home with a young companion and that they were on their way to Italy when set upon and robbed by 'certaine Outlawes', which was exactly what happened to Munday and his fellow traveller Thomas Nowell in 1578.[116] In the supposedly autobiographical work, however, the hero, Munday himself, is English and visits Italy rather than vice versa. In another, properly Protestant inversion of the 'true' narrative Munday relates in *The Englishe Romayne lyfe*, Zelauto's companion is 'so farre in love with [England]' that he could not be prevailed upon to leave (Nowell, Munday's associate in the other text, converted to Catholicism and remained in Italy).[117]

As his return to Oxford after his fall from grace suggests, Munday was generally careful with his patrons: *Palladine of England*, for instance, was dedicated to Essex in 1588, while the Earl was still in high favour. That Essex was, in Moore's words, 'primarily associated with chivalry through his skill in the tiltyard' serves to make Munday's choice of recipient for a text that describes 'Knightly deedes of Armes and Chivalrie' all the more appropriate.[118] The City Corporation was a more stable environment than the court, so the important civic sponsors that Munday increasingly gravitated towards would have been less prone to vicissitudes of fortune than high-profile courtiers such as Oxford or Essex. Thus by 1602, as we will see further below, Munday was so much oriented towards the City that he dedicated part three of *Palmerin of England*, a text 'enterlaced with the loves and fortunes of many gallant Knights and Ladies' which in the

1580s or 1590s he might have offered to some aristocrat, to John Swynnerton, alderman of London. Another motive, of course, for his many and various dedications was that they would have been a source of income for a professional writer like Munday. However, as well as multiplying his possible avenues for patronage, Munday's numerous roles could sometimes conflict with one another and as a consequence have an effect upon his literary output. For instance, in the introductory epistle to part two of *Gerileon of England* (1592) Munday ascribes the delay in publishing his text to other demands on his time which resulted from his court employments. His comment here might serve as much as a boast of his importance to the monarch as a complaint about obstacles to his writing: 'since my first entring on this Historie', he tells his dedicatees, 'I have been divers and sundrie times countermanded by her Majesties appointment, in the place where I serve, to post from place to place on such affaires as were enjoyned mee'.[119] *Gerileon* was dedicated to Ralph and Frances Marshall of Nottinghamshire, who had obviously offered the writer some patronage during its composition, for Munday reminds the couple in his dedication of their connection, stating that 'at your owne house I wrote a sheete or two, and elsewhere in your companie'.[120] Munday, true to form, was soon (as a subordinate of Richard Topcliffe) to betray their support by arresting Mr Marshall for recusancy.[121]

Munday's dedications show a clear orientation towards the City from well before the time of his numerous Jacobean civic shows. His early play *Fedele and Fortunio*, published in 1585, was dedicated to John Heardson, who was a wealthy member of the Skinners' Company. Heardson's older brother Thomas was a Warden of the Drapers, and Richard Hosley has speculated that it might have been through Thomas Heardson that Munday had a connection with the play's dedicatee.[122] It can hardly be a coincidence that the dedication in Munday's pamphlet *A Watch-woord to Englande*, published only a year before in 1584, was to another important member of the Drapers, the Lord Mayor, Thomas Pullison.[123] Munday was made free of the Drapers in the same year that *Fedele and Fortunio* was published, so dedicating to a brother of a Warden of his own livery company at this point in his life makes perfect sense for a young man trying to establish himself. *A Watch-woord*, however, was also dedicated to the Queen, from whom, unlike Heardson and Pullison, Munday would have been unlikely to have received any direct reward.[124] Munday may here have been hedging his bets, for this text appeared only a couple of years after the Campion *et al.* debâcle when his allegiance to the state came under some scrutiny. The subject matter of this pamphlet is certainly closer to national than civic matters.

From the turn of the seventeenth century onwards Munday directed himself more and more towards the City and its dignitaries. Such is the complex nature of his network of activities and associates, however, that 1599/1600 was also the year in which he and his usual collaborators (Chettle, Dekker, Drayton, Hathaway, Wilson, Haughton and Day) were entirely predominant as writers for the Admiral's Men in their last year at the Rose (more of which below).[125] If Munday's literary allegiances were on the turn at this point, they were so at a moment, ironically, when the stage was offering him consistent employment. Munday himself, we should recall, stated that his work for the City stretched at least as far back as the early 1590s. There are a number of transitional texts which demonstrate Munday trying to establish himself in a new domain. In *A breefe Treatise of the vertue of the Crosse*, a translation which was dedicated in 1599 to Sir Stephen Soame, the current Lord Mayor, and his wife, Munday alludes to 'some favours' he had previously received from Soame, which had encouraged him to present the current text to him, as a 'little remembrance' for the 'extraordinarie gentlenesse' the Soames family had shown him.[126] The immediate pretext for Munday's no doubt rather presumptuous dedication is also provided, in case Munday's gratitude for the 'favours' received seems to be inadequate cause. He tells how he had heard a Good Friday sermon at Paul's Cross delivered before the Mayor and Aldermen, the argument of which reminded Munday of the current text which he then rapidly translated and offered up to the Mayor. He concludes with a wish that 'the true sinceritie of [his] affection' might be recognised and accepted, reminding the Soames that he would 'remaine alwaies yours for any further imployment, be it even to the uttermost of all my endevours'.[127]

The word 'further' here is an obvious cue for future preferment, and indeed, a couple of years later Munday was once more seeking advancement via Stephen Soame and other civic dignitaries. Within a short period of time he would have established himself sufficiently with the City government to be involved in his first Lord Mayor's Show. At this turning point in Munday's fortunes and allegiances he deliberately targeted powerful civic patrons. *The strangest adventure that ever happened*, a 1601 translated account of the curious history of the recently deceased Dom Sebastian, the King of Portugal, was dedicated to the Mayor, William Rider, and 'all the rest of the worshipfull Senatours and Aldermen'. The story of King Sebastian evidently had some currency, for in the same year Chettle and Dekker wrote a play called *King Sebastian of Portugal* for the Admiral's Men at the Fortune.[128] This coincidence illustrates the chameleon-like diversity of Munday's output and his attempts at this juncture to represent himself as not solely a dramatist: his erstwhile colleagues wrote a play whereas Munday, although working concurrently for the Admiral's Men, presented a prose work on the same topic to civic dignitaries. In his dedication Munday mentions two aldermen – Sir Stephen Soame and John Garrarde (who became Mayor the following year) – 'particularly by name, as bound by some favours', suggesting some previous as well as hoped-for future patronage. He also singles out two sheriffs, Thomas Campbell and William Craven, who were to become mayors in 1609/10 and 1610/11 respectively and for both of whom, as it happens, Munday was to contribute to the mayoral shows.[129] He wrote a now only partly extant pageant, *Camp-bell or the Ironmongers Faire Field*, to celebrate Campbell's mayoralty in 1609.[130] Munday takes care to emphasise his general availability for the services of worthies such as these and ends his dedication to Rider and the others with the broad hint 'so shal I rest yours in anie greater employment, and remaine readie at all times with my verie uttermost service'.[131]

The tenor of this dedication leads me to believe that it was unsolicited, for, as in the 1599 text dedicated to Soame, Munday twice asks to be excused for his 'boldness' in addressing the text to Rider *et al.* and he once again emphasises his versatility for future employment. As is often the case in his works, he also takes some pains to curtail any offence his translation might cause, mentioning that the Portuguese King's story 'ha[d] bene seene before, and sufficiently authorised'.[132] His concern perhaps derived from the present text's origin in a 'discourse' written by a famous Portuguese friar, which put him in the same position of relying on a suspect religious source as had his 1587 work, *The True Image of Christian Love* (discussed above).[133] Some twenty years earlier in 1582, at the outset of his career as a pursuivant and while still under some suspicion for his religious sympathies, Munday had tried (successfully here, too) to ingratiate himself with another powerful figurehead, Francis Walsingham.[134] Indeed, at this time of considerable alarm over Counter-Reformation Catholicism, Munday dedicated primarily to influential Protestant figures such as the Earl of Leicester, Francis Walsingham and Richard

Martin.¹³⁵ Once the immediacy of the perceived threat from the continent had diminished, however, Munday began to try to exploit a more varied range of patronage, chiefly in the civic arena. For instance, William Craven received a very lengthy and obsequious dedication from Munday in *A Briefe Chronicle, of the Successe of Time*, in which Munday indulged in his habitual self-denigration. Bemoaning his many insufficiencies, he writes: 'I know right well and such as know me, have heard me daily confesse it, that I (of infinite others) was the most unmeetest to undergoe such a serious businesse [as writing this history], which required, if not the best able, yet those that therein are much better scene [seen] than myselfe'.¹³⁶ As usual, Munday had chosen his dedicatee with prudence: as well as being at that point the Lord Mayor, Craven was one of the richest Merchant Taylors in Jacobean London. Robert Ashton states that Craven was 'at his death in 1618 ... reported to be worth half a million', and amongst his debtors was the second Earl of Essex.¹³⁷

By the early years of the seventeenth century Munday's civic turn was well under way. Those texts he produced in 1602 serve as an indicator of his transition from being chiefly an itinerant playwright and general polemicist, ready to write in favour of a variety of different agendas, to becoming an established civic writer. His employment as a pageant-writer for the City dates at least to 1602, which suggests that he moved from theatre to Guildhall without a break, or maybe even with some overlap as Pafford suggests that Munday 'was a regular candidate [as a pageant-maker] from about 1600 to about 1625'.¹³⁸ Part three of *Palmerin of England* was dedicated in 1602 to John Swynnerton, a very wealthy and well-travelled Merchant Taylor. This text was the last part of a work of which part one was originally registered back in 1581, and the 1602 edition included verses by Dekker, Webster and Anthony Gybson. That Munday was able in this text to call on at least two contemporaries who were also part of the civic literary scene further indicates how far he had moved away from aristocratic circles by this date. Swynnerton, who is mentioned in Munday's 1611 *Chruso-thriambos* as one of 'three most worthy Gentlemen', was also the dedicatee of two translations by Munday of devotional works, *The Heaven of the Mynde, or The Myndes Heaven, A moste excellent, learned and religious Treatise* (a translation from Italian which exists today only as a manuscript dedicatory copy) and *The True knowledge of a mans owne selfe*, a treatise against atheism.¹³⁹ Both of these texts were also written in 1602, so Munday dedicated at least three times to this powerful Cripplegate man in the first year of his aldermanry.[140] This regular patronage from Swynnerton might stand as more evidence for Munday's (at least part) authorship of Robert Lee's mayoral Show in that year, for Lee, like Swynnerton, was a Merchant Taylor, and the latter accompanied the new mayor in the Show.[141] The year 1602 has further significance for understanding Munday's relations with various civic bodies since, as we have seen, it was the year in which he took out a lease from the City Corporation for a property in Cripplegate.

The True knowledge of a mans owne selfe refers explicitly to Munday's expectation of 'kinde patronage' from Swynnerton and his wife, which strikes an opportunistic note in the context of the otherwise effusive dedication. Here Munday, having offered the pair a lengthy and somewhat tortuous theological lesson despite his express claim 'I am loth to be troublesome by tediousness to your Worship', signs off by 'prostra[ting]' himself to their 'gentle interpretation', wishing them both and any 'hopefull issue' 'all those hapepie blessings that this worlde can or may affoord, & after the finishing of this frail terrestriall pilgrimage, a full measure of eternall tranquillitie in the land of the living'.[142] The lavishness of his address to Swynnerton might in part have been prompted by some problems Munday had experienced in bringing this text to its patron, the delay for which he apologises. He is not very explicit about these hindrances, but does say that 'the troubles of the time, & misinterpretation of the worke by some in authoritie' had delayed its publication.[143] This 'misinterpretation' demonstrates that Munday's religious texts were still causing official disquiet even twenty years after his direct involvement in religious politics. From the undifferentiated 'Reader' Munday can have had no such expectations of patronage, let alone protection from official disapproval, and he is therefore content to receive as 'a good turne' merely 'kindnes at the least, which ... is all we [i.e. Munday and the original French author] desire, and in trueth no lesse then wee have well deserved'.[144] However, despite Munday's attentions towards Swynnerton and his family he was not commissioned to write the latter's mayoral Show in 1612.[145] That honour went to Dekker, who probably got the lucrative commission because he too was a Merchant Taylor, unlike Munday or Middleton, either of whom might in 1612 have been regarded as likely candidates.

Munday did not address his texts solely to individual civic dignitaries. *A True and admirable Historie, of a Mayden of Consolens*, a translation of a French text by François Citois about a girl who reportedly lived for three years without food or drink, was published in 1603 and again in 1604 (with a commendatory poem by Dekker to its translator, 'his good friend'): it was dedicated to 'the Worshipfull, M. Thomas Thorney, Maister. M. William Martin, M. Edward Rodes, and M. Thomas Martin', the 'Governours' of the livery company of Barber Surgeons. Munday writes that he regards them as appropriate recipients for this text on the grounds that they are 'men of a misterious profession, exceeding good Anatomists, and skilfull searchers into our bodies whole faculties'.[146] Having established their scientific credentials, Munday then further justifies his choice of dedicatee:

> I could not be-thinke me, to bestowe my paines any where more desertfullie, then on such as are answerable to the first Authours qualitie: which neither I would not over-boldly presume to doo, till (by a kinde examen) of some of your selves, the worke was thought worthie your entertayning.[147]

Prompting his learned audience to remember that authors like himself cannot, unfortunately, live by science alone, he goes on to make the unambiguous plea that the work 'hath cost me good paines, and therefore may merit the kinder acceptaunce'. Inevitably, the dedication ends with a reminder of its author's perpetual availability for other work: 'I remaine yours in any more serious imployment', he suggests to his patrons.[148]

As well as the immediate personal concerns of its translator, *A True and admirable Historie* emphasises the patriotic, if not nationalistic, connotations of the work of translation *per se*.[149] Munday's dedication, for example, begins with the statement that 'things ... of never so much credit .. in other countries, beeing not bred or borne in our owne, doo surmount all compasse of beleefe'.[150] His rendering of this 'wonder' into English consequently bestows upon it a credibility its continental provenance might otherwise have denied it. The preface to the Reader puts the point of translation across very prosaically: Munday's intention, he tells the readers, is 'to let [them] have the same [history] in [their] owne familiare language'; thus even the two sonnets with which the work proper begins are 'Englished' for his domestic readership.[151] Dekker's commendatory verse reiterates the point and praises the 'magick' that Munday's translation has worked on this French maiden's narrative: 'Last day she spake no language but her owne, / Yet now shee's understood by Englishmen'.[152] Unlike his address to the esteemed scientists of the Barber Surgeons, however, upon whose knowledge Munday can rely for objectivity and whom he regards as having less 'queazie stomacks' than others, the reader is given many and various assurances of the truth of this incredible story to counteract 'all occasions of sinister suspition'.[153] 'Many worthie, grave and credible persons, such, whose truth can no way bee excepted against', along with physicians sent by 'his Majesties commaundement' are marshalled to counter any scepticism.[154] The authority of Munday's English version of the 'mayden''s history is given further strength by the fact that the text also proclaims on its title page that it was 'published by the Kings especiall Priviledge'. This is perhaps because King James had taken a particular interest in the girl's plight; he had apparently visited her in person and sent 'his best and chiefest Phisitians' to test the truth of her story. Indeed, the full title of this work accentuates the royal dimension:

> A True and admirable Historie, of a Mayden of Consolens, in the Province of Poictiers: that for the space of three yeeres and more hath lived, and yet doth, without receiving either meate or drinke. Of whom, his Majestie in person hath had the view, and, (by his commaund) his best and chiefest Phisitians, have tried all meanes, to find, whether this fast & abstinence be by deceit or no.

Munday was probably right to stress the authorised nature of this translation, for, as we have already seen, some of the texts he chose to translate had dubious provenance. The nervousness he often evinces might have been compounded by the fact that a number of his translations were printed by the highly controversial John Wolfe.[155] As an ex-printer's apprentice Munday would have been particularly aware of issues of licensing and the control of print. Munday was also responsible for two Wolfe editions of *The Coppie of the Anti-Spaniard*, an anti-Spanish and anti-Catholic text of 1589/90 which was subtitled, rather worryingly, 'made at Paris by a French man, a Catholique'.[156]

Munday's orientation towards the City was apparent not only in his choice of patrons. Even where the scene of his text was not London he often found a way of introducing a civic element. In *Zelauto*, for instance, the eponymous hero is keen to visit England because of meeting in Italy 'certayne English Merchauntes' whose account of their country impresses him greatly: Zelauto remarks 'of long time I had heard great commendation thereof'.[157] Turner Wright has noted that in *Zelauto* 'though the scene is Verona, the persons involved are like prosperous members of the London shopkeeper class'.[158] Zelauto and his new merchant friends make their way directly 'into the so famous bruted Realme of England' and thence to London, 'their cheefe Cittie', where their first port of call is naturally that emblem of mercantile London, 'their Bursse, where aboove were so many fine Shops full of brave devises'.[159] Given the future career of his author it is interesting to note that Zelauto praises a pageant put on for the Queen, and is particularly struck by its 'straunge devises', including 'a brave and comely Shippe ... [that] ran upon a Rock'.[160] The author himself evidently shared Zelauto's admiration of the ship, for the original text features a woodcut of 'an armed ship' complete with a descriptive verse.[161] Over forty years later, at the end of Munday's time as the City's chief pageant-writer, he invented another ship, 'a beatifull and curious Argoe', to perform in *The Triumphes of the Golden Fleece*.[162] Never one to waste his literary energies, Munday here re-used the 'Argoe' that first appeared in the 1615 pageant for the Drapers, *Metropolis Coronata*, and then again in the 1616 *Chrysanaleia*, where it is called 'a very goodly and beautifull fishing Busse, called, the Fishmongers Esperanza, or Hope of London'.[163]

Although *Zelauto* was written while the young Munday still appeared to be more interested in improving his prospects via court and governmental rather than civic connections, the text still associates London first and foremost as a city of trade; as such it cites London as one of the aspects of England that most excites admiration in the visitor. It does so, however, with an uneasy ambivalence. In this respect, my reading of *Zelauto* differs somewhat from Scanlon's; he asserts that *Zelauto* is not about 'the importance of London [but rather] ... a court encomium'.[164] My view is that, as in other early works by Munday, this text tries to orient itself in both directions at once. For this reason, Zelauto's benefactor Astroepho's assertion that money brings 'discencion among the commons, [and] discorde among freendes' strikes a sententious note which does not sit well with the previously positive attitude to English merchants. Bringing to mind another of Munday's 1580 voices, this time the one he utilised in *A second and third blast*, Astroepho (ostensibly the moral voice of the text) goes on to paint a highly unflattering picture of city life. He tells Zelauto: 'if in your carefull Citties, you as lyttle regarded, your coyne as I you should not have so much extorcion, so much brybing to Officers, so much wrangling and jarring among the common sort, so much encroching one upon another'. Indeed, the marginal note makes the urban context all the more apparent, stressing that 'Money *in Cities* causeth much mischeefe'.[165] As we saw with *The paine of pleasure*,

3 'The Fishmongers Esperanza, or Hope of London' device from *Chrysanaleia* (1616)

Munday's youthful writing often expresses a more sceptical attitude towards urban life and mores than his later work.

Just as Munday criticises the laxity of the City authorities in his antitheatrical pamphlet (as we will see shortly), so in *Zelauto* he also, if implicitly, attacks the theatre. According to Astroepho, who stands as the sceptical voice in this text and another side to Munday's multi-faceted literary identities, money leads to immoral conduct, culminating in the lowest of all degradations – 'many devillish devises frequented'.[166] 'Devises', celebrated earlier in the text for their innovativeness and aesthetic appeal when they appear as part of a royal entertainment, or as a feature of London's 'Bursse', are here castigated as the worst element in city life. Zelauto, in contrast, is more comfortable with theatrical modes than the ascetic Astroepho: for instance, the former calls the second instalment of the story of his travels 'a straunge and tragicall Commedy'.[167] Indeed, the form of the text itself often lapses from narrative prose into a kind of dramatic dialogue. There are some further links between Munday's prose texts such as *Zelauto* and anti-theatrical writing: Stephen Gosson, Munday's antagonist in the former's 1582 anti-stage *Playes Confuted in Five Actions*, also wrote a prose narrative of the same kind as *Zelauto* in 1579 entitled *The Ephemerides of Phialo*, and John Rainolds, the Oxford scholar and author of the self-explanatory *Th'Overthrow of Stage-Playes* of 1599, is regarded as an influence on both Gosson's and Munday's euphuistic novels.[168]

One can see that Munday's dedications trace the complex path of his flexible loyalties: from the Earl of Oxford to the Lord Mayor of London; from court and Privy Council to the City; from quasi-Catholic noblemen to ultra-Protestant aldermen. As such, they reveal the breadth of his connections and the range of his ambitions. That he should have dedicated some of his most trenchant politico-religious tracts of the 1580s to Cecil and the Privy Council, his early, more strictly literary efforts to the Earl of Oxford and his later 'civic' productions of the Jacobean period to City dignitaries shows that each type of text was directed towards what Munday evidently felt to be its most appropriate – and profitable, in all senses of the word – recipient. As Jan van Dorsten has written, 'authors dedicated books in order to gain support for a cause or to draw attention to their loyalty and personal expertise in an attempt to improve their own social position through "preferment"'.[169] Indeed, one can map Munday's career vicissitudes via his changes of allegiance and the rewards they brought him (theatrical ubiquity with Nottingham or a lucrative patent from the City Corporation, for example).

Munday's 'social mobility' can be read on a number of levels: his work straddled various stratum of early modern urban society, he himself engaged in trade, playwrighting, politics and civic entertainments as his status was consolidated, and he literally moved from one part of London, as representing some aspect of its life, to another. He is, then, a prime example of what Manley has argued is characteristic of Elizabethan and Jacobean London, for his career can be seen to demonstrate a typically versatile adaptation to 'the very different mediating institutions ... audience expectations, and linguistic strata' involved in London's various cultural forms.[170] Munday, however, might be regarded as exceptionally well connected when compared to many of his contemporaries; he thus demonstrates to an even greater extent what Manley calls the 'inter-orientation' of cultural practice in the metropolis.[171] In the 'small competitive world of London' Munday would no doubt have been well known (as the numerous references to him by his contemporaries indicate), and his unabashed self-publicity suggests that he regarded himself as a contender for any office or advantage that might come his way. As his career progressed, Munday's definitive move towards the City and away from Westminster and the Privy Council as his chief source of employment might be related to what Manley has described as the 'deepening alienation of London's merchant class from the economic practices, foreign policy, and moral and religious tone of the Stuart court'.[172] Other wider developments that might be relevant here include the end of *ad hoc* dramatic patronage by aristocrats and courtiers once James I took all theatre companies under the royal wing on his accession. Certainly, Munday's work for the Privy Council was, as far as we know, almost exclusive to the final two decades of Elizabeth's reign. He was to dedicate works to the Queen, to her favourite, the Earl of Leicester, and to other powerful members of the Privy Council during the 1580s but by the end of the sixteenth century civic dignitaries such as Alderman John Swynnerton were increasingly likely to be the recipients of Munday's literary labours. Before I move on to discuss Munday's exclusively civic writing in the final chapter of this book, I will explore more fully his writing for and against the stage, setting this in a London context.

NOTES

1 Parry, 'Literary patronage', p. 118.
2 Munday, *Zelauto*, p. 62.
3 In this respect it is interesting to note that John Pitcher cites Chaucer as the writer through whom 'the notion of an English author' was established ('Literature, the playhouse and the public', p. 359).
4 Munday, *The Mirrour of Mutabilitie*, p. 23.
5 Munday, *The second Booke of Primaleon of Greece*, sig. A4r.
6 Munday, *The Third and last part of Palmerin of England*, sig. A4r. Gybson takes the same position, saying of Munday that 'plaine poor affection hath as true a tongue' as those who write with 'richer pennes' (ibid., sig. A4v).
7 Sidney, *Selected Writings*, p. 120. See also Moore, 'Jonson, Dekker, and the discourse of chivalry', p. 136 n. 52. Jonson makes a slighting reference to *Amadis* in *Epicoene* (IV.i.50).
8 Hans Peter Heinrich notes that Munday 'often takes shallow commonplaces for wisdom' (Munday, *The Mirrour of Mutabilitie*, p. 25). Turner also comments that 'underscorings on the sole surviving copy [of *Zelauto*] show that at least one reader rolled under his tongue Mundy's homely adages' (*Anthony Mundy*, pp. 34–5). Munday's frequent use of proverbs has often been noted and has been cited as one indicator of his authorship of *Fair Em*, which features a large number of proverbs (see Henning, ed., *Fair Em*, p. 187).
9 Munday, *Zelauto*, pp. 146–7.
10 Ibid., pp. 128 and 140.
11 Heinrich, who calls Cicero 'Munday's favourite authority', has remarked on how indebted Munday was to Cicero as a literary role model, whose 'eclectic type of thinking ... was prepared to take its crumbs of knowledge wherever it

could find them' (Munday, *The Mirrour of Mutabilitie*, pp. 66n and 25n).
12 See Munday, *Zelauto*, pp. 192–3. In the *Mirrour* Munday confuses the Bible's three Herods (Munday, *The Mirrour of Mutabilitie*, p. 32n). Leah Marcus states that 'from the standpoint of even the most elementary classical scholarship', Munday's pageant *Chruso-thriambos* is 'a strange muddle' ('City metal and country mettle', p. 39).
13 Munday, *The True knowledge of a mans owne selfe*, sig. A7v.
14 Munday, *Zelauto*, p. 4. Munday uses a similar tactic in *Palladine of England*, where he compares his gift of this text to the Earl of Essex to 'a simple Heardsman [who brings] his offering on a broken potsheard'; the translator calls himself 'a simple zealous man' (sig. iiir).
15 Munday, *Zelauto*, p. 46. See Turner, *Anthony Mundy*, p. 104, for Elizabeth's reported attitude towards these romances.
16 Munday, *Zelauto*, p. 62.
17 *Ibid.*, p. 8.
18 See Beaumont, *The Knight of the Burning Pestle*, Act I, lines 211–30. Other Munday texts utilised an anachronistic language in a way that recalls parodies such as this play: for example, in *Chruso-thriambos* Munday writes that London's cathedral church '*hight* the Church of blessed Paul' (sig. B4r; my emphasis).
19 Burnett, *Masters and Servants*, p. 47 n. 4. Unlike most of his works, Munday's *Palmerin* texts were still being reprinted in the 1660s. They gained a fictional readership too, for romances including *Amadis*, *Palmerin of England* and *Palmerin d'Oliva* were implicated by Cervantes in Don Quixote's madness (see Schlauch, *Antecedents of the English Novel*, p. 165).
20 See Munday, *Palmerin d'Oliva. The first [second] part*, sig. A3v. As Hayes notes, with typical economy Munday had here re-used his previous dedication to Oxford almost verbatim when he came to re-dedicate this work to the Youngs ('Anthony Munday's romances of chivalry', pp. 77 and 79). Hayes also comments that 'the purity of [Munday's] dedications was by no means "unspotted"' ('Anthony Munday's romances: a postscript', p. 32).
21 See Hayes, 'Anthony Munday's romances of chivalry', p. 61.
22 Munday, *Palladine of England*, sig. iir.
23 Nashe, ed. McKerrow, *The Works of Thomas Nashe*, vol. I, pp. 168–9. See also Heinemann, *Puritanism and Theatre*, p. 53, and Wilson, *Will Power*, p. 42. Nashe's text is generally misanthropic, but he directs particular contempt towards those 'sprung up of Nothing' who aspire to a status that he sees as above them.
24 Nashe, ed. McKerrow, *The Works of Thomas Nashe*, vol. I, pp. 213–15.
25 Manley, *Literature and Culture*, p. 322.
26 Butler, 'Literature and the theatre to 1660', p. 572.
27 Nashe, *The Unfortunate Traveller and Other Works*, p. 54.
28 Nashe, ed. McKerrow, *The Works of Thomas Nashe*, vol. I, p. 194. Although he knew him, Jonson too was occasionally unkind about Stow (see Heywood, ed. Rowland, *Edward IV*, p. lxxxiv). This attitude is not exclusive to the period, for in 1979 Alice-Lyle Scoufos called sixteenth-century historians such as Stow 'a relatively stodgy group' (*Shakespeare's Typological Satire*, p. 17).
29 Nashe, ed. McKerrow, *The Works of Thomas Nashe*, vol. III, p. 149. See also Manley, *Literature and Culture*, p. 337.
30 Nashe, ed. McKerrow, *The Works of Thomas Nashe*, vol. III, pp. 315–16.

31 Munday, *The second Booke of Primaleon of Greece*, sig. A4r; my emphasis.
32 Baldwin, *On the Literary Genetics of Shakspere's Plays*, p. 26; see Nashe, ed. McKerrow, *The Works of Thomas Nashe*, vol. III, p. 316.
33 Nashe, ed. McKerrow, *The Works of Thomas Nashe*, vol. III, p. 312.
34 Munday, *Palmerin d'Oliva*, sig. iiiv.
35 Munday, *Palladine of England*, sig. ivr.
36 Munday, *The second Booke of Primaleon of Greece*, sig. A4v.
37 Munday, *The Third and last part of Palmerin of England*, sig. A3v.
38 See Moore, 'Jonson, Dekker, and the discourse of chivalry', pp. 155–6.
39 Munday, *The second Booke of Primaleon of Greece*, sig. A4r.
40 Munday, *Zelauto*, p. 5. Randall Anderson has noted of such 'aggressive' prefaces that one might 'wonder where the profit lies in such an apparently indecorous, hostile attack on the audience'; he concludes that 'it would have to be the experienced reader who can navigate ironic paratexts' ('The rhetoric of paratext', p. 638).
41 Munday, *The Mirrour of Mutabilitie*, p. 13.
42 Jonson, *The Case Is Altered*, I.ii.26–7. Balladino does not appear again in the play: Mann has called this 'an almost entirely extraneous scene', emphasising that its sole purpose is to satirise Munday ('Sir Oliver Owlet's Men', p. 304). Jonson's parody of Munday has been called 'prejudiced and not wholly fair' (Ashley, 'Munday, Anthony', p. 1006).
43 Jonson was probably prompted to attack Munday in 1609 partly because of the latter's recent republication in 1608 of *The admirable deliverance of 266 Christians*, a work about John Fox (or Reynard) originally published in 1579 (I am grateful to Richard Dutton for bringing this point to my attention).
44 Jonson, *The Case Is Altered*, I.ii.13.
45 *Ibid.*, I.ii.43–4. In *Palladine of England* Munday himself disclaims 'borrowed phrases' (sig. iii).
46 Jonson, *The Case Is Altered*, I.ii.54–6. This series of in-jokes includes a reference to Jonson's own two 'humours' plays performed in the late 1590s.
47 *Ibid.*, I.ii.68–71. If Onion is intended to be Nashe as some have speculated, then Jonson insinuates here, ironically, that Nashe is indebted to Munday's work as a literary model (see Moore, 'Jonson, Dekker, and the discourse of chivalry', pp. 150–1).
48 Moore, 'Jonson, Dekker, and the discourse of chivalry', p. 152.
49 Marston's own dramatic career probably started at the Rose in 1599, where he would have been a contemporary of the now-reviled Munday (see Rutter, ed., *Documents of the Rose Playhouse*, pp. 166 and 168).
50 ?Marston, *Histrio-Mastix*, sig. E4v. For the case for the 1599 date see Bednarz, 'Representing Jonson', p. 27 n. 12. A date of 1599 for *Histrio-Mastix*, however, does take us some distance from the early to mid 1580s, the time when Munday was most likely to have still been appearing on the stage as a performer, and makes the play's numerous cutting references to Posthaste's deficiencies as an improviser look a little anachronistic.
51 ?Marston, *Histrio-Mastix*, sig. D4r.
52 *Ibid.*, sig. Cr. The verses so set forth do bear some similarities to Munday's plays. Given the play's criticisms of Munday's deficiencies as a writer it is amusing to note that some early reader of this play has written 'not good' both at the beginning and at the end of the text (BL shelfmark C.34.b.23, sigs A3r and H3r).

53 *Ibid.*, sig. E4v.
54 *Ibid.*, sig. Cv.
55 *Ibid.*, sigs F2v and Hv.
56 Baldwin, *On the Literary Genetics of Shakspere's Plays*, p. 31.
57 Cited in Henning, ed., *Fair Em*, p. 67.
58 See Dillon, *Theatre, Court and City*, p. 16, and Moore, 'Jonson, Dekker, and the discourse of chivalry', pp. 139 n. 61 and 148 n. 85.
59 The Drapers' Company regularly employed dramatists for their civic shows: two Draper playwrights (Munday and Middleton), as well as Heywood and Webster, wrote for them. See also Jones and Stallybrass, *Renaissance Clothing and the Materials of Memory*, pp. 175–6.
60 See Bald, 'Middleton's civic employments', p. 66; see also Dutton, *Jacobean Civic Pageants*, pp. 138–9. Middleton, like Jonson, was the son of a bricklayer, but he was made free of the Drapers in 1626 by redemption, i.e. by purchasing his freedom.
61 See Dutton, *Jacobean Civic Pageants*, p. 141; see also Lobanov-Rostovsky, 'The Triumphes of Golde', pp. 879–80.
62 See also Lobanov-Rostovsky, 'The Triumphes of Golde', p. 879, Dutton, *Jacobean Civic Pageants*, p. 143, Johnson, 'Jacobean ephemera', pp. 164–5, and Bald, 'Middleton's civic pageants', pp. 72–3.
63 Dutton, *Jacobean Civic Pageants*, pp. 163–4.
64 See Bergeron, *Pageants and Entertainments*, pp. 31–2.
65 See Jenstad, 'Institutional uses of pageantry', p. 14.
66 Cited in Bergeron, *Pageants and Entertainments*, p. 134.
67 See Withington, *English Pageantry*, vol. II, p. 37, and Bergeron, 'Thomas Middleton and Anthony Munday', p. 474.
68 Munday, *Sidero-Thriambos*, sig. A3r. See also Bergeron, *Pageants and Entertainments*, pp. 125 and 134, and Johnson, 'Jacobean ephemera', p. 165 n. 18.
69 See Withington, *English Pageantry*, vol. II, p. 38, and Withington, 'The Lord Mayor's Show for 1623', pp. 112–15.
70 Withington, 'The Lord Mayor's Show for 1623', pp. 114–15.
71 See Bergeron, 'Thomas Middleton and Anthony Munday', p. 475.
72 See Bergeron, *Pageants and Entertainments*, p. 140.
73 *Ibid.*, p. 141.
74 See Bald, 'Middleton's civic employments', p. 73, and Lobanov-Rostovsky, 'The Triumphes of Golde', p. 893 n. 2.
75 Bergeron, *Pageants and Entertainments*, p. 19.
76 Lobanov-Rostovsky, 'The Triumphes of Golde', pp. 879–80.
77 Gurr is sceptical about the distinction between 'public' and 'private' playhouses, citing an instance of the Blackfriars being called 'a common playhouse' to indicate how uncertain these categories could be (*The Shakespearean Stage*, pp. 114–15).
78 For an alternative view see Bergeron, 'Actors in English civic pageants', pp. 25–6, and Bergeron, *Pageants and Entertainments*, pp. xii and xvii.
79 See Bergeron, 'Stuart civic pageants', p. 165. See also Kipling, 'Triumphal drama', p. 42. Kinney remarks that the printed text 'immortalizes [the show] for a potentially larger reading market [than those] who might have seen only a part of [it]', although it should be borne in mind that most pageant texts were not commercial publications and thus were not very widely disseminated (*Renaissance Drama*, p. 373).

80 Lobanov-Rostovsky, 'The Triumphes of Golde', p. 880. For a different view see Kipling, 'Triumphal drama', pp. 43–4.
81 See Jenstad, 'Institutional uses of pageantry', passim.
82 Munday, A second and third blast, sig. Eviiv.
83 CLRO Rep. 38, fol. 31. See also Forker, 'Two notes on John Webster and Anthony Munday', pp. 33–4. This right was extended in 1633 to Munday's widow Gillian, who at the same time received ten pounds from the Court of Aldermen for the printing of Munday's second edition of the Survey (see Lloyd, 'Anthony Munday, dramatist', p. 98). Some forty years earlier Stow had been similarly advantaged; Middleton, too, in 1621, 1622 and 1623, the same year as Munday (see Archer, 'The nostalgia of John Stow', p. 30, and Bald, 'Middleton's civic employments', p. 67).
84 Johnson, A History of the Worshipful Company of the Drapers, p. 3 n. 3.
85 Stow, ed. Munday, The Survay of London, sig. Av.
86 Robertson and Gordon, A Calendar of Dramatic Records, p. 176. See also Turner, Anthony Mundy, p. 147.
87 Robertson and Gordon, A Calendar of Dramatic Records, p. 176.
88 Munday, A Briefe Chronicle, sig. A2v.
89 Jenstad, 'Institutional uses of pageantry', p. 18 n. 20. This text was also dedicated to the current Lord Mayor, William Craven.
90 Munday, A Briefe Chronicle, sig. B2v.
91 Ibid., sig. B2r.
92 Ibid., sig. A2v.
93 Robertson and Gordon, A Calendar of Dramatic Records, pp. 177–8.
94 Wardens Accounts and Court Minutes of the Goldsmiths' Company, part 2, vol. P, fol. 164r (23 January 1617/18). Munday had previously sought out payment from the Goldsmiths for this text in December 1617 and earlier in January 1618. His son Richard's parish, St Botolph Aldgate, also made a payment in 1618 to Munday of 'a peece of Gold of two and twentie shillings for a Gratuitie' on receipt of a copy of his edition of Stow's Survay of the same year (see Denkinger, 'Actors' names', pp. 107–8).
95 Nichols, ed., Chrysanaleia, p. 23.
96 See Robertson and Gordon, A Calendar of Dramatic Records, pp. 180–1, and Heinemann, Puritanism and Theatre, p. 132.
97 The experiences of Richard Robinson, another would-be professional writer, illustrates the precariousness of depending upon the whims of potential patrons (see Parry, 'Literary patronage', pp. 127–8).
98 Munday, ed. Meagher, The Downfall, lines 1043–52.
99 Ibid., lines 1055–6.
100 Munday, Chrysanaleia, sig. A3v.
101 Munday, The Mirrour of Mutabilitie, p. 21.
102 Ibid., p. 11.
103 Ibid.
104 Munday, Zelauto, p. 80.
105 See ibid., p. 186.
106 The same cloud was to fall over another patron, Lord Strange, a decade on (see below).
107 Munday, Palmerin d'Oliva, sig. iir. Oxford recanted his Catholicism in 1580, the year Zelauto was published. See also Turner, Anthony Mundy, pp. 25–6, 28–30, Turner Wright, 'Young Anthony Mundy again', pp. 155–7, and, for

Howard's putative Catholicism, Kenny, 'Notes on the "Catholicism"'. It is worth noting in respect of the theory that Munday was himself a Catholic that, although his *Mirrour* was dedicated to Oxford, it also contains a verse by Claudius Hollyband, a Protestant Huguenot refugee, of whom Munday had been a 'scholler' (p. 14). In 1619 Munday dedicated an edition of *Primaleon* to the then Earl of Oxford, Henry de Vere, Edward de Vere's son.

108 Munday, *The Mirrour of Mutabilitie*, pp. 8–9. In 1582, at the height of the controversy over Munday's role in the capture and execution of Campion and other Catholic priests, Munday dedicated *A breefe Aunswer made unto two Seditious Pamphlets* to Francis Walsingham. In this response to his antagonists he emphasises his personal contribution to the salvation of the English state from Counter-Reformation Catholicism: 'not I alone', he assures Walsingham, 'but I cheefely as one, gave foorth such unproovable notice of ensuing harmes, as bewrayed their secret trayterous intent, and also notably convicted the adversary' (sig. Aiiiiv).

109 Munday, *The Mirrour of Mutabilitie*, p. 8.

110 Munday, *Zelauto*, p. 5; see Turner Wright, untitled review of *Zelauto*, p. 154.

111 Munday, *Zelauto*, p. 52; see also pp. 54–5 and 189.

112 Hamilton, 'Anthony Munday and *The Merchant of Venice*', p. 91.

113 Parry, 'Patronage and the printing of learned works', p. 177; see also Parry, 'Literary patronage', p. 123.

114 Munday, *Zelauto*, pp. ix n. 8, xiv–xv. See also Scanlon, 'Munday's *Zelauto*', p. 12.

115 Munday, *Zelauto*, p. 16.

116 Ibid., p. 21.

117 Ibid., p. 55.

118 Munday, *Palladine of England*, sig. iir; Moore, 'Jonson, Dekker, and the discourse of chivalry', p. 136.

119 Munday, *Gerileon of England*, sig. A2r. See also Bennett, *English Books and Readers*, p. 290, and Turner, *Anthony Mundy*, p. 92. In *A True and admirable Historie, of a Mayden of Consolens* Munday refers to his 'more weightie imployments' hindering his writing (sig. 3v), and in *Palladine of England* he explains that 'I beeing often absent' has resulted in many printer's errors (sig. ivr). Some further idea of the nature of Munday's work as a royal messenger can be gained from what we know about Robert Poley, a contemporary of Munday's and a man who may have played a part in Marlowe's death in 1593 (see de Kalb, 'Robert Poley's movements').

120 Munday, *Gerileon of England*, sig. A3r.

121 See Turner, *Anthony Mundy*, p. 93, and Byrne, 'Anthony Munday and his books', p. 231.

122 Hosley, 'Anthony Munday, John Heardson, and the authorship of "Fedele and Fortunio"', pp. 564–5.

123 This text revisits the recent executions of Catholic priests. The Drapers' Company itself had some history of Protestant affiliation: certain members of the Company were associated with Protestantism in the early sixteenth century, and the company had 'a cell of the brethren' in the 1530s (Brigden, *London and the Reformation*, pp. 206 and 121). During the Marian period, the Drapers 'admitted that some [anti-Marian] books had been discovered among them' (*ibid.*, p. 595).

124 Parry comments that writers 'might as well dedicate a book to the moon for

all the benefit [a dedication to the Queen] brought' ('Literary patronage', p. 125).
125 See Carson, *A Companion to Henslowe's Diary*, p. 59. The year 1599 was also the year that Heywood wrote *Edward IV* for Derby's Men, a play in which Munday may have had a hand; if so, he did not write exclusively for the Admiral's Men during this period.
126 Munday, *A breefe Treatise*, sig. A3r–v.
127 Ibid., sig. A4v.
128 See Carson, *A Companion to Henslowe's Diary*, p. 110.
129 Munday, *The strangest adventure that ever happened*, sig. A2v. See also Turner, *Anthony Mundy*, p. 138, and Foster, *The Politics of Stability*, p. 164.
130 See Bergeron, *Pageants and Entertainments*, pp. 25–34. Munday's (probably co-authored) 1610 Show for Craven has not survived.
131 Munday, *The strangest adventure that ever happened*, sig. A3r.
132 Ibid., sig. A2v.
133 Ibid., sig. A3v.
134 See the 'Epistle Dedicatorie' to Munday, *A breefe Aunswer*.
135 As Hamilton has noted, 'all of Munday's writing about Campion and on related issues, printed during 1581 and 1582, were [sic] dedicated to one or several members of the Privy Council or to the Queen' ('Anthony Munday and *The Merchant of Venice*', p. 90).
136 Munday, *A Briefe Chronicle*, sig. A3r. Preambles of this kind were one of his specialities – even the habitually indulgent Turner describes the dedication to the Earl of Oxford in *The Mirrour of Mutabilitie* as 'a masterpiece of servility' (*Anthony Mundy*, p. 11 n. 31). *The Mirrour* begins with an address wishing Oxford 'in this world a triumphant tranquillitie, with a continuall increase of Honourable Dignitie, and after this life, a Crown of everlasting felicitie, in the eternal Hierarchie' (p. 6), and concludes with a set of complimentary verses to Oxford (although there are more such verses to Munday himself than to Oxford).
137 Ashton, *The City and the Court*, p. 39. See also Sayle, *Lord Mayors' Pageants*, pp. 85–6, and Overall and Overall, *Analytical Index*, p. 211.
138 Munday, ed. Pafford, *Chruso-thriambos*, pp. 48 and 50.
139 Ibid., p. 37. See Thompson, 'The autograph manuscripts of Anthony Mundy', pp. 330 and 345–8. *The Heaven of the Mynde* was entered in the Stationers' Register in February 1602/3 by Leake, although this alone does not tell us if the text was actually published: 'Master Leake. Assigned over unto hym from Edward Aggas a booke Called the heaven of the mynd' (Arber, *Transcript of the Records*, vol. III, p. 227).
140 Munday's choice was judicious as well as parochial, for the alderman's status was considerable. Foster explains that 'even before the statute of 1601 gave him this authority, the powers of the alderman in his ward ... were certainly as great as any county justice's' (*The Politics of Stability*, p. 51). In 1608 Swynnerton and his wife were dedicatees of *The Conversion of a most Noble Lady of Fraunce*, a translation which has been ascribed to Munday.
141 See Bergeron, 'Actors in English civic pageants', p. 19.
142 Munday, *The True knowledge of a mans owne selfe*, sigs. A4v–5r.
143 Ibid., sig. A5v.
144 Ibid., sig. B3v.
145 Swynnerton was apparently parodied as a hog in the year of his mayoralty in a play performed by apprentices at the Whitefriars, *The Hog Hath Lost His*

Pearl. Sir Henry Wotton cited the incident as an example of 'how sharp-witted the City is'. A number of the apprentices ended up in the nearby Bridewell as a result (Wickham et al., *English Professional Theatre*, p. 562).
146 Munday, *A True and admirable Historie*, sig. 2v.
147 Ibid., sig. 3r.
148 Ibid., sig. 3r.
149 In this respect my reading of Munday's translations differs from that put forward by Hamilton. She cites these texts as evidence for Munday's disguised Catholicism, although she does not say which translation in particular leads her to this view ('Anthony Munday and *The Merchant of Venice*', p. 91).
150 Munday, *A True and admirable Historie*, sig. 2v.
151 Ibid., sig. 3v.
152 Ibid., sig. Br. Dekker strikes the same note in his verse to Munday in part three of *Palmerin of England*: 'For tho in courtly French [Palmerin] sweetly spake, /... A harder labour thou doost undertake / Thus to create him a fine Englishman'. Webster too celebrates Munday's achievement in bringing Palmerin via 'his owne language ... to his owne Nation' (sigs A3v–A4r).
153 Munday, *A True and admirable Historie*, sig. 3v. Munday's strategy in these two epistles is a good example of what Anderson calls a writer's 'stylization of audience status' ('The rhetoric of paratext', p. 643).
154 Munday, *A True and admirable Historie*, sig. 3v.
155 See Bennett, *English Books and Readers*, p. 69. Amongst other works, Wolfe printed Munday's translation of Lord de la Noue's *Declaration* in 1589 and the original 1590 edition of the first book of *Amadis of Gaul* (see Huffman, *Elizabethan Impressions*, p. 143).
156 Bennett, *English Books and Readers*, p. 102.
157 Munday, *Zelauto*, p. 32.
158 Turner Wright, untitled review of *Zelauto*, p. 157.
159 Munday, *Zelauto*, pp. 34–5.
160 Ibid., pp. 38–9; see also Turner Wright, untitled review of *Zelauto*, p. 153. Munday later combined his interest in ships with a fuller depiction of London's burse in 'the Shippe called the Royall Exchange' in *The Triumphes of re-united Britania* (sig. A4v).
161 Munday, *Zelauto*, p. 188.
162 Bergeron, *Pageants and Entertainments*, p. 140.
163 See ibid., p. 105. The illustrations for this Show have, uniquely, survived; the originals are kept at Fishmongers' Hall.
164 Scanlon, 'Munday's *Zelauto*', p. 12.
165 Munday, *Zelauto*, p. 64; my emphasis. In *The Admirable Deliverance of 266. Christians*, in contrast, Munday has nothing but praise for the benefits of 'marchandizing' and 'commerce', which together form a 'chayne which bindes Kingdomes in Leagues ... and teacheth nations ... to deale faithfully together as brethren' (sig. A2r).
166 Munday, *Zelauto*, p. 64.
167 Ibid., p. 65.
168 See ibid., pp. vii–ix; see also Chambers, *The Elizabethan Stage*, vol. I, pp. 252–4.
169 Van Dorsten, 'Literary patronage in Elizabethan England', p. 192.
170 Manley, *Literature and Culture*, p. 12.
171 In October 1595, the same year as some ex-members of the Admiral's Company toured on the continent under their erstwhile patron's name, Munday

himself was issued with a six-month passport to travel within the then-disputed Low Countries. Munday's reason for travelling, however, was not to perform theatrical but rather governmental business: he visited the continent to pursue 'ses particulieres affaires'. The passport says that Munday, who must have arrived without their permission, 'suppliat très humblement' for licence to stay (Schrickx, 'Anthony Munday in the Netherlands', p. 484). This journey may be the referent of Munday's complaint in the second part of *Primaleon of Greece* that he was unable to complete the first part of this romance owing to his 'urgent occasions at that time' (sig. Aiiv).

172 Manley, *Literature and Culture*, p. 369.

4

'Plaiers can not be better compared than to the Camelion'

Munday and the theatre

'THE INTOLERABLE EXERCISE OF PLAIES'[1]
CIVIC ANTITHEATRICALITY REVISITED

MUNDAY'S attitude towards the theatre was as opportunistic as one might expect. Early in his career he was employed by one employer, the City of London, to attack another, the stage. Despite his own history as a player, when sponsored by the City Corporation in 1580 to attack the stage in *A second and third blast of retrait from plaies and Theaters* he did not hesitate to condemn its failings in the most uncompromising fashion, choosing not to disguise but rather to highlight the fact that his contempt for the stage derived from an actual personal acquaintanceship with its iniquities. In the Preface to the Reader the author of the work is described as 'a great affecter of that vaine Art of plaie making ... yea ... as excellent an Autor of those vanities, as who was best'.[2] Rather than undermining the legitimacy of such an attack, this only serves to demonstrate, Munday claims, that plays are so abominable that they 'stirreth up the verie Autors themselves to inveigh against them'.[3] Indeed, his turn away from the stage is a cause for celebration, not embarrassment: it is 'a joie to the children of God, and griefe to the servants of Satan ... to heare, that he, who was so famous an Autor, was now become a religious dehorter from plaies'.[4]

This recanted player then takes the opportunity to chastise the government of those areas where the playhouses were located. These authorities, he claims, are too lax in their treatment of the theatres and ought to learn from the example of their continental neighbours. 'The citie Marsiles [Marseilles]' is singled put for praise in this respect, for it apparently 'kept so great gravitie, that it would receave into it no stage-plaiers'. Munday expresses the wish that his own city would do likewise: 'I would to God the magistrates of our citie of London would have the like foresight.'[5] In case any of his readers have failed to connect his diatribe to their own city, the text emphasises in a marginal note that it is 'London' from whence the players ought to be 'banished'.[6] In this polemic, however, there is an underlying ambiguity about the identity of the 'magistrates' who are regularly identified in this text with 'London' itself rather than Middlesex or Surrey, their actual areas of jurisdiction. Indeed, Munday elsewhere in his works uses the term 'magistrate' in a more general sense to mean 'governor of London' (in *Sidero-Thriambos*, for instance, the Lord Mayor himself is London's 'chiefe Magistrate').[7] Alongside the reference to Marseilles which I have just quoted, Munday exclaims in a marginal note 'Harke Magistrates of London', and then goes on to claim that 'the permission of plaies so long a time hath alreadie corrupted this citie and brought the Name of the citizens into slander'.[8] Indeed, these errant magistrates are one of his major targets: 'this booke was made', he explains, 'that the Magistrats being informed might take such good waies, that the intolerable exercise of plaies might be utterlie put downe'.[9] His references to 'this citie' and 'the citizens' have the effect of eliding the difference between the City of London proper and the wider London domain including the suburbs and liberties. Such rhetoric might be regarded as somewhat self-defeating when one considers that Munday's pamphlet bore the arms of the City Corporation on its first page.

As well as demonstrating Munday's own personal duplicity, this text also complicates any straightforward notion of civic antitheatricality. When he writes for different purposes in other works the governors of London are applauded rather than criticised. There is a contrast between Munday's antitheatrical text and the way in which he eulogises magistrates in the 1610 entertainment *Londons Love*, presented to a civic audience and intended to celebrate the City as much as the Prince of Wales. Here he writes in positive terms that 'Plato termeth Magistracy, to be the Anchor, Head, and Soule of any Citty: and holdeth it for the same thing in any commonwealth, as the Heart is in the body of a living creature'.[10] Given the additional fact that *A second and third blast* is overtly sponsored by the City Corporation, one might find Munday's criticisms of the City, its judiciary and, implicitly, its citizens rather hard to account for.[11]

However, it is always risky to read such polemics on their own terms. In the context of Munday's other works, this text raises questions about the intended recipients of such antitheatrical polemics. As Munday's reference to the endangered integrity of the citizens implies, Londoners themselves frequented playhouses and the London authorities (with provisos) sanctioned playgoing within their boundaries – so who might be the 'Christian reader' whom Munday's preface addresses? Is the Corporation – whose coat of arms is positioned directly opposite this preamble – thereby putting its imprimatur upon his text and instructing its population to desist from playgoing? There would, after all, hardly be any point in preaching to the converted, those already convinced of the vices of the theatre and unlikely ever to go near the place. Unlike Steven Mullaney, who states that Stow's 'fellow citizens [made] drama the scapegoat for … [social] ills', Patrick Collinson argues that 'it cannot have been the case that in [London] society some people (Puritans, or "the godly") "gadded" to sermons … while others flocked to plays. People went to both. Had that not been the case, the preachers would not have wasted so much breath in telling their congregations that they should rather be seen dead than at the theatre.'[12] By consistently referring to 'we', Munday's rhetoric

4 The arms of the Corporation of London, from *A second and third blast of retrait from plaies and Theaters* (sig. A1v)

certainly suggests that he is enjoining those who *do* attend plays to cease doing so; in the process he includes himself in the category of deluded citizenry. 'Let us consider what is done', he writes: '*wee* run forthwith unto playes, *we* flie unto madnes, *the people* disperse themselves in Theaters, the whole multitude revel it out at stages'.[13] That this is a specifically civic problem is exemplified by the fact that the author of this 'third blast' is called 'a worshipful and zealous Gentleman' on its title page, two adjectives that Munday and others were to use regularly in respect of city dignitaries.

Munday's representation of 'Anglo-Phile Eutheo', the third blast's ostensible author, as a moral voice in the wilderness is only too accurate, for the City authorities, as I go on to discuss below, had little by the way of ingrained disapproval of playgoing in its early days before the 1580s. Indeed, antitheatrical preachers sometimes addressed a specifically civic audience, including the Lord Mayor, whom some commentators might assume already to be apprised of the evils of playgoing.[14] Even Stephen Gosson in his 1579 denunciation of playing *The Schoole of Abuse*, which is otherwise hostile towards the stage upon which he himself had so recently been employed, represents players almost as worthies of London and in terms that reflect the usual civic virtues: 'it is well known, that some of them are sober, discreete, properly learned honest housholders and Citizens well thought on amonge their neighbours'.[15] Ironically, given his attack on Munday in this text as one who had 'returned to his first vomit' by recommencing his theatre career, Gosson's 'housholders and Citizens' would have included Munday in their number.

Far from being entirely at odds at all times, the City and the theatres were closely associated in a number of ways. The geography of the city and the multiple roles of many of its inhabitants, Munday included, could hardly have made it otherwise. Nevertheless, it has long been a given of much dramatic criticism and even stage history that the City held a deep-seated and uniform antagonism towards the theatre.[16] The reality is that the two bodies had a long, if sometimes vexed, relationship. When in May 1574 James Burbage was for the first time granted a royal patent for his troupe to perform plays as Leicester's Men within the City and its liberties, the patent broke with the existing role of *civic* authority, whereby would-be players had to petition the Lord Mayor for a permit to perform, naming the venue, which would have been as likely to be the house of a prosperous city merchant as an inn yard.[17] The 1574 patent therefore explicitly and provocatively permitted theatrical performance under certain conditions 'within oure Citie of London and liberties of the same', as well as 'within the liberties and fredomes of anye oure Cities, townes, Bouroughes &c ... throughoute oure Realme of England'.[18] Previously, plays and masques, even if not enacted by professional companies, had regularly taken place in the halls of the livery companies during the early sixteenth century.[19] This infringement of the Corporation's longstanding and probably lucrative authority was compounded by the expansion by patent of the court role of the Master of the Revels in 1581. From that point on the Master of the Revels had more power over the theatres than the Corporation.[20] Prior to 1581 and the rise of Tilney, in December 1574 the City, via an Act of the Court of Common Council, decreed that the Mayor and the Court of Aldermen should be responsible for seeing and approving all stage plays. As Glynne Wickham has noted, this Act represented the City's attempt to regain the initiative over the control of playgoing from the acting Master of the Revels, Thomas Blagrave, in the aftermath of the patent of May 1574.[21]

This civic document is well worth the perusal. As a kind of rhetorical preamble, the City authorities rehearse all the usual arguments against theatregoing – such as its tendency to foster unchaste assignations, crime, the waste of money, and seditious words – but they also stress that their intention is to *permit* 'the lawfull honest and comelye us [use] of plaies pastymes and recreacions in good sorte'. The Act continues:

> no Inkeper Tavernekeper nor other person whatsoever within the liberties of thys Cittie shall openlye shewe or playe ... anie playe, enterlude, Commodye, Tragidie, matter, or shewe, which shall not be firste perused and Allowed in suche order and fourme and by suche personnes as by the Lorde Maior and Courte of Aldermen for the tyme beinge shalbe appoynted.[22]

Ingram points out that gaining powers such as these would enable the City to gather in substantial income in fees for licensing, since not only the text but also the venue for its performance had to be scrutinised and allowed; as he comments, 'another layer of permissions, of course, meant more fees and more hassle'.[23] Wickham too has argued that 'the City's determination to retain control over ... playing places was not ... wholly altruistic ... the taxation of admission receipts [was] in order to subsidise some of the City's costs for the relief of the sick, the aged and the unemployed'.[24] Indeed, the City had written into its self-imposed role considerable income in the form of licence fees, which 'shalbe ymployed to the reliefe of the poore in hospitalles of this Cittie, or of the poore infected or diseased in this Cittie of London, as the lord Maior and Courte of Aldermen for the tyme beinge shall adjudge meete to be distributed'.[25] The judgement of the Mayor and Aldermen was based on their assessment of what the putative playing establishment should afford; there were also heavy fines consequent upon non-compliance with these complicated arrangements. The Act specifically (and, as Wickham suggests, 'tactfully') excluded from its provisions 'anie plaies, Enterludes, Comodies, Tragidies, or shewes to be played or shewed in the pryvate hous, dwellinge, or lodginge of anie nobleman, Citizen, or gentleman … withowte publique or Commen Collection of money of the Auditorie or beholders theareof'.[26] It is interesting to see that the mercantile Corporation explicitly exempted dramatic productions not staged for profit from its strictures. Only a month earlier the Privy Council had sent letters to the Surrey and Middlesex magistrates 'to restraine all plaiers and other unnecessarie assemblies, in respect of the plague, within x miles of London untill Esther [Easter] next'.[27] With this background in mind, the City's contingent sanction of playgoing looks more liberal than repressive. Even as late as 1594 Lord Hunsdon requested that his company, the Chamberlain's Men, be permitted by the Lord Mayor to perform at the Cross Keys inn, in the heart of the City in Gracechurch Street.[28] This is a significant context within which to place Munday's 1580 *Second and third blast*, for when he attacks the City government for its laxity towards playgoing he is writing at a time when the Corporation still had considerable sway over the few purpose-built theatres and the other playgoing venues closer to the centre of the City, for in 1580 the city inns would still have constituted a set of major venues for playgoing (as, to a more limited extent, did the legal Inns of Court outside the City). The date of this text, one should note, also makes the City's sponsorship of Munday's polemic all the harder to understand.

How to interpret documents such as the 1574 Act is a major point of contention. For Ingram, the Act demonstrates the City's provisional tolerance of playgoing and its related attempt to profit from its popularity. For Hawkes, in contrast, it is 'the first act passed *against* plays by the London City Council'.[29] If one approaches antitheatricality with the assumption that it was a one-dimensional phenomenon encompassing letters from the City authorities to magistrates and the Privy Council, along with propaganda pieces such as Munday's *A second and third blast*, then the latter reading is inevitable. Mullaney too has bracketed all elements of 'the city' together in order to be able to claim that this undifferentiated entity 'reserved its most strident outrage for the newly emerged companies of professional players'.[30] Hawkes's otherwise interesting account of antitheatrical writing implies that the Corporation shared antitheatrical writers' apparent hostility towards 'a consumer economy ... [and] popular taste', which is an implausible charge given the mercantile activities which the City's livery companies existed to protect and foster, not to mention the 'popular taste' so lavishly indulged by the Lord Mayors' Shows.[31] It seems unlikely that the City and its constituent bodies, famed for their wealth and commercial acumen, would wish to put forward, in Hawkes's words, 'a coherent and sophisticated critique of the ideological and psychological effects of a commodity culture', let alone participate in what he calls 'the taboo against commercialism'.[32]

Contrary to the usual construction placed upon the City's motives in issuing the 1574 Act, Ingram's revisionist account argues that the prime rationale for the City's action was to establish 'the profitable granting of exemptions ... and the equally profitable issuing of licences', rather than stemming from a moralistic objection to playing *per se*.[33] Given the sums of money that might have been forthcoming from such a set-up, it is certainly possible to argue that the City's aim might actually have been to encourage playgoing within its environs, not prohibit it. As Ingram suggests, this would make the theatre building in the suburbs from 1576 an unexpected and perhaps unwelcome move on the part of the players for another reason than that of the problem of civic control – one of financial interest.[34] It is, of course, still the case that the City authorities did try on a number of occasions to prevent or at least to inhibit playgoing. However, these instances should not automatically lead one to the view that the City alone was sometimes hostile to the stage, for there are also a number of documents from the Privy Council too, on an almost annual basis, instructing the magistrates and/or the City Corporation to forbid playing within their areas of jurisdiction, even if only temporarily. These inhibitions were normally due to – or purported to be due to – outbreaks of plague or other unusual moments, such as the death of Prince Henry in 1612, or incidents of unrest within London.[35] Conversely, the orders from Westminster to *permit* playing could also be provisional, as in April 1582 when the Privy Council requested that the players should be allowed to recommence playing on the understanding that their activities could be inhibited again on receipt of a recommendation to that effect from the City.[36] Ambivalence over moral, social and financial considerations pervades attempts to control playgoing. Freedman argues that plague ordinances were sometimes used to cloak the chief reason for the closure of the theatres – the fear of social disorder. She cites a number of examples as illustration, such as one from April 1580 (the year when Munday's antitheatrical pamphlet was published) where the Mayor's pretext for closure ('many [a]ffrayes, querells, and other disorders and inconveniences') was transformed for politic reasons by the Privy Council into a plague prevention measure.[37]

All of this is evidence to support the case that control of the theatres was not simply a one-way process of support from the court facing up to repression from the City. Much of the business to do with the theatres, one can surmise, was carried out on a more *ad hoc* basis and with the use of personal contacts and politic influence rather than stereotypically 'moral' and inflexible opposition on the part of the City. For instance, the civic record has survived of an order from March 1592 by the Court of Aldermen that (as a lobbyist might wine and dine a cabinet minister nowadays) Edmund Tilney, Master of the Revels, should be 'treated' by two City dignitaries (one of whom was the influential Richard Martin, to whom Munday had dedicated a text in 1582) 'for some good order to be taken for the restrayning of the playes and enterludes within this citie'.[38] This brief minute is all that remains of this putative encounter but that Martin was at this juncture both an alderman and the Master of the Mint, a court post, would indicate that some beneficial use of his 'foot in both camps' position was intended. Liaison rather than conflict between the City and the Master of the Revels is also indicated by a precept which was issued from the Lord Mayor in 1592 asking the City Companies to contribute towards an annuity for Tilney, 'for the putting down of plays'.[39] In a letter to Whitgift of March 1592, the then Mayor, Cuthbert Buckle, requests precisely this kind of liaison: 'for the better effecting and continuance of this restraint of the sayed playes in and about this Citie, wee have appointed certein of our Brethren the Aldermen to conferre with [Tilney] forthwith'.[40] One can usefully compare this initiative to the projected Commission of Censorship of 1589, which was to comprise Tilney, Whitgift (the Archbishop of Canterbury) and the Lord Mayor.[41]

The latter body was proposed in the immediate aftermath of the Marprelate controversy, and it is clear that urgent circumstances sometimes led to a unanimity of policy on both supposed 'sides' towards the theatres. Similarly, an outbreak of unrest in June 1584 which started 'very nere the Theatre or Curten' prompted a delegation of aldermen from the City to the court there to obtain 'a lettre to suppresse' the theatres, which 'all the LL [Lordships, i.e. the Privy Council] agreed thereunto, saving my Lord Chamberlen [Howard] and mr. Vizchamberlen'. James Burbage, the owner of the Theatre, who was, in William Fleetwood's words 'a stubburne fellow', protested that he was 'my Lo. of Hunsdons man', and refused to obey the order, saying that he would take the matter up with his patron – who was, of course, a member of the Privy Council that had co-issued the letter in the first place, and who had put his hand to the document. Burbage was then confounded when Fleetwood showed him the letter bearing his lord's signature, although he continued to claim, even after Fleetwood threatened him with imprisonment in Newgate, that despite the evidence on the letter 'the Court wold not bynd hym being a [Privy] Counselers man'.[42] As Scott McMillin and Sally-Beth MacLean conclude after retelling this series of events, 'exactly what was going on was anyone's guess'.[43] To put it another way, this incident presents quite a profusion (or perhaps confusion) of competing authorities and, ultimately, a challenge to simplistic court-versus-City accounts of the status of the theatres.[44]

Some playhouses and theatre companies, as Dutton has argued, received greater indulgence from both conciliar and civic authority, and the intricate patronage arrangements of this period were a prime factor here.[45] Tilney, too, had calls on his allegiance from both the Privy Council and from his relative and erstwhile sponsor, Charles Howard, who himself was a member of the Council and of course the patron of the Admiral's Men, one of the most important theatre companies in the 1590s and for whom Munday wrote for some years.[46] Howard, as we see from the extract cited above, had dissented from the majority line in the Council over the closure of the playhouses. The governance situation was, as Dutton puts it, 'less homogenous and univocal than its public image liked to suggest ... [and] there were levels of policy and personality where the issues were far from clear-cut'; this incident, featuring Howard's dual and conflicting roles, illustrates the point extremely well.[47] When the need arose, courtiers and theatre patrons could deal with the City authorities in a perfectly equitable manner: Howard, for example, had cause to thank the Mayor and Aldermen for granting the freedom to one of his servants in 1581.[48] Where tensions between aristocratic patrons and the City authorities did occur, they can be explained in part as the City's resistance to wider incorporation and modernisation of its structures emanating from the court, represented in this context by powerful Privy Councillors. Here, as elsewhere, the City clung jealously to its ancient prerogatives.

It is crucial to temper our understanding of such conflicts with a reminder that a number of theatre men (such as Henslowe and Munday, for example) were also 'of' the City as members of livery companies, for instance. Those involved in the theatre had had connections with city tradesmen at least as far back as the establishment of the Red Lion in 1567. Indeed, as Carol Rutter points out in relation to the Rose's initial investors, 'once solid citizens began investing in the young enterprise, detractors must have found it increasingly difficult to diagnose the playhouse as an unnatural growth on the face of society'.[49] As Douglas Bruster notes, the building of the Red Lion in 1567 coincided with the construction of Gresham's Royal Exchange – thus two institutions essential to London's cultural *and* economic life in this period were chronologically, if not geographically, siblings.[50] As far as Henslowe's Rose is concerned, the City's livery companies were fully involved with the playhouse from its very outset. The Deed of Partnership drawn up before the theatre was built in 1587 was an agreement between two trading partners, both described in the usual convention as citizens of London and members of livery companies: 'Phillip Hinshley [sic] cittizen and Dyer of London one thonne partye and John Chomley cittizen and grocer of London one thother partye'.[51] Part of Chomley's benefit from the arrangement was definitely mercantile, as he thereby gained 'the exclusive right to sell his produce to the playgoers' at the Rose.[52] It is almost impossible to imagine a theatre venture in this period that could have got off the ground without the support of the City and its financiers and tradesmen, who dominated London's economic life. Why, after all, did men such as Henslowe and Burbage initiate these enterprises, if not for profit? As Foakes and Rickert put it, 'the evidence suggests that they were all capitalists'.[53] The distaste of many scholars for any juxtaposition between art and commerce has resulted in, for instance, the poor reputation of Henslowe as an exploitative businessman with no aesthetic sense, which is related to Munday's categorisation as simply a hack writer.[54] With rare and problematic exceptions such as Nashe and Jonson, there is little to suggest that most people in early modern London shared these prejudices.

In fact, as the players had no livery company of their own, it actually *aided* them to have membership of these companies amongst their number, for, although the suburban theatres were outside of the livery companies' ambit, younger players could thereby be apprenticed, by a legal fiction, to a senior member of the company.[55] Livery company membership was after all widespread amongst those who worked for the theatres, even if the two forms of urban identity were to become separate as the theatre became more professional and autonomous.[56] As Dillon has commented, 'the hierarchy of sharers, hired men and apprentices was clearly modelled on that of master-craftsmen, journeymen and apprentices'.[57] This may well have been how the system worked for Munday himself, who, having been apprenticed initially to the Stationers' Company but never having fully served his time with Allde, may have continued his period of de facto 'apprenticeship' in the early 1580s as a player. He would therefore have been quite familiar with these conditions when he moved from John Allde's shop in the Poultry to Oxford's Company. Much as an apprentice would be indentured for seven years or so, or a journeyman, even once 'free', was obligated to serve his master, Thomas Heywood's covenant of exclusivity (witnessed in 1598 by Munday, amongst others), renders him as a player a 'searvante for ii yeares' to Henslowe.[58]

As Heywood and Munday's careers indicate, probably the most notable connection between the City and the theatre is the way in which both dramatists and actors were regularly called upon to play a part in civic entertainments, even the most high-profile such as the royal entry written by Dekker, Jonson and Middleton to celebrate James's accession.[59] Indeed, as Bergeron notes, the Corporation and its Companies would not have taken any risks with a show performed before the monarch and his family – clearly they thought it best to call in the professionals.[60] Edward Alleyn, the chief actor of the Admiral's Men, performed the role of 'Genius Urbis' (the Genius of the City) in James's royal entry into London. The part in this entertainment performed by 'Mr Allin (servaunt to the young prince [Henry])' was spoken, according to Dekker, 'with excellent Action, and a well tun'de audible voyce'.[61] Royal entries may have been infrequent but the annual Lord Mayor's Show was a regular and important means of bridging any 'gap' between the stage and the City: after all, writers for both these forms of theatre included Munday, Webster, Dekker, Jonson, Middleton and Heywood. These annual entertainments demonstrate that the City's opposition to all that the theatre stood for was perhaps rather more contingent than some have allowed. As Lobanov-Rostovsky has conceded, the bringing together of the professional stage and the city authorities that the mayoral pageants facilitated stands as an acknowledgement of 'the guilds' annual compromise with the moral ambivalence of the public theatres'.[62] For his 1611 pageant for the Goldsmiths Munday, belatedly revisiting his theatre days, called upon John Lowin, then a well-known actor in the King's Men and a member of the Goldsmiths himself, to perform the important speaking role of 'Leofstane' in the Show.[63] Indeed, Bergeron writes, 'Munday boast[ed] that three members of the King's Men – Richard Burbage, John Rice and John Lowin – performed in his pageants'.[64] Burbage and Rice had taken part the year before in Munday's *Londons Love*. In this latter text Munday singles out these two players (who had several roles in the entertainment including the only speaking parts) as 'two absolute Actors, even the verie best our instant time can yeeld'.[65] Burbage and Rice were well reimbursed for their civic duties, receiving 'seaventeen pounds tenn shillings six pence by them disbursed for robes and other furniture ... and they shall receyve to their owne uses in lieu of their paynes therein taken all such Taffety, silke, and other necessaries'.[66] Jones and Stallybrass have suggested that the gift of such expensive clothing was a generous one and one likely to be especially appreciated by these men of the stage, given the extremely high cost of rich fabric such as silk for theatrical costumes.[67] Bergeron, in contrast, suggests that this would have constituted scant payment and speculates that the actors might have taken part for reasons more of 'prestige and recognition'.[68] Munday himself was conferred a total sum of 'six pownds thirteene shillings and eight pence' by the Corporation for 'the devising of two speeches ... [and] for divertions when my Lord Maior and Aldermen attended the prince'.[69]

Bergeron instances the use of famous players for civic entertainments such as James's 1604 royal entry as demonstrating that 'the usual distinctions between the professional theatre ... and the amateurish street theatre do not obtain [but rather] the line that ordinarily separates the two is blurred, if not erased'.[70] My view is that the fact that such a temporary 'erasure' of this 'line' might take place should give us cause to re-examine what we think we know about these very 'distinctions'. Bergeron himself concedes as much when he ponders Burbage's participation in *Londons Love*: 'our minds may need some adjustment to think of one who created the roles of Hamlet and Lear ... at the Globe also busying himself along the Thames in this slight, undramatic role of Amphion ... there may have been more diversity in the actor's career ... than we normally think of'.[71] When Burbage, as Amphion, addresses Prince Henry 'on behalfe of Londons Lord Major, his worthie Brethreren, and this goodly Fleete of well affected Cittizens' the actor himself is speaking of (and to) his own civic community – he is not a marginal outsider as Mullaney, for one, might have claimed.[72] Moore argues that 'celebratory drama' such as the Lord Mayor's Show, and the fact that writers such as Jonson and Munday moved across various forms of literary production, 'forces a reassessment of ... such traditional boundaries as "courtly" and "popular"'.[73] Leinwand has commented that the City's 'willingness to retain playwrights ... to write their celebrations suggests an uneasy alliance between capital and those who articulate its ideologies'.[74] Although Leinwand does not mention Munday explicitly in this regard, 'an uneasy alliance' seems a fine characterisation of Munday's typically ambivalent relations with both theatre and City Corporation.

Inside the City itself during the late sixteenth century, one should recall, there were a number of playing spaces: for instance, the Bel Savage on Ludgate Hill, the Bull on Bishopsgate Street, and the two inns on Gracechurch (or Gracious) Street, the Bell and the Cross Keys.[75] These inns were used in poor weather and/or in the winter so that Londoners did not have to travel so far for their entertainment. In *The Downfall of Robert, Earle of Huntington* Munday himself emphasised the proximity of these playing spaces to the heart of the City and their consequent appeal to the citizenry as handy local venues. At the beginning of the play, when Little John arranges for Marian to meet Robin after he has been outlawed, John says to Robin:

> your horses at the Bell shall readie bee,
> I meane Belsavage, *whence as citizens*
> *That meant to ride for pleasure come small way,*
> You shall set foorth.[76]

The juxtaposition of these two inn names and the suggestion that they are places where citizens go a short distance for pleasure (rather than further afield to Southwark, for instance) might be regarded as controversially nostalgic in a 1598 play, as these city inns had been closed four years previously. It certainly serves as a salutary reminder that the City had its own theatrical venues, and it also reiterates the underlying message of Munday's *Second and third blast* that Londoners comprised the majority of theatre audiences.

As well as attending plays London citizens gave the theatre further support. John Swynnerton, to whom Munday dedicated at least three texts, was also the dedicatee in 1613 (the year of his mayoralty) of a play by Wentworth Smith called *The Hector of Germanie, or, The Palsgrave*. Palsgrave's (or the Elector Palatine's) Men had been reformed in that same year after the death of their previous patron, Prince Henry, and were based at the Fortune in Cripplegate. *Hector of Germanie* is 'highly anomalous', in Dutton's words, because it was written for a performance at this playhouse which had been 'rented for the occasion' by an amateur company composed of citizens. Indeed, the play may well have actually been sponsored by the Merchant Taylors, Swynnerton's company. The play, according to its dedication, was 'made for citizens, who acted it well', so much so that its writer 'deemde it fitte to be Patronizde by a Citizen'.[77] Here we find a play written by a popular playwright, performed at a suburban theatre, written on a royal theme, and performed by London citizens: it therefore stands as a demonstration of how Bergeron's 'distinctions' can be readily collapsed. Swynnerton was evidently a man of culture as well as commerce: in 1607 he was 'entreated to conferr with Mr Benjamyn Johnson the Poet about a speech' performed before the King at a Guildhall dinner given by the Merchant Taylors.[78] Swynnerton was not entirely exceptional for his interest in drama, as another wealthy citizen, Robert Keysar, a Goldsmith, was a financial backer of the company based first at the Blackfriars theatre, then at the Whitefriars, at around the same time. The satirical *Knight of the Burning Pestle*, a Blackfriars play of c.1607 which mocked Munday's prose romances, was dedicated to Keysar by its publisher.[79]

Those who assume that the theatres and the City were always and entirely at odds are often obliged to manipulate both the evidence and the categories they bring to bear upon it. Although Lobanov-Rostovsky does Munday's civic shows the rare service of paying them extended critical attention, it is Middleton and Dekker who are his main concern. He focuses on these two writers because their productions apparently demonstrate the sophisticated 'literary' virtues to which critics are commonly drawn, regardless of the fact that Munday was by far the most successful pageant-maker of this period. To sustain his view Lobanov-Rostovsky tries to establish a split between 'literary' values and economic and political realities; success in one sphere does not necessarily entail success in another, for 'critical and popular taste', he admits, 'rarely coincide'.[80] Although Munday's old competitor, Middleton, was to be commissioned to write *Civitatis Amor*, the civic entertainment celebrating the investiture of Charles as Prince of Wales after Henry's early death, it is still the case that again Middleton was reliant on Munday, for part of the latter's recent Lord Mayor's Show, *Chrysanaleia*, was re-used by the Fishmongers' Company for Middleton's work, which took place only a few days later.[81]

As with the contentious distinction between the so-called 'private' and 'public' theatres, the level of literariness that some modern commentators discern in the civic shows has an inverse relationship to the popularity they held in their day. Thus as Middleton sits within the literary canon then his shows in turn reside at a different level of literary hierarchy than those by Munday, who does not. In the seventeenth century Munday's were the favoured shows; nowadays, although Lobanov-Rostovsky concedes that the way in which the 'literary values' of Middleton's pageants have been privileged 'obscures the political realities reflected in the patronage decisions of the guilds', how quotidian works like those by Munday might be made to speak to us is not his prime concern.[82] Our retrospective categorisation of 'the popular', 'the literary' and 'the theatrical' is not itself subjected to scrutiny, despite the ways in which Munday's sheer existence testifies to the merging of these terms. Theatricality, especially in relation to pageantry, is regarded by Lobanov-Rostovsky as a mode set apart from civic life, not part of the continuum of London culture that Munday's career habitually indicates.[83] The problem with this strict demarcation of the theatrical from the civic is exemplified when Lobanov-Rostovsky summarises his view of pageantry. He first establishes as a given that 'the guild oligarchs, in their role as civic authorities, lost few opportunities ... to express their distaste for theatrical representation', then discusses the city pageants as 'carefully scripted, emblematic spectacles, for which professional actors were retained'. Of course the latter description could stand very well for stage plays themselves, were it not for the fact that by his interpretation the two entities must always remain distinct.[84] It is rather the case, as Jenstad has commented, that 'theatricality ... was already an intrinsic part of [the livery companies'] institutional self-definition'.[85] In their own day, these writers regularly traversed what we now regard with the questionable benefit of hindsight as canonical and generic confines. We do the complexity of London life in this period no favours by pretending that its inhabitants recognised these graduations as little as we often do.

'NO DOUBT A CALLING OF SOME CREDITT'

Munday's work in civic pageantry is fairly well documented, but tracing his earlier theatrical life is no simple matter. Were it not for Henslowe's *Diary*, an essential source of information on the working practices of Munday and his contemporaries, it would be even more difficult to reconstruct the theatrical environment within which Munday and the other dramatists and players worked. Even so, despite the best efforts of stage historians from Chambers onwards, much is still uncertain, although via Henslowe's records Munday is known to have been employed at the Rose and the Fortune.

Prior to the building of the Fortune north of the City in Cripplegate, Munday wrote for the companies based at the Rose, which had been established in 1587 by Henslowe in partnership with John Cholmley, a Grocer. Henslowe's *Diary* was kept from 1592 to March 1603. The first recorded company at the Rose, from February 1592, was Lord Strange's (renamed Derby's Men for a six-month period from September 1593). They produced, amongst other plays, the suppressed anti-Marprelate play of c.1592, *A Knack to Know a Knave* (which has been ascribed to Munday) and, according to McMillin and a number of other scholars, *Sir Thomas More*. Strange's Men were, according to Rutter, 'undoubtedly London's premier company in 1592' with unusually frequent performances at court.[86] Concurrently Munday dedicated his 1593 translation *The Defence of Contraries* to his theatrical patron Ferdinando Stanley, recently made Earl of Derby on the death of his father (Stanley himself died in the following year), whom Munday calls 'the right Noble, vertuous, and worthy minded Lord, Ferdinando Stanley: the great and puissant Earle of Derbie'. Munday goes on to offer 'my selfe, and my uttermost habilitie to your Honors service' to his Lord in his time of 'just conceived greefe' for his recently deceased father.[87] Given Stanley's dubious religious affiliation it is interesting to note that the title page of this text calls its author 'A. M. one of the Messengers of her Maiesties Chamber', alluding to his role as a pursuivant, rather than Munday the playwright, which might have been regarded as more relevant to Munday's position in Stanley's Company in 1593.[88]

During the 1590s Lord Strange's Men gave way to the Admiral's Men under the patronage of Charles Howard, the Earl of Nottingham. It was under the aegis of the Admiral's Men that Munday was to be involved in a large number of plays in the later 1590s; indeed, it has been calculated that in the single year of 1597 he had a hand (with Chettle and Dekker) in at least twenty-six.[89] Howard's own connections and political interests had an impact on Munday's plays. In relation to the brouhaha over the depiction of Oldcastle in Munday's very successful play of 1599, Rutter identifies Nottingham (and hence, by implication, his Company) with 'the [court] Establishment', in contrast to the Chamberlain's Men, whose patron, George Carey, Lord Hunsdon, flirted in the 1590s with dangerous courtiers such as Essex.[90] Furthermore, as Paul Whitfield White points out, Nottingham himself was then 'a political ally' (as well as being the putative father-in-law) of Henry Brooke, Lord Cobham, a member of the family with which Oldcastle had become associated. Indeed, White suggests that the 'bonus' that Munday and his collaborators received from Henslowe for this play may have been the gift of 'an outside party'; thus the play may in effect have been commissioned, or at the very least was rewarded, by a member of the Cobham faction.[91] Andrew Gurr's view of this theory is that Nottingham himself may have 'suggested the subject to his company', given Lord Cobham's betrothal to his daughter, although Roslyn Knutson cautions that 'there is no document in Henslowe's papers to support the claim of a company commission'.[92] Relatedly, it has been suggested that Munday's *Huntington* plays might have been prompted by Howard's recent rise in status to the Earldom of Nottingham. *The Downfall of Robert, Earle of Huntington* was played at court in December 1598 after some 'mendinge' by Henry Chettle, although the extant text probably does not contain any of Chettle's revisions.[93] If the play was indeed intended in part as a celebration of the recent elevation of the patron of the Admiral's Men then a court performance seems all the more appropriate.

The controversy over his *Oldcastle* plays aside, apart from various entries in Henslowe's *Diary* Munday's stage years have left little trace. However, we do know that as well as his disputed turn to acting before and after the publication of *A second and third blast*, Munday is on record as having been involved in writing for the stage from the mid-1580s (the entry in the Stationers' Register for *Fedele and Fortunio* is in 1584) until around 1602.[94] Despite the much-cited claim in Thomas Alfield's 1582 'Caveat' that before his apprenticeship to Allde Munday was 'first a stage player' and then 'did play extempore' on his return from Rome in 1581, there is unfortunately scant concrete evidence about Munday's acting career or early play-writing. Given Munday's age at the time of Alfield's text, his acting days may have been as a boy player, possibly for the Children's companies, or for those players based at the Red Lion or Newington Butts in the late 1570s to early 1580s. The Newington Butts playhouse may have been a venue for Oxford's Men in the early to mid-1580s; as such it might also have featured Munday as an actor 'ruff[ling] on the stage', as Alfield put it.[95] In 1584 there were only a few companies in existence: they included the Paul's Children and the Chapel Children (founded in 1575 and 1576 respectively) who acted at Paul's or the first Blackfriars.[96] These two children's companies were united in 1583 (the year of the creation of the Queen's Men by Tilney) under the patronage of the Earl of Oxford, Munday's patron during this period.[97] As Munday dedicated to Lord Strange when he was in Strange's Company, it is certainly possible that he might have dedicated to Oxford on the same basis. This suggests that Munday was associated with Oxford's Men, perhaps first as a player and then as a writer; McMillin and MacLean list Munday as one of the writers 'we can be fairly sure of' being in Oxford's Company in 1583.[98]

Munday's adaptation of *Fedele and Fortunio*, one extant edition of which has a epilogue for a court production, may well have been performed at court before its publication in November 1584.[99] Lord Howard's Men, as the company who were to become the Admiral's were then known, did not perform at court until 1588/9, so *Fedele* is unlikely to have been written for them, but rather for another company, possibly Oxford's if Munday was indeed active in his Company at that time.[100] The chronology of Munday's theatrical career from the 1580s until c.1592 is obscure: as well as uncertainty over the provenance of *Fedele* it is not known for which company he wrote *John a Kent and John a Cumber* in 1590, although it has been speculated that it may be the same play as the successful Admiral's production of 1594–97, *The Wise Man of Westchester*.[101] However, Gurr claims that the 'plot' of *The Seven Deadlie Sinns*, which he believes to be a Strange's play from the 1590/1 period when they were at the Theatre, shortly before they moved to the Rose, 'is in the same hand as the scribal hand that wrote the *More* manuscript' – Munday's hand, which it certainly closely resembles.[102] The subject matter of this play, with its exemplary ancient anti-hero personifying sin, does bear some resemblance to Munday's 1579 prose work *A Mirrour of Mutabilitie*, suggesting that Munday's hand in this play may have been as much authorial as scribal.

Once the Admiral's Company was established at the Rose a number of writers, Munday included, began to feature regularly in its repertory.

Jonson, Dekker and Heywood all began their theatrical writing careers at Henslowe's Rose; indeed, Jonson and Munday both first appear in Henslowe's *Diary* in 1597. Middleton's first (co-authored) play was *Caesar's Fall*, which was played at the Fortune in 1602 for the Admiral's Men, although Middleton, unlike Munday, was not associated with any one company for long.[103] In 1599/1600 when the Admiral's Men moved to the Fortune Munday was one of the seven writers who dominated their repertory. Neil Carson has surmised that Munday was in that year part of a regular writing 'syndicate' with Drayton, Hathaway and Wilson (his co-authors on *Sir John Oldcastle*), all of whose names regularly appear with Munday's in Henslowe's entries.[104] Munday's work for the Admiral's Company at their new venue included the now lost *The Rising of Cardinal Wolsey*, written in 1601 and performed the following year.[105] According to the available evidence, Munday had probably retired from the stage by 1603, when he was in his early forties.[106] The last entry in Henslowe's *Diary* for payment to Munday is for *A Set at Tennis* in December 1602, although of course the *Diary* itself finishes shortly afterwards anyway, in March 1603.[107] Another dramatic text from 1602 is the now-lost collaboration with Dekker, *Jephtha*, for which Munday may well have drawn on his earlier work *The Mirrour of Mutabilitie*, where Jephthah's story features.[108] The year 1602 looks like a crucial transitional year for Munday as he shifted his self-identity as a writer from the professional stage to the civic domain proper.

Carson has calculated that the average yearly earnings of playwrights on the whole barely exceeded 'a working-class wage'. Thus it is possible that Munday diversified his literary activities at this stage at least in part for financial reasons, for he had a number of dependants and the status of 'gentleman' to support. However, in 1602 it appears that Munday earned more through his playwrighting at the Fortune (a total of £7) than he had for a number of years; this sum compares favourably with the figure set by proclamation in 1589/90 for the wages for 'the best and most skillful workmen and journeymen' of the Drapers' Company of £4, for instance, and gives an indication that Munday may have taken to writing as a more profitable occupation than the drapery trade.[109] If Munday did earn £7 per year he was fortunate, for Carson states that 'to live like a "gentleman" would require two or three times' the likely annual income of one of Henslowe's writers.[110] There certainly is no evidence that Munday took on the more lucrative role of 'sharer' in his theatre company, as the younger

Thomas Heywood was to do. Alternatively, it is feasible that Munday was too busy writing for the City from the end of 1602 onwards to concentrate on writing plays; he certainly stressed the arduous nature of the historical research that underpins many of his civic texts. His income notwithstanding, it would appear that Munday left active employment with the stage shortly before the major reorganisation of the theatre companies under royal patronage from 1603 onwards and before the move towards 'private' theatres such as the Blackfriars in the Jacobean period. At this pivotal point in his career, having been only very recently one of Henslowe's most ubiquitous writers, Munday seems to have elected to put his eggs in the civic basket, so to speak.

Playhouses such as the Admiral's Men's Fortune are often supposed to have appealed specifically to a civic audience. The usual distinction between the so-called 'citizen' or 'public' playhouses such as the Fortune and the Red Bull and the apparently more elite and erudite plays at the Globe and Blackfriars establishes a hierarchy of both play-texts and playwrights, with Munday at the bottom end in all respects. Doubtless if Shakespeare had written for the former companies rather than the Chamberlain's/King's Men the standings would be reversed.[111] As it is, the Admiral's Men, together with Munday and their other chief writers, are made to stand in opposition to the Chamberlain's Men and their most celebrated playwright. However, as Foakes points out, in the 1590s in particular the hierarchies that we have belatedly applied to the stage companies, their writers and their plays cannot really be sustained. During this decade, he argues, 'the Admiral's and the Chamberlain's Men ... seem to have had equal standing at court, and, probably, with the public', so the 'rivalry' between them was more commercial than aesthetic.[112] Munday and some of his less well-known collaborators are forced to suffer from their connection with Henslowe and all he is supposed to stand for. As with so many aspects of the material history of the theatres, the reality seems to be resistant to watertight categorisation. Munday himself, of course, in the case of *Sir Thomas More* may have had a hand in the same dramatic text with the one playwright whose place in the literary canon is unassailable.

As I have already established in respect of civic attitudes to the stage, in terms of their subject matter too the plays and writers of the Rose and the Fortune cannot be said to have been indifferent to the City. The repertoire of these theatres in the 1590s and the early years of the seventeenth century featured a number of plays 'based on stories from Foxe's *Book of Martyrs*', the so-called 'Elect Nation' plays.[113]

White has written that 'the Admiral's troupe ... established an identity with the more advanced Protestant party by staging a series of plays based on Protestant heroes'; as well as *Oldcastle*, White also mentions Munday's *Huntington* plays in this category.[114] In relation to the so-called 'Oldcastle controversy' White argues that the Admiral's Men 'reaffirmed an identity with London's puritan-leaning audiences' via Munday et al.'s *Sir John Oldcastle*, which was in part a defence of the Lollard martyr's reputation.[115] From the evidence of repertory that has survived, it also seems that plays with a specifically London setting were popular.[116] As well as Munday, both Dekker and Heywood produced a number of plays that mediated national history through a metropolitan lens, such as Heywood's 1598 Rose play *Edward IV*, which features civic heroism of the kind that Munday also celebrated in his civic shows. All three of these writers worked together on one play that foregrounded the London dimensions of social and religious conflict, *Sir Thomas More*.

However, as with types of play, it would be unwise to make firm distinctions between audience types at different playhouses and thus to associate the Fortune with a narrowly defined idea of 'citizen culture', for there was a visit to the Fortune in 1621 by the Spanish ambassador Gondomar, who 'afterwards banqueted with the players'.[117] Gurr also comments about the Rose's repertoire that 'Henslowe's lists of titles certainly indicate more plays that seem to come from the academic and learned community than from the popular and rural tradition'.[118] He singles out Munday's *Huntington* plays as examples of lively 'innovation' towards 'old material'.[119] Peck asserts too that Munday's version of the Robin Hood story 'sought a higher tone in setting and content, and made very little use of the popular tradition'.[120] Indeed, the play establishes itself in contradistinction to 'popular' treatments of the Robin Hood story, for in response to John Eltham's desire in *The Downfall of Robert Earl of Huntington* for 'jeasts' and 'merry Morices', Skelton/Friar Tuck implies somewhat dismissively that the old-fashioned style of representation of Robin Hood is now hackneyed and out of date, 'for merry jeasts, they have bene showne before'.[121] The *Huntington* plays raise other questions about a simplistic notion of the 'popular' dramatic form practised by the Admiral's Men, for Munday's additions and revisions to the Robin Hood legend are noted primarily for the way in which they *gentrify* their eponymous hero. Certainly, this is an important aspect of the texts, for unlike some other contemporary dramatic treatments of this semi-mythical figure, let alone the various ballad versions of his story, Munday's plays do not feature the name 'Robin Hood' in their titles.[122] Although Munday did not invent the tradition that Robin Hood was a displaced aristocrat of high rank rather than a mere yeoman (the idea was put forward, unsourced, in Richard Grafton's *Chronicle*), his plays certainly helped to establish it more firmly and worked to dislodge the extant idea that 'Robin' was a plebeian yeoman or even a subversive outlaw more in the Jack Cade mould.[123] As we will see, Munday was not even averse to adding a specifically civic dimension to Robin Hood's identity when the occasion demanded it.

If the Fortune really was a 'citizen' playhouse, this in itself raises questions about how it was regarded by those citizens' governors. As Munday's *Second and third blast* inadvertently demonstrates, Londoners' attitudes to the stage were by no means univocal. The prolonged contention over the opening of the Fortune in 1600 is significant for Munday in more ways than one. The theatre was located in his own parish, and he was simultaneously at that date both one of the Admiral's Men's most productive playwrights as well as addressing himself increasingly to civic dignitaries, some of whom clearly had mixed feelings about the appearance of a new playhouse so close to the boundary of their jurisdiction.

'SOE FARR DISTANT AND REMOTE FROME ANY PERSON OR PLACE OF ACCOMPT': CRIPPLEGATE AND THE FORTUNE

In 1600 Munday's theatrical employer arrived in his own Cripplegate neighbourhood when the Admiral's Company moved north of the river from Bankside to their new purpose-built theatre, the Fortune. The contract for the building of the Fortune was drawn up between Henslowe and 'Edwarde Allen' of Southwark, 'gentlemen', and 'Peeter Streete, Cittizen and Carpenter of London'. Street, who had been employed to take down the Theatre and rebuild it as the Globe the previous year, was to be paid £440 for building the Fortune.[124] Unfortunately for Henslowe and his associates, the building of the Fortune playhouse was to be anything but unproblematic.

As with the Red Lion in Mile End, we know more about how the Fortune was to be built than we know about precisely where it was built, although, as we will see, its location has more implications for the material history of the playhouse and its companies. Although she does not discuss the Fortune explicitly, Dillon has argued that the metropolitan playhouses in the suburbs were not simply or uniformly 'marginal' in their locations, as Mullaney has previously claimed. She writes that 'their location and status is more complex than that, and different playhouses stand in different relation to the city'.[125] The Fortune is a case in point. It is very clear from the playhouse's vexed early history that Cripplegate was not regarded in the same way as Southwark, which, despite the 1550 charter which extended the City's jurisdiction across the river, was still quite distinct from the City and caused many headaches for the Corporation.[126] Dillon's comment that 'theatres therefore stand at a cross-roads between the city and the non-city' has an almost literal relevance to the Fortune, one which certainly teaches us to be wary of casual assertions of 'marginality'.[127]

The Fortune was to be located between Golden Lane (then 'Golding Lane') and Whitecross Street, just north of Cripplegate itself: the contract between Henslowe, Alleyn and Street concerns 'a certeine plott or parcell of grounde ... scytuate and beinge nere Goldinge lane in the parishe of Ste Giles withoute Cripplegate of London'.[128] It was

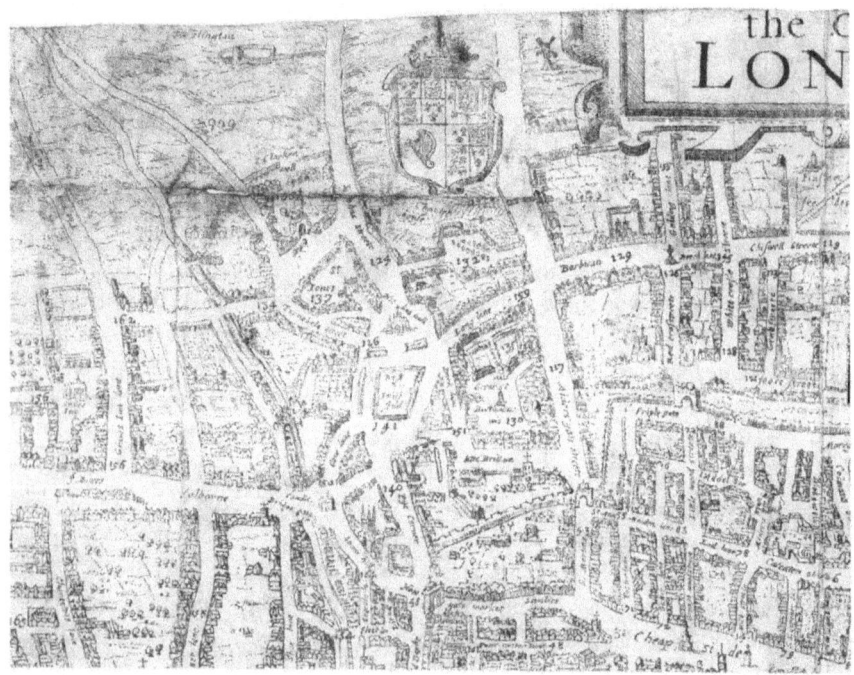

5 Map of 'The Cittie of London' (undated).

therefore located within Munday's home parish at the time. Some literary critics do not seem to realise that the boundary of the *parish* of St Giles Without Cripplegate (which extended as far north as Old Street, on the edge of Islington) was not identical to the City boundary, i.e. the limits of the *ward* of Cripplegate Without. It is significant that the Fortune was built within the parish of St Giles Cripplegate, in the liberty of Finsbury under the jurisdiction of the Middlesex justices; it was thus located outside, although probably very close to the edge of, the ward of Cripplegate Without.[129] It was much nearer to the City limits than most of the other northern playhouses such as the Theatre, the Curtain and the Red Bull. The Cripplegate ward boundary zigzags across Golden Lane northwards for some distance before crossing back in a westwards direction. Like Southwark, the ward of Cripplegate Without, especially on its eastern side towards Moorfields, was renowned for its lawlessness: 'the civic authorities ... looked upon the Outer Ward [of Cripplegate] as a pestilential nuisance better left to its own devices'.[130]

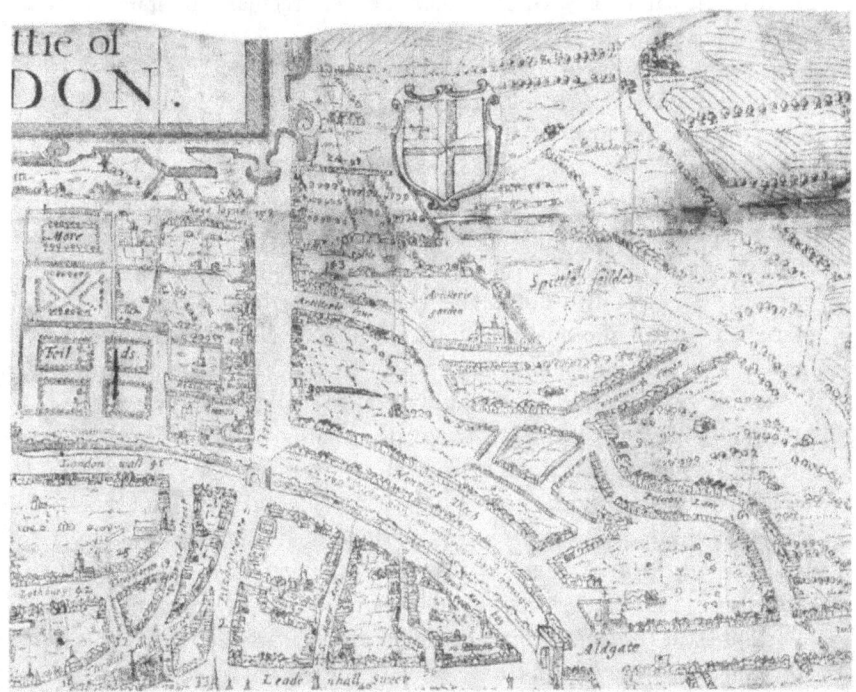

The Fortune playhouse is shown below the bottom left of the cartouche.

The Fortune bears out what Henri Lefebvre has argued about boundaries generally: their arbitrariness 'give[s] rise ... to an appearance of separation between spaces where in fact what exists is an ambiguous continuity'.[131] In this respect the Fortune can be likened to Munday himself, whose spheres of activity overlapped and at times conflicted. Without the distinct physical barrier of the Thames (as was the case with Bankside) between the City and its outer northern regions, the Fortune's position at the limits of the City can be interpreted as both threateningly close to and outside of the City proper, being within sight of its ancient wall. The ward of Cripplegate was bisected by London Wall; indeed, the larger part of the ward was extra-mural.[132] Even the presence of the walls was no guarantee of civic integrity for those places that lay within them, as the case of the Blackfriars theatre within its liberty demonstrates; as Dillon has argued, 'the emphasis on the city wall as fixed boundary may be read as a sign of ... strain rather than of real fixity'.[133] No 'natural' boundary, then, marked the city's limits in the contested area of Cripplegate. It is not for nothing (as we will see further in the next chapter) that the limits of the parish of St Giles Cripplegate were regularly re-stated in the ceremony known as 'beating the bounds'.

The place of this particular stage can be seen to be overdetermined in both the spatial and ideological senses of the term.[134] Rather than being the simple antithesis of the 'inside' of the intra-mural area, the suburbs and their theatres regularly reached inside and compromised the identity of the purely civic area. Both the ward and parish of Cripplegate stretched in part beyond the walls and, in the case of the latter, beyond civic control too: consequently Cripplegate was a space bisected by various institutions and individuals. It brought those ideo-spatial differences into close proximity, making the distinction between inside and outside all the more difficult to sustain. Cripplegate is therefore a fine example of what Moretti has called 'the generalized spatial proximity unique to the city'.[135] As with the location of the Fortune – as we will see, sometimes said to be remote from the City, in other contexts fortuitously proximate – the city walls could sometimes be used *rhetorically* to encompass the City. Indeed, in Munday's pageant *Himatia-Poleos*, as Andrew Gordon has commented, the walls are transformed into the 'protective clothing of the city', or, in Munday's own words, its 'best garments [that] do preserve it from all dangerous annoyances'.[136] Munday, of course, would have known full well that the walls did not inevitably constitute the boundary of the City – at least not in Cripplegate: he simply used their appearance as a convenient metaphor with which to celebrate the Drapers in their Lord Mayor's Show.

As the knotty case of the Fortune suggests, one can see attitudes towards the theatres and theatregoing in a more dialectic light: contrary to Mullaney's overheated claims, the extra-mural areas of London were not necessarily experienced as 'liminal', threatening or overly licentious by their residents nor by their visitors.[137] It is equally clear from the complicated narrative of the Fortune's early days that the local residents were by no means uniformly antagonistic to the theatre in their midst. As we have seen, some of the Fortune's writers and players were inhabitants of Cripplegate parish, attending the same church (in Munday's case, even claiming familiarity with the vicar) and quite probably undertaking the same kind of parochial duties as some of their less apparently 'socially disreputable' neighbours. As the protracted negotiations over the building of the Fortune indicate, those who lived in these supposedly 'subversive' areas were as likely to regard the theatres as convenient local providers of poor law relief as they were to dread them as dangers to social order.[138] Indeed, as Mark Bayer argues, some citizens might have 'view[ed] the "civilised" west end with the same apprehension that Londoners travelling to Clerkenwell, Finsbury, or Southwark for dramatic performances would view these unfamiliar neighbourhoods'.[139]

Despite its relative neglect by literary scholars, the Fortune playhouse was described by a contemporary, John Chamberlain, as 'the fairest playhouse in this town'.[140] It was certainly spacious when compared to the Bankside theatres; furthermore, it has been calculated from Street's plan for the Fortune that the bulk of the space in the playhouse was intended for the more expensive (and more lucrative) gallery seating, rather than the one-penny standing-only playhouse yard.[141] Carson has calculated from Henslowe's *Diary* that the Admiral's Company's weekly receipts increased after their relocation to the Fortune.[142] Furthermore, Dutton has recently established a close connection between this new playhouse and the court, a connection first made probable in respect of Dekker's 1600 play *Old Fortunatus*. This play was rewritten for court performance (with an unusually high payment from Henslowe to Dekker) only a few months after the Fortune itself had been completed in mid-1600. Dutton suggests that Dekker's play was that rare artefact, a playhouse text written, or rewritten, specifically for a performance at court, since there is no evidence from Henslowe's records that it played at the Fortune subsequently. He goes on to argue that this together with other examples of plays from the early 1600s indicates a theatre company at the height of their status and full of confidence in the likely success of their new venue.[143]

Notwithstanding the hopes with which the Admiral's Men moved north of the river, many and various bodies had a role to play during the Fortune's difficult early days. The Privy Council intervened in March 1600 over the building of the Fortune because of complaints from St Giles inhabitants headed up by Lord Willoughby. Munday was, of course, a St Giles parishioner at this point as well as being an Admiral's Men's playwright. The Council issued an injunction to prevent the completion of the playhouse, stating baldly that 'no soche theatre or plaie-howse be built there ... wee require you not to fail forthwith to take order that the foresaid intended building maie be staied, and yf any be begone [begun], to see the same quite defaced'.[144] The theatre's neighbours were not all opposed to the plans, however, for twenty-seven other local residents of Finsbury petitioned the Privy Council in April rather to *permit* the completion of the playhouse on the grounds that it was located 'neere unto the [Finsbury] ffeildes' and thus 'soe farr distant and remote frome any person or Place of accompt, as that none can be Annoyed thearbie'.[145] Here the Fortune is rhetorically described as far removed from the City, or at least from those City inhabitants that mattered. The 'remoteness' that the letter stresses is not geographical at all, but rather ideological, since the playhouse site was actually only a couple of hundred yards from Cripplegate itself and certainly in sight of the City limits. In contrast to this, the Privy Council letter to the Middlesex magistrates upholding Willoughby *et al.*'s complaint against the proposed theatre describes the Fortune's position as 'in white crossstreete *neere unto the Barres* in that parte that ys in the countie of Middlesex'.[146] When opposing the building of the Fortune the Council chooses to represent the location of the disputed playhouse in terms of its nearness to the margin of City and county (symbolised by 'the Barres', the markers of the City boundary) although they do concede that it actually lies within the jurisdiction of the county of Middlesex.[147] This conciliar letter also uses the moralistic lexicon usually associated with the City Corporation to condemn the playhouse (which it calls 'an offence and a scandall'), reminding the Middlesex magistracy that 'soche occacions ... breed increase of base and lewde people and divers other disorders'.[148]

What is striking about all these various interventions is that the location of the Fortune is represented with a different emphasis depending on the agenda of the writer(s). Nottingham's own warrant, written from Court at Richmond in January 1600 to the Middlesex JPs and any other interested parties requesting them to 'permitt and suffer my saide Servant [Alleyn] to proceede in theffectinge and finishinge of the saide New howse, without anie your lett or molestation, towards him or any of his woorkmen', places the proposed playhouse 'neere Redcrossestreete *London*' and, in contrast to its putative 'remoteness', says that it stands '*verie convenient* for the ease of People', much as the City's playhouse inns (such as the Cross Keys) did until the mid-1590s.[149] The Privy Council echoed Nottingham's words in April, when instructing the Middlesex JPs that it had been persuaded by those Cripplegate residents who wrote to them in favour of the playhouse. Their letter states that 'the *conveniencie* of [the theatre site] ... ys testified unto us under the handes of manie of the Inhabitantes of the Libertie of Fynisbury, wheare it is'.[150] This playhouse, it would seem, could perform the miraculous feat of being both 'remote' *and* 'convenient' simultaneously, depending on the argument to be made at a given time. The debate about its precise distance from the City notwithstanding, as with the City's attempt to gain control over the licensing of playgoing back in 1574, another consideration had due priority: poor relief. Those Finsbury residents who pleaded for the playhouse to be allowed stressed that their chief reason for doing so was that 'the Erectours of the saied howse are contented to give a very liberall porcion of money weeklie, towards the releef of our Poore'. For a large and impoverished parish such as Cripplegate this would have been no small consideration; indeed, their letter makes this quite plain. They write that 'wee are the rather Contented to accept this meanes of releif of our Poore, because our Parrish is not able to releeve them'.[151]

Those few records of Finsbury that survive indicate that it was a place composed largely of semi-rural and small-scale industrial properties where, Cerasano writes, 'property value was poor ... and tenant restrictions oppressive'.[152] It is unclear from the documents whose best interests were really being served by the prospect of a new playhouse in the area. Rutter, for one, speculates that the second group of residents (which included many of the local parish officers) may have been prompted to make their intervention by a person or persons involved in the playhouse itself who could have 'canvassed the community'.[153] She suggests Henslowe as a candidate for this role, but it could potentially have been Munday who had more local links in

Cripplegate than Henslowe. There is a precedent for this earlier in Henslowe's career, for in 1598, in the face of attempts by local parish officers to draw up a petition against the Southwark playhouses (including the Rose), Henslowe used his own parish status to dissipate this threat to his livelihood.[154] Although this makes it likely, as Rutter speculates, that Henslowe later took on the same role in Cripplegate, it certainly does not rule out Munday, who as we have seen was busy cultivating the patronage of influential civic figures at precisely the same time as the Fortune was being debated. In addition, he had only recently simultaneously been involved with both the Privy Council and the Admiral's Men.

Like the attempted suppression of playing in 1584 that I have already discussed, this is another complex chain of events, since Nottingham, the Fortune company's patron, was present at the March 1600 Privy Council meeting where the policy to suppress the Fortune was decided only a couple of months after he had written a warrant to the Middlesex justices to *support* the new theatre.[155] Still more inconsistently, Nottingham then only a month later encouraged the Privy Council finally to recommend to the Justices of Middlesex that they should allow the theatre to be completed. The Council duly sent the magistrates a letter signed by Nottingham himself plus Lord Hunsdon, the Lord Chamberlain (another players' patron) and Robert Cecil to express her majesty's 'pleasuer' that this by then nearly completed playhouse should be permitted, 'scituat' as it was 'in a verie remote and exempt place neere Goulding lane'.[156] In its phrasing the letter echoes the pro-theatre residents' letter that prompted it quite closely. The distance of the Fortune from the city was stressed too by Henslowe, who described it as being 'in the contrey'.[157] It seems a common tactic of the various pro-theatre forces to emphasise the lack of potential offence to Londoners that would result from the playhouse's so-called remoteness. The conciliar letter, which seems to have had little enforceable status but was rather a 'private initiative', according to Rutter, owing to its theatrically complicit signatories, was followed up by a Privy Council order of June 1600, only a month before the theatre was due to be completed and the final sally in this convoluted, six-month-long saga of toing and froing.[158] This latter document, clearly the result of much debate and amendment, shows classic Elizabethan political compromise, paying lip service to the accepted dangers of 'the ydle ryotous and dissolute livinge of great nombers of people' caused by the playhouses whilst at the same time preserving a place for the theatre, which is described as 'not beinge evill in yt self' so long as it exhibits 'good order and moderacion'.[159] It is worth noting here that this final Privy Council intervention over the establishment of the Fortune addresses both the county magistrates and the Lord Mayor as responsible for ensuring good order: 'it is ordered that severall Copies of these orders shalbe sent to the Lord Maior of London and to the Justices of the peace of the Counties of Middlesex and Surrey and that lettres shalbe written unto them from their Lordshippes [the Council] straightly charginge them to see to the execucion of the same'.[160]

The sense one gains from this and some of the other documents produced in 1600 is of a political stitch-up; the definitive Privy Council intervention of June 1600 explains that 'there Lordshippes have bin enformed by Edmond Tylney Esquire ... that the howse now in hand to be builte ... is not intended to encrease the number of the Plaiehowses, but to be in steed of an other, namelie the Curtaine'.[161] What may or may not have been 'intended' is not necessarily what actually happened, although in this case the assurance served a purpose. Of course, what this decision ensured was that Nottingham's company, who were as much indebted to their patron as was Tilney himself, retained their privileged position in the London theatre world (in 1597/8 Langley's Swan had already suffered from being outside of this duopoly). This was a position which Privy Council policy on the theatres over the next few years seemed determined to underline, even when the Admiral's and the Chamberlain's Men had been replaced by direct royal patronage under James I and his family.

Although one of the chief preconditions for the Fortune's existence was the simultaneous destruction of the other northern suburban theatre, the Curtain, which was ordered to be 'either ruynated or applied to some other good use', this precondition was never met, despite a series of ferociously worded letters from the Privy Council to the magistrates, and from thence to the Mayor and aldermen, over the next eighteen months asking why this was so.[162] The June 1600 conciliar order also stipulated that no 'stage plaies shalbe plaied (as sometimes they have bin) in any Common Inn for publique assemblie in or neere about the Cittie'.[163] Given what Ingram has discovered about the beneficial financial arrangements around the licensing of City inns (as discussed above) it is even probable that this prohibition would have financially damaged rather than gratified the City. As Dillon argues, the three-way relationships between theatre, City and court were never straightforward: 'players endlessly renegotiate[d] ... their double orientation towards these ... locations, themselves necessarily in dialogue with each other as well as with the theatre'.[164] At this level of local knowledge the inter-relationships are very complex, if not contradictory; counter-examples can always be found to complicate a simple reading of the stage–City–court nexus.

This contested Cripplegate neighbourhood also has a tangential role to play in Munday's other dramatic works, his Lord Mayors' Shows. Whitecross Street, which like the neighbouring Golden Lane lies both within and outside of the city boundary, crops up again in the more unlikely context of civic documentation as there was a barn there in which properties for civic entertainments were made. In another of the parallels that make Munday's contribution to civic culture so suggestive, a record has survived of a payment to Munday in 1623 for his final pageant, *The Triumphes of the Golden Fleece*. This show was written for the Drapers, a fact which Munday alludes to in his usual fashion by describing himself as their 'poore loving Brother'.[165] The Drapers' records for this show include an item reimbursing Munday for the sum of forty shillings: 'item paid to Mr Monday for the hyer of a barne in Whitecrossestreete to make the Argoe in'.[166] It was in the year 1623 that Munday received the right of 'nomination of a freeman' and the year after his lease in Cripplegate was 'surrendered', suggesting an end to his lengthy sojourn in that parish. Here, on the street adjacent to the recently rebuilt Fortune, Munday also concluded his theatrical productions for the City, which are the subject of the next chapter.

NOTES

1. Munday, *A second and third blast*, sig. Eir.
2. *Ibid.*, sig. Aivr.
3. *Ibid.*, sig. ivv.
4. *Ibid.*, sig. Avr.
5. *Ibid.*, sig. ivv.
6. *Ibid.*, sig. Hiv.
7. See Munday, *Sidero-Thriambos*, sig. A4r.
8. Munday, *A second and third blast*, sigs Iiiiv–ivr.
9. *Ibid.*, sigs Dviiiv–Eir.
10. Munday, *Londons Love*, sig. A4v.
11. Unlike most of those who cite *A second and third blast*, Ingram has noticed that Munday's attack on the stage 'may be more formulaic and fashionable than fervently felt' and he also makes the point that Munday 'was capable of turning his pen to either side of an issue' (*English Professional Theatre*, p. 162).
12. Mullaney, *The Place of the Stage*, p. 46; Collinson, 'Saints on Sundays', p. 16.

13 Munday, *A second and third blast*, sig. Avv; my emphases.
14 See Lake, *The Antichrist's Lewd Hat*, pp. 426–7.
15 Cited in Ingram, *The Business of Playing*, p. 41. Ingram remarks that 'this strand in [Gosson's] thought is not normally given its due' (*English Professional Theatre*, p. 161).
16 In her study of civic theatre Anne Lancashire comments on 'the misperception ... of many Renaissance theatre scholars that the London authorities at all times were implacably opposed to the theatre' (*London Civic Theatre*, p. 3). Lancashire links this ingrained assumption to 'the general prejudice' of such scholars 'against pageantry and in favour of playtexts', leading them to deny that pageantry is a form of theatre (*ibid.*). As an example of the approach Lancashire critiques, Jean Howard found it 'surprising' that the City sponsored civic entertainments (*The Stage and Social Struggle*, p. 41).
17 See Ingram, *The Business of Playing*, pp. 73–5 and 83, and Rutter, ed., *Documents of the Rose Playhouse*, pp. 7 and 11.
18 Cited in Gurr, *The Shakespearean Stage*, p. 31.
19 See Robertson and Gordon, *A Calendar of Dramatic Records*, pp. xlviii–xlix, and Lancashire, *London Civic Theatre*, pp. 73–94 and *passim*. Lancashire comments that the Drapers (Munday's company) were especially active in sponsoring players.
20 Tilney was first appointed by the Privy Council in 1577, the year after the building of the Theatre. See Rutter, ed., *Documents of the Rose Playhouse*, pp. 16–17, and Chambers, *The Elizabethan Stage*, vol. IV, pp. 285–7.
21 Wickham *et al.*, *English Professional Theatre*, pp. 70–4.
22 Chambers, *The Elizabethan Stage*, vol. IV, p. 274; see also Wickham *et al.*, *English Professional Theatre*, pp. 73–7, and Ingram, *The Business of Playing*, pp. 130–4.
23 Ingram, *The Business of Playing*, p. 131.
24 Wickham *et al.*, *English Professional Theatre*, p. 75.
25 Chambers, *The Elizabethan Stage*, vol. IV, p. 275. As we will see, this poor relief issue was also mobilised in the debate about the building of the Fortune theatre in 1599/1600.
26 Chambers, *The Elizabethan Stage*, vol. IV, p. 276; Wickham *et al.*, *English Professional Theatre*, p. 76. See also Ingram, *The Business of Playing*, p. 134. Other civic authorities also exhibited ambivalence towards the theatre: Bristol, for instance, 'banned all playing in the city's guildhall in 1585, on the grounds that playing was too frivolous an activity'; in 1596, however, both Derby's Men and the Queen's Men performed in that same guildhall (Gurr, 'Privy Councilors as theatre patrons', p. 221).
27 Chambers, *The Elizabethan Stage*, vol. IV, pp. 272–3.
28 See Wickham *et al.*, *English Professional Theatre*, p. 304.
29 Hawkes, 'Idolatry and commodity fetishism', p. 256; my emphasis.
30 Mullaney, *The Place of the Stage*, p. 45.
31 Hawkes, 'Idolatry and commodity fetishism', p. 257.
32 *Ibid.*, p. 258.
33 Ingram, *The Business of Playing*, p. 135.
34 *Ibid.*, p. 146.
35 See Freedman, 'Elizabethan protest', pp. 39–43, and Overall and Overall,

Analytical Index, pp. 350–7 and *passim*.
36 Chambers, *The Elizabethan Stage*, vol. IV, p. 288.
37 Freedman, 'Elizabethan protest', pp. 36–7.
38 Chambers, *The Elizabethan Stage*, vol. IV, p. 309.
39 Robertson and Gordon, *A Calendar of Dramatic Records*, p. xlix; see also pp. 166–7.
40 Quoted in Dutton, *Mastering the Revels*, p. 79.
41 See *ibid.*, pp. 77–8.
42 Chambers, *The Elizabethan Stage*, vol. IV, p. 298.
43 McMillin and MacLean, *The Queen's Men and Their Plays*, p. 47.
44 See also Gurr, 'Privy Councilors as theatre patrons', pp. 222–4.
45 See Dutton, *Licensing, Censorship and Authorship*, p. 22.
46 Tilney's superior (the Lord Chamberlain) in 1596, before the appointment of Lord Hunsdon in 1597, was Lord Cobham, whose wife was a descendant of Munday *et al.*'s dramatised martyr, Sir John Oldcastle.
47 Dutton, *Mastering the Revels*, p. 45.
48 See Overall and Overall, *Analytical Index*, p. 151. In 1594 Howard 'begged' the City to confer the freedom on another of his servants (*ibid.*, p. 157).
49 Rutter, ed., *Documents of the Rose Playhouse*, p. 37.
50 Bruster, *Drama and the Market*, p. 3; see also Dillon, *Theatre, Court and City*, pp. 64–5.
51 Rutter, ed., *Documents of the Rose Playhouse*, p. 37.
52 Gurr, 'The authority of the Globe and the Fortune', p. 261; see also Carson, *A Companion to Henslowe's Diary*, p. 14.
53 Foakes, *Henslowe's Diary*, p. xxxvii.
54 See also Rutter, ed., *Documents of the Rose Theatre*, pp. 1–5, Carson, 'Literary management', pp. 187–8, and Foakes, *Henslowe's Diary*, pp. viii–x and xxix–xxx.
55 See Jones and Stallybrass, *Renaissance Clothing and the Materials of Memory*, pp. 175–6; see also Dillon, *Theatre, Court and City*, p. 156 n. 23, Forse, *Art Imitates Business*, pp. 13–14, and Baldwin, *The Organization and Personnel*, p. 37 n. 127.
56 See Ingram in Wickham *et al.*, *English Professional Theatre*, pp. 154–5.
57 Dillon, *Theatre, Court and City*, p. 35; see also Baldwin, *The Organization and Personnel*, pp. 25–6 and 32–8, and Knutson, *Playing Companies and Commerce*, p. 27.
58 Rutter, ed., *Documents of the Rose Playhouse*, p. 138; see also McLuskie, *Dekker and Heywood*, p. 2, Carson, *A Companion to Henslowe's Diary*, pp. 33 and 65, and Munday, *John a Kent and John a Cumber*, pp. 47–51.
59 This was the first civic production with which Middleton was involved.
60 Bergeron, 'Actors in English civic pageants', pp. 21–2.
61 Withington, *English Pageantry*, vol. I, p. 224 and 224 n. 2; see also Cerasano, 'Edward Alleyn', p. 22.
62 Lobanov-Rostovsky, 'The Triumphes of Golde', p. 891.
63 Munday, ed. Pafford, *Chruso-thriambos*, pp. 13 and 54. See also Denkinger, 'Actors' names', pp. 96–7, and Bergeron, *Pageants and Entertainments*, p. 68. Bergeron has explained the reason for Lowin's participation (and, by implication, for the degradation of his dramatic fame) as allegiance to his livery company ('Actors in English civic pageants', pp. 24–5).
64 Bergeron *Pageants and Entertainments*, pp. xii and xiv.

65 Munday, *Londons Love*, sig. B4v. See also Withington, *English Pageantry*, vol. I, p. 231, and Bergeron, 'Actors in English civic pageants', pp. 22–3.
66 Withington, *English Pageantry*, vol. I, p. 231.
67 See Jones and Stallybrass, *Renaissance Clothing and the Materials of Memory*, pp. 176–9 and *passim*.
68 Bergeron, 'Actors in English civic pageants', p. 23.
69 Withington, *English Pageantry*, vol. I, p. 231. Withington states that Munday was probably responsible solely for the show itself, since his account of the ensuing 'water-fight and fireworks' is only a 'reporte' (*ibid.*, p. 232 n. 3; see Munday, *Londons Love*, sigs A2r and D2r).
70 Bergeron, 'Actors in English civic pageants', p. 22.
71 *Ibid.*, pp. 23–4.
72 Munday, *Londons Love*, sig. C4v.
73 Moore, 'Jonson, Dekker, and the discourse of chivalry', p. 149.
74 Leinwand, 'London triumphing', p. 138.
75 The Cross Keys is the inn where Strange's Men defied the instruction to cease playing in 1589, at the height of the Marprelate crisis (see Chambers, *The Elizabethan Stage*, vol. IV, p. 305, Wickham et al., *English Professional Theatre*, p. 302, and McMillin et al., 'Reading the Elizabethan acting companies', p. 127 n. 14).
76 Munday, ed. Meagher, *The Downfall*, lines 294–7; my emphasis.
77 Dutton, *Licensing, Censorship and Authorship*, p. xv. It is important to remember that individual Lord Mayors would have had differing attitudes towards the theatre; Gurr, for one, mistakenly brackets all the Lord Mayors of this period into an undifferentiated entity with a uniform view (see 'The authority of the Globe and the Fortune', p. 256).
78 Robertson and Gordon, *A Calendar of Dramatic Records*, p. 169. Gordon and Dewhirst call Swynnerton as 'an unusual man' (*The Ward of Cripplegate*, p. 73).
79 See Beaumont, *The Knight of the Burning Pestle*, p. 3. Keysar himself may have come in for satirical treatment from Middleton, for whom he had been a creditor, in the character of Yellowhammer in *A Chaste Maid in Cheapside* (see Kinney, *Renaissance Drama*, p. 440).
80 Lobanov-Rostovsky, 'The Triumphes of Golde', p. 893 n. 3.
81 See Withington, *English Pageantry*, vol. I, pp. 233–4, and Bergeron, 'Thomas Middleton and Anthony Munday', p. 474. Note here that Middleton chose an equivalent title in Latin to Munday's vernacular *Londons Love*.
82 Lobanov-Rostovsky, 'The Triumphes of Golde', p. 893 n. 3.
83 See, for example, *ibid.*, p. 888.
84 *Ibid.*, p. 891.
85 Jenstad, 'Institutional uses of pageantry', p. 1.
86 Rutter, ed., *Documents of the Rose Playhouse*, p. 24.
87 Munday, *A Defence of Contraries*, sig. A2v.
88 See *ibid.*, sig. A1v. Stanley was from a largely Catholic family and had run into some political difficulties in the early 1590s (the family was to do so again in 1598). Gurr suggests that *Sir Thomas More* was written because of this patron's religious affiliation (*The Shakespearian Playing Companies*, pp. 34–5, 264; see also Heywood, ed. Rowland, *Edward IV*, p. xxvii).
89 See Turner, *Anthony Mundy*, p. 113, and Rutter, ed., *Documents of the Rose Playhouse*, p. 27.

90 Rutter, ed., *Documents of the Rose Playhouse*, p. 171.
91 White, 'Shakespeare, the Cobhams, and the dynamics of theatrical patronage', p. 87.
92 Gurr, 'Privy Councilors as theatre patrons', p. 242; Knutson, *Playing Companies and Commerce*, p. 53. In 1596 Munday dedicated *The Orator* (via the alias of 'Lazarus Pyott') to John St John, Baron of Bletso, whose daughter was then about to marry the Lord Admiral's son (see Hamilton, 'Anthony Munday and *The Merchant of Venice*', p. 96).
93 See Rutter, ed., *Documents of the Rose Playhouse*, pp. 153–5, and Munday, ed. Meagher, *The Downfall*, pp. vi–vii.
94 Curiously enough, *Fedele and Fortunio* was once attributed by Chambers to Munday's recent antagonist and fellow turncoat playwright, Stephen Gosson (Chambers, *The Elizabethan Stage*, vol. IV, p. 14; see also Hosley, 'The date of "Fedele and Fortunio"', p. 386, and Haaker, 'Anthony Munday', p. 131). See below for further links between Munday and Gosson.
95 Ingram, *The Business of Playing*, pp. 174–5 and 236; see also Turner, *Anthony Mundy*, p. 28.
96 The Paul's Children's company 'performed regularly at court [from 1584] up to 1590' (Gurr, *The Shakespearean Stage*, p. 33). Sebastian Westcott, the Paul's choirmaster from 1547 to 1582, 'was an open Catholic' (ibid., p. 35; see also Ingram, *The Business of Playing*, pp. 146–7).
97 McMillin and MacLean, *The Queen's Men and Their Plays*, p. 3. John Lyly, another of Oxford's servants whom Munday mentions in *Zelauto*, wrote a number of plays for Oxford's amalgamated boys' company (as, probably, did Oxford himself).
98 McMillin and MacLean, *The Queen's Men and Their Plays*, p. 4.
99 See Turner, *Anthony Mundy*, p. 69, and Turner Wright, 'Young Anthony Mundy again', p. 156. Munday dedicated one edition of this play to 'M.R.', believed to be Sir Roger Mostyn, a Welsh nobleman; Pennell suggests that Munday 'may have visited Mostyn Hall [in North Wales] and investigated its library' (Munday, *John a Kent and John a Cumber*, p. 1). It was during the early 1580s that Munday was most active as a recusant-hunter so he may well have reached North Wales in the course of his travels around the country.
100 Gurr, *The Shakespearian Playing Companies*, p. 231. According to Michael Shapiro, only the Chapel Children and Oxford's Boys (both children's companies) and the newly formed Queen's Men performed at court between 1583 and 1585 ('Patronage and the companies of boy actors', p. 285).
101 See Munday, *John a Kent and John a Cumber*, pp. 27 and 53. Pennell dates the play to 'probably the late 1580s', partly on the basis of the 'John a Cant' line in the Marprelate tract, *The Protestatyon* (ibid., pp. 43–5).
102 Gurr, *The Shakespearian Playing Companies*, p. 264.
103 See Rutter, ed., *Documents of the Rose Playhouse*, p. 26, and Heinemann, *Puritanism and Theatre*, p. 63.
104 See Carson, *A Companion to Henslowe's Diary*, p. 59, and Foakes, *Henslowe's Diary*, p. 85 and *passim*; see also Moore, 'Jonson, Dekker, and the discourse of chivalry', p. 148.
105 Also playing in 1601 at the Admiral's Men's new theatre was a play about John of Gaunt co-written by Hathaway, Munday's regular collaborator, and another man with a less than consistent attitude towards the stage, William Rankins – the author of the virulently anti-stage tract *A Mirrour of Monsters*,

published in 1587. Rankins is first recorded as a writer in Henslowe's *Diary* in 1598, which makes him an immediate contemporary of Munday, although there is no evidence that the two ever collaborated (see Rutter, ed., *Documents of the Rose Playhouse*, pp. 81–2 and 154).

106 See Turner, *Anthony Mundy*, pp. 124 and 142.
107 Carson, *A Companion to Henslowe's Diary*, p. 114.
108 Munday, *The Mirrour of Mutabilitie*, p. 85n; see also Greg, *Henslowe Papers*, p. 59.
109 Carson, *A Companion to Henslowe's Diary*, p. 140; see also Hughes and Larkin, *Tudor Royal Proclamations*, vol. III, p. 40. See also Baldwin, *The Organization and Personnel*, pp. 26–7.
110 Carson, *A Companion to Henslowe's Diary*, p. 66.
111 Foakes and Rickert parody the prevalent view of the supposed distinction between the 'lower-class appeal' of the Admiral's Men versus 'the fashionable gallants and ladies ... [who] frequented the Globe in anticipation of a kind of Third Programme' (*Henslowe's Diary* (second edition), p. xxx).
112 Foakes, 'Henslowe and the theatre of the 1590's', p. 6. In relation to the so-called 'rivalry' between the Rose and the Globe companies Knutson has also commented that 'the teleology of [the Shakespeare-centred] story is the commercial and artistic triumph of the Chamberlain's Men' (*Playing Companies and Commerce*, p. 36).
113 Gurr and Ichikawa, *Staging in Shakespeare's Theatres*, p. 18; see also Heinemann, 'Rebel lords, popular playwrights, and political patronage', pp. 75–7.
114 White, 'Shakespeare, the Cobhams, and the dynamics of theatrical patronage', p. 88.
115 *Ibid.*
116 See Stevenson, *Praise and Paradox*, p. 20.
117 Gurr, *The Shakespearean Stage*, p. 200.
118 Gurr, *The Shakespearian Playing Companies*, pp. 247 and 241.
119 *Ibid.*, pp. 241–2.
120 Knight and Ohlgren, *Robin Hood*, p. 297.
121 Munday, ed. Meagher, *The Downfall*, line 2221.
122 Henslowe, however, calls the first *Huntington* play 'the firste parte of Robyne Hoode' and refers with characteristic imprecision to the other play as the 'seconde parte of the downefall of earlle huntyngton surnamed Roben Hoode' (Rutter, ed., *Documents of the Rose Playhouse*, p. 130). See also Singman, 'Munday's unruly Earl', p. 73.
123 See also Dobson and Taylor, 'The legend since the Middle Ages', p. 163, and Singman, 'Munday's unruly Earl', pp. 64–5, 69 and 73–4. Robin Hood was also mentioned in Stow's *Summary of English Chronicles* (1565). Carol Levin notes that, like Munday, Stow's wider historical works represented Robin Hood as an 'heroic' figure from the reign of Richard I (*Propaganda in the English Reformation*, p. 212).
124 See Rutter, ed., *Documents of the Rose Playhouse*, pp. 174–5; see also Hodges, *The Globe Restored*, pp. 163–6.
125 Dillon, *Theatre, Court and City*, p. 33.
126 See Johnson, *Southwark and the City*, p. 114, and Birch, *The Historical Charters*, pp. 110–27.
127 Dillon, *Theatre, Court and City*, p. 33. Butler, too, makes the point that 'Jacobean London lacked a simple opposition between ordered centre and

disorderly periphery; rather, the playhouses were increasingly part of that metropolitan scene to which, superficially, they seem opposed' ('Literature and the theatre to 1660', p. 570).

128 Chambers, *The Elizabethan Stage*, vol. II, p. 436.

129 Although the contemporary documents make it clear that the Fortune was within the parish of St Giles, the map in Knutson's recent book on the playing companies seems to have mistaken the ward boundary for the parish boundary, for it places the theatre outside of the latter (see Knutson, *Playing Companies and Commerce*, p. 31). The Boar's Head on the eastern side of the City at Whitechapel was similarly 'located exactly at the City boundary' (Gurr, *The Shakespearean Stage*, p. 130; see also Wickham *et al.*, *English Professional Theatre*, p. 452).

130 Gordon and Dewhirst, *The Ward of Cripplegate*, p. 113. See also Cerasano, '"More elbow roome, but scant better aire"', p. 70. In 1607 the Privy Council had cause to write to the Mayor about 'the decay of the ways in Golding Lane ... and other parts of the suburbs, in the parish of St Giles without Cripplegate'; the Mayor then 'called before him the chief inhabitants of the parish within the City, who denied their liability to contribute to the mending of the same' (Overall and Overall, *Analytical Index*, p. 480). The Cripplegate inhabitants' denial of their responsibility for the parish's infrastructure compares interestingly with the equivocal attitudes of those same residents towards the building of the Fortune a few years earlier.

131 Cited in Dillon, *Theatre, Court and City*, p. 21.

132 Gurr nevertheless makes a point of locating the various playhouses in relation to their proximity to the city walls, thereby implying that he considers the wall itself to be the city boundary (Gurr, *The Shakespearean Stage*, p. 115); Twyning wrongly states that 'the City of London ... strictly and legally defines the place ... "within the walls"' (*London Dispossessed*, p. 202 n. 6).

133 Dillon, *Theatre, Court and City*, p. 99.

134 Sullivan has argued that 'the suburbs were profoundly overdetermined for most Elizabethan Londoners' (*The Drama of Landscape*, p. 208).

135 Moretti, *Atlas of the European Novel*, p. 129.

136 Gordon, 'Performing London', pp. 79 and 82; Munday, *Himatia-Poleos*, sig. Br.

137 See, for example, Mullaney, *The Place of the Stage*, pp. 45–51 and *passim*.

138 Queen Anne's Men made the contribution of the large sum of £500 towards highway maintenance in Clerkenwell (see Bayer in McMillin *et al.*, 'Reading the Elizabethan acting companies', p. 144).

139 *Ibid.*, p. 143.

140 Cited in Cerasano, 'Edward Alleyn', p. 27.

141 Stevenson, *Praise and Paradox*, p. 72.

142 Carson, *A Companion to Henslowe's Diary*, p. 43.

143 Dutton, *Licensing, Censorship and Authorship*, pp. 31–2; see also Gurr, 'The authority of the Globe and the Fortune', p. 252, McLuskie, *Dekker and Heywood*, pp. 10–14, and Rutter, ed., *Documents of the Rose Playhouse*, pp. 171–3.

144 Chambers, *The Elizabethan Stage*, vol. IV, pp. 326–7. A letter from Blackfriars residents, including Hunsdon, the patron of the Chamberlain's Men, was apparently sent to the Privy Council in 1596 opposing Burbage's new playhouse (see Chambers, *The Elizabethan Stage*, vol. IV, pp. 319–20, Dillon, *Theatre, Court and City*, pp. 98–9, and Wickham *et al.*, *English Professional Theatre*, pp. 507–8).

145 Chambers, *The Elizabethan Stage*, vol. IV, p. 328.
146 Rutter, ed., *Documents of the Rose Playhouse*, p. 183; my emphasis.
147 C. Walter Hodges places the theatre along the right-hand side of Golden Lane literally only a few yards north of the city boundary. Most theatre historians locate the playhouse where Fortune Lane is now (see figure 6, where 'Playhouse Yard' occupies some of the site); unfortunately, unlike the Rose and the Globe, no archaeological exploration has yet been undertaken here.
148 Chambers, *The Elizabethan Stage*, vol. IV, p. 327.
149 *Ibid.*, p. 326; my emphasis.
150 *Ibid.*, p. 328; my emphasis.
151 *Ibid.*, p. 328. See also Ingram, *The Business of Playing*, pp. 45–6, Rutter, ed., *Documents of the Rose Playhouse*, pp. 184–6, and Freedman, 'Elizabethan protest', p. 21 n. 7. Until 1671 the St Giles vestry was responsible for all parish matters in St Giles Without, including the Liberty of Finsbury where the Fortune lay.
152 Cerasano, '"More elbow roome, but scant better aire"', p. 75. As noted below, Stow does not mention the Fortune in the 1603 edition of the *Survay*: all he has to say of Golding Lane is that it 'is replenished with many tenements of poore people' (Stow, ed. Kingsford, *A Survey of London*, vol. II, p. 79).
153 Rutter, ed., *Documents of the Rose Playhouse*, p. 184.
154 See *ibid.*, p. 146.
155 *Ibid.*, p. 182; see also Gurr, *The Shakespearian Playing Companies*, p. 242, and Chambers, *The Elizabethan Stage*, vol. IV, p. 326.
156 Gurr, *The Shakespearian Playing Companies*, p. 243.
157 Rutter, ed., *Documents of the Rose Playhouse*, p. 187.
158 See *ibid.*, p. 185.
159 *Ibid.*, p. 192.
160 Cited in *ibid.*, p. 193.
161 Chambers, *The Elizabethan Stage*, vol. IV, p. 330.
162 Despite its intended destruction, the Curtain playhouse outlived both the Fortune and the Globe: it was extant as late as 1698 (Wickham *et al.*, *English Professional Theatre*, p. 418; see also Rutter, ed., *Documents of the Rose Playhouse*, p. 192, and Wickham *et al.*, *English Professional Theatre*, pp. 108–9).
163 Chambers, *The Elizabethan Stage*, vol. IV, p. 331. Despite this complicated story of civic animosity and deal-brokering, it is instructive to note that in 1622, the year after the playhouse burnt down, Thomas Sparkes, 'citizen and merchant taylor', was granted 'a lease of one share of the Fortune Theatre' (Robertson and Gordon, *A Calendar of Dramatic Records*, p. 179).
164 Dillon, *Theatre, Court and City*, p. 4.
165 Bergeron, *Pageants and Entertainments*, p. 139.
166 Robertson and Gordon, *A Calendar of Dramatic Records*, p. 106; see also Bergeron, *Pageants and Entertainments*, p. 142, and Withington, 'The Lord Mayor's Show for 1623', pp. 112–13. The same 'barne' in the Golding Lane area was probably used for 'the little shipp' from Webster's 1624 pageant, *The Monuments of Honour* (Sayle, *Lord Mayors' Pageants*, p. 111).

5

'The Mother of authenticke memory'[1]

Munday and civic history

MUNDAY'S contribution to civic culture transcended his writing for London's theatres to encompass texts about the City itself. Once he had ceased to write for the professional stage he concentrated increasingly over the last three decades of his life on writing of a historical and sometimes topographical nature. Such writing was often informed by the work of his illustrious predecessors such as John Stow. Stow, who has been described as one of London's 'most civically aware historians', had been free of the Merchant Taylors for nearly fifty years when the *Survay of London* was first published in 1598.[2] It is likely that Munday and Stow had worked in different roles on the same civic text in 1602 (giving their acquaintanceship a duration of at least three years by the time of Stow's death) as both men are recorded as receiving various payments by the Merchant Taylors Company in this year. In this instance Munday was given at least £30 for some props and speeches for a pageant and Stow received the sum of ten shillings for his historical research into past mayors, sheriffs and aldermen of his company.[3] With his work on two subsequent editions of Stow's *Survay* Munday has long been considered the antiquarian's 'literary executor'. Munday did at times acknowledge his indebtedness to his predecessor: for instance, there is a marginal reference to Stow as an authority on Henry Fitz-Alwin in Munday's 1611 pageant *Chruso-thriambos* at the point where the character of Time expounds on London's history and the venerable lineage of the role of Lord Mayor, although (as we will see in more detail below) Munday was later forced to retract his faith in Stow's account of Fitz-Alwin.[4] Munday's *Briefe Chronicle* of the same year is also extensively based on Stow's historical works and cross-references its source in places; indeed, this work can be considered as Munday's attempt to emulate Stow's national, rather than local historical writing.[5]

Stow's work for the City was never very generously rewarded (his poverty was legendary). Around 1590 he wrote two drafts of a petition to the Lord Mayor and Aldermen asking for a pension for his long service to the City, one of which begins:

> Pleasethe it your honor and worships to understond that where your orator Iohn Stowe citizen &c. ... hathe for the space of almost xxx yeres long past ... set forth divars somaries dedicated to the lord maiors, his brithren thaldarmen, and comoners of the Citie. In the whiche he hathe specially noated the memorable actes of famows Citizens by them done to the greate benefite of the comon welthe, and honor of the same Citie.[6]

In the second draft, Stow stresses that the expenses he has incurred over the years in researching and writing his histories 'hathe bene altogethar of his owne charges'.[7] When Munday came to take on the job of extending and updating Stow's *Survay* he made a similar complaint, telling his dedicatees: 'I have (to my great cost, care, and no meane labour, both of body and mind, and for the space of above twelve yeeres) done my diligent endevour, to effect the full scope of that which I had set downe to my selfe.'[8] He echoes Stow's representation of his arduous efforts by calling his predecessor's work 'these painefull labours'.[9] It would appear that the city chroniclers were expected to subsidise their own research, which might explain Munday's frequent recourse to various livery companies in search of recompense for his civic texts. Stow's role as London's 'chronicler', never made fully official, led after his death to the creation in 1620 of the office of City Chronographer. This was a post first held by Middleton until his death in 1627, whose background as a pageant-maker would have served him well as an introduction to the importance to the City of its historical record.[10] Munday had equal if not greater credentials for such a post. Jonson then succeeded to the role but he made such an indifferent job of it that he was not paid between 1631 and 1634 because he had done no work in the post during that time. This might only have been expected, given Jonson's mixed feelings towards the City and his poor sight and infirmity by that point in his life (he had become paralysed in 1628).[11]

The 1604 edition of Stow's *Summarie of the Chronicles of England* (first published in 1566) was dedicated to the Lord Mayor and aldermen. As its dedicatees suggest, Stow's text had a distinctly 'civic character', not least because as well as its general history of England it listed all the officers of the City of London since the Norman Conquest.[12] Laura Stevenson comments of Stow's *Summarie* that 'each of its successive editions contained more London history than its predecessors, and offered detailed portraits of eminent Londoners ... [written] in an obvious attempt to give London's wealthiest and most important citizens a dignified history'.[13] As we will see further below, Munday incorporated sections of Stow's *Summarie* in his editions of the *Survay*. A large number of Munday's works continue in the same urban tenor; like Stow, Munday relished the opportunity to combine history with topography, particularly when it was the history of London. Like the *Summarie* Munday's *Briefe Chronicle* also had a bias towards London despite its broader historical range. Munday frequently uses London as a prism through which to represent a range of topics; for instance, his early text *A View of Sundry Examples* adopts the local scene for its admonitory moral exemplars: the murder of 'Maister Temple', a merchant, in his shop near the Royal Exchange, for instance.[14] Likewise, in Munday's 1618 *Survay* the murder of 'M. Saunders' in 1572 when 'his wife, Browne, Mistris Drewry, and trusty Roger [were] executed' is cited in the marginal commentary as a notable event for that year, alongside and on equal terms with the rather less parochial event of the beheading of the Duke of Norfolk.[15] Munday often switches from a larger to a more circumscribed notion of history, sometimes with inadvertently comic effect: a particularly 'domesticated' example appears in *Chruso-thriambos* when, at the point where 'Time' is expounding on the history of the Goldsmiths, the previous prices of various foodstuffs from 'a fat stalled Oxe, 24s' to '24 Egges a peny' are cited in the margin as demonstrating the 'plentie' that resulted from Faringdon's mayoralty.[16]

Stow's *Survay* itself, naturally, was dedicated to the Mayor and the 'Comminalty, and Citizens' of London; both of Stow's editions were printed by the current printer to the City (John Wolfe printed the 1598 edition and John Windet the 1603 edition).[17] Stow had a large part to play in the remaking and improving of the image of city dignatories towards the end of the sixteenth century: in his historical works, Stevenson writes, 'the pale figures from earlier London histories became the heroes of the 1590s'.[18] Her statement is equally true of Munday's Jacobean civic pageantry. Barrett Beer emphasises Stow's exceptionally civic background, education and social orientation compared to other Tudor historians and topographers, many of whom, such as Richard Grafton and William Camden, had court and/or Parliament links.[19] Like Munday, Stow had not been educated either at university or at the Inns of Court. This, Beer argues, makes Stow a 'particularly valuable' historical witness: he was 'closer to the ordinary men and women of Tudor England than to the political elite ... [and] his London included the small crowded houses ... as well as the fine homes'.[20] In contrast to contemporaries such as Foxe, his outlook was predominantly secular and local which, as we have seen, prompted scorn on the part of more controversial writers such as Nashe.

As many commentators have pointed out, it is noticeable that Munday did not add to Stow's terse account of the London theatres in either of his editions. Only the Theatre and the Curtain were mentioned in the 1598 original, and their names were deleted in Stow's 1603 edition; in his 1618 edition Munday puts them back in but makes only one inconsequential change to Stow's original text.[21] This is a seemingly deliberate omission, for Stow as a careful topographer must have been aware of the playhouses which, given the increase in the number of theatres between 1598 and 1603 (including the Fortune) would have formed an conspicuous part of the London landscape.[22] For Munday, as an ex-playwright, it is even harder to account for, except for the possibility that in this text he is writing in another guise, like his antitheatrical pose in *A second and third blast*. Manley links Stow's virtual silence on the subject of theatres to his taciturnity about the Lord Mayors' Shows, 'whose leading writers were also being commissioned by the City for the scripts of the mayoral pageants'.[23] Although Manley does not explicitly connect the two individuals here, it is certainly suggestive of a slight, even if an unintended one, towards Munday, Stow's so-called literary executor, and in 1603 a practitioner of both of the cultural forms towards which Stow is so unexpansive. By the year of Stow's death, 1605, Munday may have ceased to work in dramatic circles, but he was well on the way to becoming one of the major pageant writers of the early Jacobean period, a fact of which Stow cannot have been unaware, especially given their work on the same pageant in 1602.

Given his personal history of Catholic sympathy Stow had to tread carefully when it came to matters of religion. He habitually underplayed religious tensions and changes in London; indeed, Foster has written that 'one has to read carefully between the lines [of the *Survay*] to become aware that there was a Reformation in England'.[24]

With his nostalgia and his latent Catholic sympathies Stow was generally hostile towards what Michael Berlin has called 'the secularisation of space', and often criticised the appropriation of previously sacred sites for more prosaic uses, or where such places had either deliberately or by indifference been allowed to decay. He mourns the decrepitude and defacement of the Eleanor Cross on Cheap at length, for example, and blames 'contempt' for its fate.[25] One ought to ascribe Stow's taciturnity on such dangerous topics to caution rather than indifference. His associations with men such as Fleetwood and William Camden, not to mention Munday, took him into the heart of the Protestant establishment, regardless of some official dubiety during the religious crisis of the 1560s, such as when his study was raided by Bishop Grindal's men in 1568 and he was then reported to Cecil for a large collection of thirty-eight Catholic publications that had been discovered.[26] In the *Survay*, Stow mentions the extreme Protestant Crowley's name without comment in a list of extant memorials in St Giles. In his *Memoranda*, however, he is more expansive, and writes that Crowley was responsible for a book called 'Ye Unffoldynge of ye Popyshe atyr', a contribution to the anti-surplice movement.[27] Munday, then, was the kind of protean character capable of boasting friendship with both of these two opposed figures, Stow and Crowley. Indeed, as one might expect from what we know about his acquaintance with Crowley, he adds the cleric's epitaph (along with John Foxe's) to the Cripplegate section of his 1618 *Survay*.[28] Munday incorporated other more explicitly Protestant elements into Stow's text in a number of places. Hamilton cites Munday's *Survay* to support her claim that he was a lifelong Catholic, but she does not explain how this text can be said to demonstrate specific Catholic sympathies on Munday's part.[29] Indeed, the fact that Munday inserted into his 1633 edition of the *Survey* an account of 'the three Brethren appointed to preach at Saint Maries Spittle at Easter 1632' might actually suggest the opposite, as might his entry in the 1618 edition on 'The Christian and charitable workes of Robert Rogers', where a marginal note emphasises that Rogers's benevolence, which did not extend to either 'Atheists nor Papists', was 'an especiall note of a *godly* disposition'.[30]

Civic history could not only be found in the pages of the *Survay of London*; it was also performed on the City streets. There is a general consensus that from the accession of James I, who was relatively uninterested in such entertainments compared to Elizabeth, in Dillon's words, 'urban pageantry thrived ... in increasing isolation from the court ... leaving a space in which the lord mayor's show, with its sole focus on London, could flourish'.[31] Early in James's reign, however, civic pageantry made some attempt to combine royal and metropolitan concerns. As well as James's royal entry into London, Bergeron says that Munday's 1605 show *The Triumphes of re-united Britania*, unusually for a civic pageant, has a 'timely' focus on the new monarch and stresses its theme of national unity in a way likely to appeal to him.[32] *The Triumphes of re-united Britania* did indeed attempt to trade explicitly on James's accession and the *de facto* union of nations that his reign brought about. However, as Bergeron writes, Munday's own civic productions from 1610 onwards became more and more 'centre[d] on the city and guilds' rather than national or monarchical history, suggesting perhaps that Munday 'joined the increasing ranks of those disillusioned with James by the end of his first decade in England'.[33] Indeed, Marcus writes that there was effectively a 'rivalry' between the court masque and City pageant during James's reign.[34]

Despite Bergeron's view that 'no other Lord Mayor's Show so consciously, explicitly, and unrelentingly refers to the sovereign', one cannot really characterise Munday's 1605 pageant as wholly concerned for its royal guest.[35] It certainly differs in this respect from the previous year's *Magnificent Entertainment*, where James and his family are the sole focus for the City's applause and where, as Gordon has commented, the 'static figures [of the livery companies] are inscribed within a monarchical viewing of the city'. For Dekker and his collaborators, as Gordon has argued, 'the ceremonial city [is performed] in relation to the presence of the monarch', not the other way around.[36] In Munday's pageant, in contrast, the emphasis upon the civic persists regardless of the metaphorical presence of the king – indeed, Sir Leonard Holliday, the new Mayor, is effectively 'king for the day'.[37] As with other of his pageants, as we will see, where Munday's attention to the interests of the livery company which sponsored it can sometimes interfere with historical accuracy, he attempts here to balance monarchical and metropolitan glory in the same text. One of the show's main figures, Brutus, performs the dual role of the founder both of Britain and of her capital city 'New Troy' (which for Munday is Britain's chief glory). Similarly, of all the rivers Munday cites to create a picture of the newly reunited realm, the Thames remains 'Queene of all Britanes rivers'; her royal title implicitly reappropriates absolute power for the City, not the monarch.[38]

Munday's concern to reconcile the potentially conflicting interests of gratifying both the new king and the Merchant Taylors, sponsors of the Show, results in some awkward moments of transition from a national to a strictly civic frame of historical reference. After his attention has shifted back to his city, the procession of kings that Munday presents subjugates them all to their various roles of making and keeping the Merchant Taylors great. As Thomas Corns has stated, Munday 'is at pains to make associations between the City of London in general (and the sponsoring Merchant Taylors' Company in particular) and more recent royal patronage'.[39] Thus Richard II, for instance, is noteworthy only because he 'grant[ed] them power to have a Lyverie, / And hold a Feast on saint John Baptist day'.[40] By wearing the livery of the Merchant Taylors in a 'milde and gracious' fashion Henry VI actually gained stature, for, Munday claims, 'Princes loose no part of dignity, / In beeing affable, it addes to Maiesty'.[41] Despite this text's ostensible desire to please the current monarch, only seven kings are cited from Edward III onwards because only these seven played any significant part in the history of the livery company, as did 'fourteene great Dukes', all of whom are listed.[42] In fact, *eight* previous monarchs had been free of the Merchant Taylors, but Munday, still in 1605 deferential to the Tudor myth of history, omits the benighted Richard III.[43] The pageant's characters discuss the most noticeable lack of a current monarch quite openly. When 'Pheme' asks why 'that seat is unsupplied, / Being with the most eminent and chiefest place, / With State, with Crowne and Scepter dignified?', the question is answered with another: 'may not time bestow / an eight[th king], when Heaven shall appoint the same?' Once again the recourse is to *civic* history for the answer: according to the Merchant Taylor's 'Register' only 'seaven Kings have honord this Society'.[44] Service to the Merchant Taylors is the dominant concern of Munday's text, and the message seems to be that James will take his place in the company's hall of fame only when he has done something of the same kind to deserve it: until that point the vacant chair on the chariot pageant will remain empty. In the same fashion, in the list of mayors and other civic dignitaries in Munday's 1618 *Survay* the beginning of James's reign in 1603 is relegated to a marginal comment: 'This yeere dyed good Q. Elizabeth, and our Sovereign K. James rightly succeeded.'[45] The names, dates and notable deeds of the mayors, sheriffs and other London worthies, about whom this section of the text is mostly concerned, are given at least equal prominence: in 1615, for instance, 'two Brethren Sheriffes and the yonger Brother [were] first chosen'.[46]

Later in Munday's civic output his confidence in the importance of London's mayor is yet more apparent, even to the extent of this civic dignitary entirely displacing the monarch.[47] In *Metropolis Coronata* Munday relates that 'the order of march' of the Show appears 'even as if it were a Royall Maske, prepared for the marriage of an immortall Deitie, as in the like nature we hold the Lord Maior ... by representing the awefull authoritie of soveraigne Majestie'.[48] In Munday's hyberbolic account, London's ruler takes the place of both monarch and God, and both are relegated to the status of a metaphor. Even in *Londons Love, to the Royal Prince Henrie*, which was written for no other reason than to celebrate the Prince of Wales's arrival in the City, Munday does not seem entirely comfortable with the task in hand. He twice reminds his readership (who are, implicitly, the London citizenry and the prince himself) that he and the City Corporation were given 'very shorte and sudden intelligence' from which to prepare the entertainment, remarking prosaically that 'they determined to meet [Henry] in such good manner as the brevitie of time would then permit them'.[49] Furthermore, the proposed 'water Fight & Fireworkes' which were to form the culmination of the day's festivities were unaccountably postponed to the following week. Munday explains rather dismissively that 'whether [this delay was] by the violent storme of rayne, or other appointments of his maiestie, I knowe not'; he himself, it is clear, did not witness the performance when it did eventually take place.[50] To compound the somewhat grudging note (and with an uncanny prescience given Henry's own untimely death two years later), Munday concludes his brief survey of the history of Henry's precedessors as Prince of Wales with some who experienced 'hard and disaster fortune' such as 'Richard the third [whose] Sonne dyed with in three moneths after, as a just judgement of God for his Fathers wickednes'.[51]

Despite Munday's probably opportunistic interest in representing the monarch in his 1605 Show, the City became increasingly important to him after his busiest period working for the Privy Council as a Messenger of her Majesty's Chamber in the 1580s and 1590s had come to an end.[52] As a consequence, his later Jacobean pageants show an intensified focus on the civic rather than the courtly arena. If urban pageantry was thriving under James regardless of the King's indifference, its chief manufacturer was evidently keen to get his share of the action, at times receiving payment from the Corporation even when his bid for that year's show proved unsuccessful.[53] That Munday had largely moved into a different sphere from the theatrical in the Jacobean period is further exemplified by the fact that he was employed by the City Corporation in 1610 to write *Londons Love* for Henry, Prince of Wales whereas in 1612, after Henry's death, the theatres were ordered to be closed, leaving his erstwhile colleagues without employment.[54] Jonson's career took an alternative turn to Munday's, moving from 1605 onwards away from the civic towards more courtly forms of entertainment.[55] For example, Jonson's court masque from 1615, *The Golden Age Restored*, attempts, according to Marcus, to 'demonstrate the superiority of royal policies, poetry and pageantry over the industrious but menial arts of London', which can be seen to be exemplified by Munday's Shows.[56]

One gains a strong sense from Munday's civic productions not only of a geographical but also of a temporal 'home' with which he is comfortable. Thus one can find in many of these texts a representation of medieval history in and for a still quasi-medieval city which tried to exploit the same civic taste as did his medieval-style romances. As the title page of Stow's *Survay* has it, London is a city of both 'antiquity' *and* 'moderne estate'; indeed, the 1603 edition was published to enhance the original 1598 edition with 'divers rare notes of Antiquity'.[57] Munday's 1618 edition of this work continues the same note, being, as Munday puts it, 'continued, corrected and much enlarged, with many rare and worthy Notes both of Venerable Antiquity, and later memorie'.[58] Munday's emphasis upon history, evident in so many of his other texts, is here so pronounced that even the recent past is a matter of 'memorie'. Manley has written that 'the successful government of London did not call for a break with the past but for a reaffirmation of it'.[59] If the same can be said about the successful *representation* of the City too, then Munday's civic shows certainly provided that necessary affirmation of historical continuity for more than twenty years. 'London's ritual significance', Manley has argued, 'lies in the saturation of the traditional civic order by ritual and ceremonial observance'.[60] As articulated by Munday and his contemporaries, London's ceremonial life bears out Clifford Geertz's claim in *Local Knowledge* that governing elites tend to 'justify their existence and order their actions in terms of a collection of stories, ceremonies, insignia, formalities and appurtenances that they have either inherited ... or invented ... The gravity of high politics and the solemnity of high worship spring from liker impulses than might at first appear.'[61] Manley too has discussed the 'sacral' dimension of civic ceremony.[62]

As we will see, something of that element of solemnity and worship pervades Munday's civic-sponsored works.

Such an emphasis upon continuity should not, however, imply a simple transition from the past into the present. The representation of merchants in Munday's civic work was similarly complex in its historicity; as Stevenson puts it, 'it reflected a mentality that saw service to the realm in traditional, chivalric, quasi-feudal terms'.[63] The livery company system, which still governed so much of London's social and economic life, was becoming increasingly anachronistic in the later sixteenth century, but this did not prevent the City's propagandists from highlighting the antiquity of these and other civic traditions. The *Survay* itself had a dual function: it was both an annotated history of the city and of its past practices and places (complete with sporadic moralistic observations) and also, effectively, a guide book for the city as it then was, carefully prepared, like a sixteenth-century *A–Z*, for the use of other perambulators. Munday himself called the *Survay* 'a Booke of such needfull use' in his 1618 edition, underlining its contemporary as well as its antiquarian function.[64] The *Survay*'s potential usefulness to the average citizen was replicated by Munday's 1611 *Briefe Chronicle*, which was clearly intended to be employed as a reference book for busy city types, for the handily summarised marginal chronology would have cut down on the labour of perusing its 611 densely printed pages.

Munday's Lord Mayors' Shows, however, habitually emphasised the historical over the contemporary. More generally, one can see what might be called 'the invention of tradition' taking place regarding the Shows, enabling one William Smythe to express an almost nostalgic view of the shows that took place in the 1560s as early as 1575.[65] However, despite the stress put within these productions on the long lineage of the city's institutions, the Lord Mayors' Shows in the specific form in which Munday, Middleton and the other pageant writers presented them had been in existence only since the mid-sixteenth century, and had been produced in printed form only since 1585.[66] Nevertheless – or perhaps because of this dearth of tradition – history itself was a prevalent theme, if not the dominant theme, in the Lord Mayor's Show, which as an annual event (and one appropriating a longer-standing religious date, the feast of St Simon and St Jude) stood as a marker of time in its own right. This theme was particularly pronounced in those Shows written by Munday, who (in Bergeron's phrase) had 'a profound interest in history'.[67] Paula Johnson has commented similarly that Munday habitually 'dwells on ... historical context'.[68] Munday went to some lengths in his civic writing to establish the long-standing historical credentials of the City, its livery companies and its various traditions; as a result, his Lord Mayors' Shows and other civic-oriented works bear out Paster's view that 'time is the essential medium for expressing a city's identity and greatness'.[69] Furthermore, these texts produce, in Sullivan's words, not simply history but 'a history that places citizen culture at centre stage'.[70]

One gains a foretaste of what was to be Munday's historical methodology in his pageants in *The Downfall of Robert, Earle of Huntington*. Here Munday presents two dumb-shows in the induction scene of the play, which are, as Skelton puts it: 'purpose[d] to expresse / The ground whereon our historie is laied'.[71] The dumb-shows that follow these words resemble the kind of historical procession characteristic of civic pageantry; indeed, one wonders why Munday might have felt the need for *two* such 'shows' unless to emphasise precisely this aspect. Thus, after the first dumb-show has taken place, Skelton requests a repeat performance so that he can 'explane them all' to Sir John Eltham, and implicitly, of course, to the audience.[72] Such historical didacticism was to reappear extensively in Munday's civic shows, where his main interest (as in the *Huntington* plays, garbled though it might have been) was in the medieval period. This from a vantage-point of the Jacobean city could perhaps be regarded as the heyday of London. In this respect he shared Stow's nostalgia for a time when London's institutions seemed, retrospectively, to be so much more stable and unquestioned, but Munday would on occasion make even bolder historical claims for his city. *Chruso-thriambos* for instance, written in the same year as Munday's more comprehensive *Briefe Chronicle*, begins by setting the Lord Mayors' Shows in a historical context dating back to the Romans, who, Munday informs his readership, 'used yearelie triumphall showes and devises, to grace [their senators'] severall Inauguration. From which famous and commendable Custome, London ... hath ... both devised and continued the like love and carefull respect.'[73] The use of the term 'triumph' points up the supposedly ancient lineage of the civic shows; in the same fashion, Munday elsewhere in his civic output often called London's aldermen 'Senatours', reaffirming their Roman equivalents.[74] As Gail Kern Paster states, 'the comparison of civic officials to their ancient Roman counterparts' in civic pageantry is a way 'of magnifying the importance of the men and the entertainments'.[75]

The use of Roman terminology such as 'senator' also alludes to a republican rather than monarchical form of government, in the context of which London could be represented as self-ruling and largely independent of royal subjection. Indeed, the City's entitlement to nominate its own officials was regularly celebrated in the civic entertainments written by Munday and his contemporaries. Gordon has called London's much-lauded self-governance 'the fiction of elective autonomy', adding that it is 'a fiction dependent upon repeated performance'.[76] An annual restatement of the City's longevity and independence was performed in front of its inhabitants on 29 October. From the 1610s onwards, the emphasis upon the City's autonomy might relate in part to James's indifference towards civic entertainments, as well as alluding to the increasing breach between the City and the court. Marcus argues that, taking this separation into account, one can see in Munday's 1611 pageant 'an assertion of independence from the king', one which might be said to contrast with Munday's ambivalent and short-lived attempt to reconcile civic and national histories in *The Triumphes of re-united Britania*.[77]

In his sole civic Show, the 1624 *Monuments of Honour* (which was written for his own company, the Merchant Taylors), Webster refers to the historiographical tradition previously established by other writers as a mode he is unable to follow. Dutton remarks on Webster's 'anxiety' throughout this pageant not to taint his reputation as 'a learned poet' through his turn to this constraining artistic form: for instance, where Munday habitually 'devises' his shows, Webster 'invents' his.[78] Webster, unlike his predecessor, clearly found to be irksome the limits on his art of the brevity of time and space associated with pageant-writing. His explanation singles out the most obvious characteristics of Munday's style of pageantry as those which he would otherwise preserve 'to all posterity' as he bemoans the fact that he is 'confined in too narrow a circle' to give his creativity full rein. Webster tells his readers:

> I could in this my preface (by as great light of learning as any formerly employed in this service can attain to) deliver to you the original and cause of all triumphs ... I could likewise with so noble amplification make a survey of the worth and glory of the triumphs of the precedent times in this honourable City of London.[79]

Unlike Middleton before him, Webster establishes an authorial identity in his pageant which has a positive attitude to that of his literary forebears and which contrasts markedly with the negative criticism discussed above of other writers such as Munday. Webster avers that all of those who have previously produced Lord Mayors' Shows – and by 1624 Munday was one of the most prolific – demonstrated considerable familiarity with the City's ancient heritage.

In his civic texts Munday took great pains to display what Webster called his 'light of learning', which in Munday's case generally constituted his knowledge of London history. That knowledge was regularly made explicit: in *Chruso-thriambos*, for example, the role of collective memory in the perpetuation of the City's ancient traditions is overtly celebrated. The initial pageant or 'Orferie' includes the figures of 'two beautifull Ladies' who represent 'Antiquity and Memory', here brought forward to demonstrate 'the Golde-Smiths ancient facultie'.[80] These two are identified as the attendants of, and implicitly, the necessary preconditions for Justice herself, the emblem of the Goldsmiths and the referent of the livery company's motto. To reinforce the general point about the continuity of London custom, 'Time' himself is given a lengthy speaking role in this Show.[81] His description of his own identity can be read as a representation of Munday's practice of history-making as a contingent activity rather than the exercise of absolute truth. Here Munday was once more following the precepts of his preferred classical authority, Cicero, whose view was that history is not an exercise in accuracy or truth-telling, as such, but rather a matter of moral instruction. When challenged to introduce himself by Leofstane, Time states that he is 'he that survaies what ever deedes are done, / Abridges, or gives scope, as likes me best'.[82] 'Time', by this token, may have a magisterial overview, but the subsequent recording of history is more dependent upon pragmatic factors such as the specific interests of the text's patrons, who here serve as the elided agent of Time's words 'as likes me best'. Where, one might ask, *are* the Goldsmiths Company, the text's chief begetter, in Time's statement? Erased though they might have been in this preamble they do recur, however, in the detail of Time's argument, as one of his main topics is the distinctly parochial one of 'the ancient love and cordiall amity' between the Goldsmiths and Fishmongers. This relationship, Munday claims, 'have long time gone, and nothing could divide / the rare continuance of that loving band; / which (doubtlesse) to the end of time will stand'.[83] He hastens to point out, however, somewhat spoiling the celebratory note, that the eternal friendship between these companies does not mean that the Fishmongers shared in the expense of the Show; the Goldsmiths' Company 'in this triumph beares the Pursse for all'.[84]

Despite this fleeting admission of the influence upon historical truth of a sponsor's own exigencies, as Johnson has argued, 'Munday sets his entire discourse [in the pageants] in the context of origins and continuity', unlike Jonson, who tended to use history 'to support a dimension of eternal meaning'.[85] Indeed, Munday stresses ancient antecedents in this Show down to what might be considered the most bathetic level. The Mayor of that year, James Pemberton, is privileged to hear a pseudo-historical derivation of his own name, which according to Munday 'derives it selfe from the aunceint Brittish, Saxon, and eldest English'.[86] Munday notes in *Chruso-thriambos* that the names of Pemberton and of his sheriffs Middleton and Swynnerton all end in '-ton' or 'town'.[87] One might be tempted to regard this is a banal observation when taken literally, but it links implicitly with Munday's strong sense here and elsewhere of his own and others' 'London-ness' – indeed, Munday associates this coincidence with London's own alternative name, 'Ludstun, or Luds-Towne'. Munday was later employed, probably by Pemberton's widow, to write the tombstone inscription when Pemberton was buried in St John Zachary, Aldersgate; Munday then recorded the epitaph in his 1618 edition of the *Survay*, concluding the transcription with his initials in order to underline his own authorship. This lengthy memorial, part of what Munday calls 'a very goodly monument', is written partly in dialogue form and, as Pafford has commented, 'reads something like an extract from a pageant', not least in its invocation of civic virtues and institutions.[88] As in Pemberton's inaugural Show, the epitaph foregrounds his moral qualities, as one might expect it to, particularly emphasising their connectedness to his status in the City: for instance, Munday writes of Pemberton's 'upright soule in that high dignitie, / Which *London* gives her chiefest Presidents'.[89]

Munday's Shows strive to represent London's particular history as having an authoritative status quite dissimilar to that of any other (especially foreign) ancient past. Although the whole of *Metropolis Coronata* is founded on the myth of Jason and the Argonauts, Munday makes it clear that the immediate pretext for the myth's use – celebrating the traditions of the Drapers' Company – is much more significant as well as more historically valid than such pagan narratives. 'This well-knowne storie', he announces, somewhat dismissively, has merely been 'borrowed' to 'helpe' the progress of the important matter in hand, which is 'to honour the day of our London Jason'.[90] Greek mythology is thus valuable only to the extent to which it is possible to transfer it as a metaphor to illuminate its London setting, in the process of which, naturally, it loses its original meaning. In the same way, Neptune is relocated to the Thames to lend his gravitas to the progress of the Lord Mayor, in order to 'make his triumph more majesticall'.[91] For Munday, all forms of classical and other ancient mythology are subordinated to the extraordinary and primordial history of the City and its dignatories. It is hardly surprising, then, that one finds the same legendary material being used and re-used in a number of Munday's pageants – Jason's Argoe is, as we have seen, a case in point.

Only in *Metropolis Coronata* does Munday express an explicit intention to eschew his habitual approach, probably because, as an experienced playwright and, by then, an equally experienced pageant-maker, he was aware of the risk of repeating himself in his second consecutive show for the same company. 'I held it not fit', he therefore explains, 'to runne again the same course of antique honour: but rather to jumpe with the time, which evermore affecteth novelty'.[92] At the same time, as ever he cannot resist emphasising continuity over novelty, for the very next sentence describes the mayor's river journey to Westminster as taking place 'after such manner as formerly hath been observed'.[93] Indeed, that he says, somewhat ambivalently, that the present time 'ever *affecteth* novelty' indicates, as the text itself goes on to demonstrate, that he might have reservations about the merits of innovation over tradition. 'Novelty', Munday's text suggests, is sufficiently demonstrated by the usage of classical rather than metropolitan mythology: Jason's 'argoe' opens the show, striking what its author no doubt hoped would be a different note of antiquity to the preceding year's pageant's unhappily contentious preamble (further discussed below). The supposed originality of *Metropolis Coronata*, however, is somewhat compromised by Henry Fitz-Alwin's first speech, which commences with lines explicitly intended to bring the preceding year's Show *Himatia-Poleos* to mind: 'It is now a complete yeere, / Since in the borrowed shape I beare / Of olde Fitz-Alwine, I was raysed from rest.'[94] Even the current Lord Mayor is identified primarily as the temporary bearer of long-standing traditions; similarly, Munday foregrounds the livery companies' 'Escutchion of Armes' as an emblem of 'auncient Heraldrie' which at the same time remains 'still in firme force' – continuity is the keynote, once again.[95] In contrast to the way in which Munday constantly foregrounds historical continuity, as Lobanov-Rostovsky has argued,

Dekker's 1612 *Troia-Nova Triumphans* 'discards the past', emphasising the future deeds of John Swynnerton as the source of his 'Fame' rather than his place in an historical procession.[96]

Regardless of all the antiquity that Munday invokes in his pageants the contemporary moment is never far away. In *Sidero-Thriambos*, for instance, rather than the conventionally benign celebration of magistracy, one of the devices has a marked emphasis on the dangers of 'disorder' and the necessity for vigilance on the part of the City fathers. Treason and Ambition are figured in the text as 'vile Incendiaries ... which seeke the subversion of all estates'. Munday goes on to explain that immediate necessity has influenced his representation of these dual threats: 'because *this yeare* may be the better secured, against all their violences and treacherous attempts; they sit gyved, and manacled together in Iron shackles'.[97] 'This yeare' acts as a prompt towards current events and present dangers: one such immediate context, one that surely cannot have been far from the minds of the audience or the author of this Show, was the execution of Sir Walter Raleigh for high treason which took place at Westminster on the very same day. Indeed, Raleigh's execution was deliberately held to coincide with the Lord Mayor's show to distract the peoples' attention from the former event. In Middleton's *The Triumphes of Truth*, however, Error, presented as the chief threat to civic wellbeing, is hardly shackled and silent as Treason and his associates were in Munday's earlier show, since they are here, in contrast, physically impersonated by actors in the pageant and given full rein to seduce the new mayor to corruption. Thus the dangers that Middleton invokes are not external to London and generally subversive of 'all estates', as they are in Munday's Show, but much closer to home – they might well emanate from the actions of the City's own leader if he were to succumb to their enticements to 'Error'.[98]

Munday's attention was more habitually directed towards the past, however, and there he could find plenty of home-grown threats to represent being defeated. His version of certain individuals and symbols from the City's past in his mayoral Shows demonstrates again the role of myth-making in London's account of its own history. It also offers an example of where his concern to promote the particular livery company's greatness leads him to historical error. The dagger which forms part of the arms of the City Corporation had consistently been wrongly associated (by Holinshed, amongst others) with the dagger used by William Walworth, Lord Mayor of London, to kill the famous rebel Jack Straw (rather than his real victim Wat Tyler), one of the leaders of the fourteenth-century Peasants' Revolt. This mythical emblem of civic identity, which actually relates to St Paul, patron saint of the City's chief church, was described by Launcelot Andrewes in a Mary Spittal sermon as 'a memorial ... in [the] city scrutcheon'.[99] It also featured in the same fashion in Thomas Nelson's 1590 Lord Mayor's pageant for the Fishmongers' Company (since Walworth himself had been a Fishmonger he regularly appeared in this company's iconography).[100] Stow, naturally, is scathing about what he calls 'a meere fable' that Walworth killed Straw, and, probably referring to Nelson's pageant for the Fishmongers, castigates the Company as 'men ignorant of their Antiquities', referring those who wish to read the correct version to his own *Annales*.[101] As far as the purported connection between London's heraldic dagger and William Walworth is concerned, Stow is equally contemptuous. He writes that it 'is now growne to a common opinion that in reward of [Walworth's] service done ... King *Richard* added to the armes of this Citie ... a sword or dagger ... whereof I have read no such recorde, but to the contrarie'.[102]

Despite its disputed provenance, Munday could not resist including the story of Walworth's dagger when he was commissioned to write the mayoral pageant for a Fishmonger, John Leman, the 1616 Show *Chrysanaleia*. Walworth's role in the defeat of the Peasants' Revolt in London in 1381 was, after all, one of the Fishmongers' Company's finest hours. Unlike Nelson, however (perhaps learning from his predecessor's mistake), he does not try to establish a link with Jack Straw (or even Wat Tyler) in the pageant, although he does, despite Stow's extant criticism of this 'common' mistake, replicate the myth about the dagger being added to the City's arms as a result of Walworth's actions. He has Walworth himself boast that:

> as my dagger slew the Rebell then,
> So to renowne the deede; And I dare say,
> To honor London more (if more it may)
> The Red-crosse, in a Silver-field before,
> Had Walworth's Dagger added to it more.[103]

Munday represents Walworth accompanied by 'Londons Genius, a comely youth', who 'sits mounted on Horsebacke by [Walworth's] Bower ... bearing the Rebels head on Walworths Dagger'.[104] Walworth's antagonist is never named in the Show, but is only referred to somewhat vaguely as 'a proud Rebel', 'the proud insulting Rebell', 'their chiefest Captaine or commanding head' or such like.[105] The essential message that Munday wishes to get across is that slaying the strangely anonymous ringleader of one of the most notorious moments of plebeian unrest gave both Walworth and his livery company 'Fame for ever'.[106] Historical veracity notwithstanding, it clearly was important to the City's propagandists that that Walworth should kill Straw rather than Tyler, as it was equally crucial to them that the dagger in the coat of arms should celebrate a local rather than a biblical figure (albeit one who was London's patron saint). As Leinwand has argued, the interest of writers such as Munday and Nelson is 'controlled' by the context of their representations: as he says, in the case of civic pageants, 'we are concerned less with the fact that national peace was preserved [from the rebels] than with the recognition that it was a Londoner who accomplished this deed – never mind which Londoner'.[107] The integrity of London, especially in the face of internal threats, is also a theme of Munday's 1616 Show, which celebrates Walworth, 'fam'd both to Citie, and the Land', for his contribution to preserving the realm from its two 'enemies', which are 'forraine Hostilitie [and] home-bred Trecherie'.[108]

Despite such occasional dangers to London, more often than not continuity, if not stasis, is expressed in Munday's seventeenth-century texts. As well as stressing London's historical chronology in both his Lord Mayors' Shows and his editions of Stow, Munday is also concerned for the historical credentials of particular civic roles and individuals, himself included. The dedication to the Lord Mayor and Aldermen in the 1618 edition of the *Survay* places a special significance on native Londoners, those who can trace their habitation and family connections back more than one generation. Here Munday describes his current task as being to make good the outstanding lack of a comprehensive civic history, and to redress this he proposes to 'ranke downe in formall order, the successive line of the Sheriffes, Maiors and Aldermen'. The chief purpose of this exercise, Munday explains, is to record the latters' birthplace and parentage, especially those 'of them this most Honourable Citie itselfe then yeelded, as challenging them to bee her owne native Children'.[109] As one might expect, his own credentials for undertaking such an onerous work, and his personal investment in it, are highlighted. He writes: 'being a Citie-Child my selfe I hold it an attribute of credite for me to record ... that this ancient, famous and renowned Mother Citie of London, never wanted ... Sonnes of her owne bearing and breeding ... borne and bred in this worthie City, some to the fourth, others the third, but many the second generation.'[110] That the great men of London history are themselves Londoners is further highlighted by the marginal note at this point, which stresses to the reader that it is 'a perpetuall glory to London, to produce her own native sons to be her Magistrates'. In a circumlocutory way Munday is here recording and praising himself, for he has already fully established his own roots in the city of his birth at the very beginning of the dedication when acknowledging Stow, where London is named as 'this Royall Citie ... Birth-place and breeder to us both'.[111] Munday was also, as we have seen, at least a second-generation Londoner. The second dedication to John King, Bishop of London, reiterates Munday's close connection to the City and again uses his Londoner status to authenticate as well as to authorise his imprimatur upon Stow's text. 'Being a Free-borne Son of this Honorable City, even as Master STOWE', Munday writes, gives him both a 'dutie' *and* a right to revise this book; indeed, he himself 'deserved to claime no meane interest therein'.[112] The 'interests' of London's fame and antiquity are emphatically merged in this text with that of the ubiquitous editor, the one dependent upon the other in a mutually rewarding relationship.

Despite his efforts in this regard, however, Munday's emphasis upon the historical continuity of the City's officers and institutions came at a time when these practices were under considerable pressure. In particular, the livery company system was struggling to retain its medieval hegemony in the face of uncontrolled economic activity in areas such as Southwark, and the social order that their hierarchies represented was equally under strain. One would not think so, however, to witness the solemn conservatism with which Munday presents the Mayor, the Aldermen, the livery companies and their responsibilities. Indeed, the bulwark of tradition that he and his fellow pageant-makers shore up is so resolutely self-contained and so assured in its historical lineage that one cannot help but regard the shows as a covert response to their increasing irrelevance, trying to put forward an ideological alternative to the sprawling, unrestrained and fractured reality of London in the early decades of the seventeenth century.[113] In the same way, Sullivan has recently argued that Heywood's *I Edward IV* presents a London shaped precisely *by* threats to its geographical and economic integrity, however much it struggles to exclude those threats: 'the symbolic meaning' of the city, for Heywood as for the city pageants, 'resists shifts in spatial practice that underlie the development of suburban industry and the erosion of livery-company influence'.[114] The following complaint from the City Corporation to the Privy Council from 1632 expresses the reality of their situation rather more freely than the more one-dimensional pageants, showing a consciousness that the ancient privileges of the City are becoming increasingly endangered: 'the freedom of London which is heretofore of very great esteem is grown to be of little worth, by reason of the extraordinary enlargement of the suburbs, where great numbers of traders and handicraftsmen do enjoy, without charge, equal benefit with the freemen and citizens of London'.[115] It may, then, be ironic that the period that saw the zenith of the Lord Mayor's Show was precisely the one that accelerated the decline of the oligarchy of the twelve great livery companies. In the Corporation's lament, 'the suburbs', demonised once more, stand for all that is physically and conceptually outside of 'London'. The expansion in terms of building and population in these extra-civic areas coincided with the growth of the purpose-built theatres from the 1580s onwards.

Stow's famously nostalgic *Survay* with its scrupulousness over London's historical dates, names and places was a major resource for Munday and others' Lord Mayors' Shows. However, as with his reluctance to highlight London's playhouses it is noteworthy that despite his almost obsessive attention to detail Stow omits to discuss the Lord Mayors' Shows in the *Survay*. Archer puts forward the suggestion that Stow regarded them as a 'poor substitute' for the more inclusive pre-Reformation festivities of the past.[116] Manley offers an alternative interpretation and ascribes this omission to 'the relative novelty' of the shows, not fully established on the London scene by 1598, although it could be argued that by 1603, the date of Stow's second edition, they would have been.[117] Stow's reticence is all the more difficult to account for when one recalls that he actually had been paid ten shillings only the year before the second edition of the *Survay* by the Merchant Taylors for 'great paynes by him taken in serching for such as have byn maiors, Shereffs and Aldermen of this Companie' – in order to assist the writing of that year's mayoral pageant.[118]

In his 1633 edition of Stow's text, in contrast to its predecessors, Munday foregrounds the Lord Mayors' Shows. In the section bearing the coats of arms of consecutive mayors, he comments in relation to Thomas Campbell (the father of one of the dedicatees of the 1633 *Survey*) that 'the Lord Maiors Shews, long left off, were now [i.e. in

1609, the year of Campbell senior's mayoralty] revived againe by order from the King'.[119] He neglects to mention, however, although doubtless some of his readers would have been able to make the link for themselves, that he himself had been responsible for Campbell's triumph in 1609, *Camp-bell, or the Ironmongers Faire Field*, as well as dedicating his civic entertainment for Prince Henry, *Londons Love*, to Campbell in the following year. As his readers would have been aware, Munday dominated the civic entertainments that took place in the first decade of the seventeenth century. One reason for this uncharacteristic show of modesty might have been the Ironmongers' displeasure with Munday's production, so much so that shortly after the Show took place Munday was brought before the Ironmongers' Court. Amongst other complaints, it appears that the child actors 'weare not instructed their speeches', 'the Musick and singinge weare wanting', and, shamefully for a Draper poet, 'the apparrell [was] most of it old and borrowed'.[120] Munday's deficiencies on this occasion relate to two of his 'trades', drapery and playwrighting, and as a consequence he failed to be granted the additional five pounds he had requested from the Company.[121] In the preamble to the Show itself, Munday hints that he experienced unusual difficulties in bringing it to completion and describes the 'weightie enforcements' he was working under: 'our time for preparation hath bene so short', he explains, 'as never was the like undertaken by any before, nor matter of such moment so expeditiously performed'.[122] The role of the child actors also appears to have caused him an especial headache, and he took what must have been unsuccessful steps to ensure that their 'weake voyces' should not be overused, because 'in a crowde of such noyse and uncivill turmoyle, [they] are not any way able to be understood'.[123] As Bergeron remarks, Munday took no chances with poor actors in the more court-oriented *Londons Love*, employing, as we have seen, Burbage and Rice, two of the chief actors of London's then most significant company, the King's Men.[124] For this later entertainment Munday was not stinted as in 1609, for he received forty-seven shillings for his expenses and 'foure pounde six shillinge and Four pence for his paines and labour taken', despite the brevity of time for preparation that he had once again experienced.[125]

The importance of myth and history – or mythic history – to the City's representation of itself in pageantry is thoroughgoing. Civic pageantry thus presented homilectic history, 'a storehouse of "the examples of virtue and vice"'.[126] There is an emphasis in both dramatic and non-dramatic histories upon utility, an emphasis with which Munday would have been in sympathy given his fondness for Cicero. The reading of history, Heinemann has argued, was represented in many works of this kind as especially instructive for 'the middling sort'. She cites Richard Braithwait's view from 1614: 'what fitter for the householder to train his children, servants and attendants in ... than the reading of profitable stories, such as excite to virtue, and stir up their minds to the undertaking of something worthy a resolved spirit'.[127] History was also a popular mode for ballads and broadsides, the most despised cultural form in London: as Manley writes, 'eulogies on virtuous citizens ... appealed especially to Londoners, as did praises of the city ... tributes to heroes like Dick Whittington ... and exhortations and warnings to apprentices'.[128] Ironically, given their progenitor's own past history, in the ritual mode of Munday's pageantry, especially the presentation of past civic worthies as pseudo-'patron-saints' of guilds, there is some mimicry of certain aspects of the Catholic ritual.[129] Ironic too was the frequent presentation of classical and medieval history in a medium which, as we have seen, was first recorded in its present form as far back only as 1535.[130] By invoking the ancient traditions of the City's constituent livery companies, Munday and his contemporaries are implicitly bringing to the foreground the increasingly anachronistic foundation of these companies as religious entities in the medieval period. As Stevenson notes, even if economic development was progressing towards a more 'modern' mode of production, this did not necessarily entail that cultural production in this period had entirely left behind older modes of self-identity. The further paradox, in Stevenson's terms, of playwrights' employment by those civic authorities who at other times tried to suppress their dramatic livelihoods is described by Manley as 'an unlikely and perhaps uneasy' juxtaposition between 'the enterprising capitalism of the dramatists' and 'the theatrical self-consciousness of the merchant class'.[131] This juxtaposition neatly encapsulated Munday himself, as does the unusual combination of traditions that he embodied.

It could, however, be a matter as much of parallelism (or even triangularism) as juxtaposition. Thus, for instance, one should recall that the première of Jonson's *Bartholmew Fair* took place only two days after *Himatia-Poleos* was presented along and on the other side of the river from the Hope on Bankside; as if to complete the third part of this equation Jonson's play was then performed at court the following day. Although the play is of course *set* in West Smithfield (which itself is barely outside the city walls in what had once been, but was no longer, a city liberty), in the induction the scrivener makes the point that it was *performed* outside of the City proper, 'at the Hope on the Bankside, in the county of Surrey ... the one and thirtieth day of October 1614'.[132] Indeed, Jonson's dating of the play's first performance is so very precise that it is almost as if he is expecting us to make the connection between his production and Munday's, which itself took place on a date which all Londoners would have recognised. This kind of 'local knowledge' enables us also to understand more fully the contexts for Jonson's satirical presentation of civic antitheatricality in the induction of this play, with its complex accumulation of different forms of urban culture.

Munday's civic texts, however, with their predominant concern for tradition and continuity, were considerably less likely to represent cultural tensions than Jonson's plays. London had its own form of mythology, and the originary moment of the City's current hierarchical structure could be traced back to the late twelfth century when Henry Fitz-Alwin was created London's first Lord Mayor – a moment Munday himself calls that of London's 'full perfection' in his 1618 edition of the *Survay*.[133] It would therefore have been essential for Munday in all his civic productions to be careful to be correct over the dating and, especially, the guild identification of Fitz-Alwin. However, just as Stow attacked Thomas Nelson's early pageant for the Fishmongers for its historical inaccuracies over William Walworth, another of the City's heroes, so Munday was later to apologise to the Drapers, his own company no less (which must have been humiliating), for misrepresenting the lineage of Fitz-Alwin, one of the City's most famous figures, in his 1611 Show for the Goldsmiths' Company, *Chrusothriambos*.[134] In this Show Munday had originally associated Fitz-Alwin with the Goldsmiths in the most unambiguous and public fashion. Fitz-Alwin, as Leofstane, has the first speaking part in the pageant and declares in his greeting to the Mayor and the other assembled spectators that he is 'a Golde-smith by my profession'.[135] He is subsequently described as a Goldsmith by no less an authoritative figure than Time himself, emphasising the role Fitz-Alwin plays in the glorious antiquity of the Goldsmiths' Company. Time asks his audience, 'Shall I tell ye what that first Lord [Mayor] was?', and then answers his own rhetorical question with: 'A Gold-Smith, of thine own profession, / Henrie Fitz-Alwine, Fitz-Leofstane'.[136]

This is a significant error that Munday was keen to put right when the opportunity arose so he tried to remedy it in an extensive and clearly disconcerted digression in *Himatia-Poleos* (1614). This section is worth exploring and quoting at length (not least because it is reminiscent of previous occasions when Munday was reproved for inaccuracy, way back in the early 1580s).[137] Even if, as Bergeron has suggested, when rendering the show's event in print pageant-writers were sometimes inclined to introduce 'digressions, descriptions and discourses on sometimes arcane topics', many of which 'call[ed] attention to [themselves]', Munday's intervention here, albeit atypical of this genre, is characteristically self-obsessed.[138] Whereas others (such as Robert Crowley) who attempted quasi-historical accounts only to be reproved over mistakes about the dates of royal reigns, say, Munday's error here, and the weight it is given, is typically parochial. This part of Munday's Show also belies Bergeron's claim that Webster's *Monuments of Honour* is exceptional in its use of first person pronouns.[139] Munday's text is as preoccupied with the status of its author as so many of his other works. Where one might expect to find at most a dedication and other brief prefatory matter in a printed text of this kind, here the author addresses a lengthy preamble to some unspecified readership (the Drapers? the Goldsmiths?), highlighting his own 'discredit'. Munday writes:

> Heere before I passe any further, it may appeare as a blemish on mine own browe, because in my Booke in the worthie Company of Goldsmiths, I did set downe Henrie Fitz-Alwine, Fitz-Leofstane to be a Goldsmith, and the first Lord Maior of London, alleadging my authority for the same in the margent of the same booke, out of John Stowe, which now I may seem to denie, and affirme the same man to be a Draper, to the disgrace of the forenamed Company, and mine owne deepe discredit.[140]

Chruso-thriambos indeed bears the marginal comment 'Ex John Stow' against the line which calls Leofstane, 'that first Lord', 'a Gold-Smith'. A few lines further on Munday reiterates the error with his reference to Leofstane as 'this grave Gold-Smith'.[141] A sense of uncertainty (probably engendered by his embarrassment) pervades the later text at this point, not least because Munday only 'seems' to deny Stow. Furthermore, the syntax of that very denial is sufficiently ambiguous as to indicate, contrary to his stated intention, that the act of now affirming Fitz-Alwin to be a Draper might cause 'disgrace' to the 'forenamed Company' - in this sentence, of course, the referent of 'forenamed' is the Drapers rather than the Goldsmiths - *and* lead to his 'owne deepe discredit'. Ostensibly, however, poor Stow, by then long since dead, bears the brunt of the blame for the mistake and is used as Munday's alibi, if not his scapegoat. Munday continues 'what then I did was by warrant of my fore-alleaged Author, who ... set [Fitz-Alwin] downe to bee a Goldsmith; which was no error in me to do the like, being thereto secured by him, and knowing (as then) no other proofe to the contrary'.[142] His readiness to blame the conveniently deceased Stow for his mistakes in this pageant contrasts with his treatment of Stow as the more senior historian in his 1618 edition of Stow's own *Survay*, which, to compound the irony, was the work by Stow from which Munday originally drew his mistaken description of Fitz-Alwin.[143] In Munday's own revised version of this latter text, Stow is still, if subtly, charged with unreliability, although Munday states rather more respectfully that his predecessor had actually explicitly charged him with remedying any deficiencies in his work. Munday represents their collaboration as a truly joint venture: 'much of [Stow's] good mind he had formerly imparted to me', he relates, 'and some of his best collections lovingly delivered me'. Indeed, Stow's awareness of his own failings was (by Munday's account) so pronounced that he actually requested the younger man's assistance, 'preuailing with me so farre, by his importunate perswasions', as Munday puts it, 'to correct what I found amisse, and to proceed in the perfecting of a Worke so worthy ... and to supply it where I found any thing wanting'.[144] Munday, of course, reportedly out of loyalty as much to his city as to his 'good friend', willingly made good Stow's deficiencies: 'being overcome by affection to him, but much more by respect and care of this Royall Citie ... I undertooke (so farre as my ability would extend) to further a Booke of such needfull use'.[145]

The error in *Himatia-Poleos*, however, is more ungratefully finessed as a 'blinde misleading by a blinder guide' and by the end of his long explanation Munday has made every effort to divert attention away from his own hideous mortification on to Stow's deficiencies as an historian (although he concedes these might have been involuntary rather than 'wilful' nor 'willing'). From thence he moves the topic on to a more general account of how he came to learn that there were in fact *two* Henry Fitz-Alwins, one of whom was more securely a Draper; for this correction Munday is indebted to 'divers other good Antiquaries beside', including 'Maister Clarentius Camden'.[146] Unfortunately, Munday's willingness to correct one of Stow's supposed errors did not extend to his later work on the 1618 edition of the *Survay*, where the text categorically states that 'the first Maior of London was a Goldsmith' and then names the said Goldsmith as 'Henry Fitz Alewin, Fitz Leafstane'.[147] In this particular case it would appear that Stow *is* to blame for the mistake, if blame is the right word, for Munday has simply reproduced Stow's original text at this point without noticing, remarkably perhaps, the very same error that recently had caused him such discomfort.[148] Clearly his vainglorious pronouncement at the beginning of the *Survay* that he will remedy anything he finds 'amiss' in Stow's original was not thoroughly carried out. Indeed, Munday himself introduces further confusion – or perhaps his allegiance to the Drapers misled him once again – for towards the end of his 1618 edition of the *Survay*, in the section on the 'Temporall Government' of London, he states that the 'first maior of London' was 'Henry Fitz-Alwin, Draper'.[149] Here Munday deliberately alters Stow's original text, where Fitz-Alwin is consistently described as a Goldsmith: 'their 1. Maior was H. Fitz Alwin Fitz Liefstane, *Goldsmith*'.[150]

In *Himatia-Poleos* he also tries to reorient his reader's focus away from Fitz-Alwin on to the relatively uncontroversial figure of the undenied Goldsmith Nicholas Faringdon, in order quite explicitly 'to cut off all such contentious questions'.[151] Both the Mercers and the Fishmongers, Munday argues, labouring the matter somewhat peevishly, had mistaken Fitz-Alwin and Walworth respectively for others of the same name without causing undue offence: the Mercers, for instance, might be equally chastised for 'mistaking Peter Fitz-Alwine (a Mercer indeed) for Henrie Fitz-Alwine, the olde Draper'.[152] This example, Munday does not seem to have noticed, does not help his case as it duplicates the very ascription of a mayor called Fitz-Alwin to the Drapers that is the contention he here tries to evade. Nevertheless, on the basis that everyone can make an honest mistake he defends himself very robustly: 'I answere freely for my selfe and appeale to an especiall Gentleman in the imagined injured Companie of Goldsmiths (who took no meane paines to be resolved in this case) that no certaine assurance could be had therein, but that it remained doubtful between both the Societies.'[153] The 'imagined injured' Goldsmiths, as he so churlishly puts it, were unlikely to have been mollified by this mediation because Munday, as we have seen (evidently learning nothing from his experience), immediately proceeds to invoke the controversial name of Fitz-Alwin in relation to the Drapers anyway despite what he has just said about the 'doubtfulness' of his claim. That this is actually *another* Henry Fitz-Alwin, who coincidentally was also a mayor, and one, mercifully for Munday, who was indubitably a Draper, does little to alleviate his discomfort. Munday ascertained the identity of this other, unfortunately named Fitz-Alwin largely on the basis of his own historical research in Drapers' Hall, which stands for Munday as a 'more assured authority' than Stow, whose other 'mistakes' about Fitz-Alwin are now rehearsed.[154] His explanation is however thoroughly undermined by the assertion *prior* to his apology that 'out of this list or band of Drapers issued Sir Henrie Fitz-Alwine ... [who] had the first honour to be stiled ... Maior of London'.[155] When appealing to the Goldsmiths he is prepared to admit uncertainty about Fitz-Alwin; however, when promoting the honour of his own company he does not hesitate to repeat the controversial claim. Despite his clear discomfort about discrepancies between *Chruso-thriambos* and the present text, he shows no consciousness that he has actually contradicted himself *within* the latter. It seems that for Munday there is something so compelling about celebrating the Drapers that it overrides all common sense. Thus his final word on the subject attempts to shield his embarrassing failings behind the undoubted grandeur of the Drapers, 'seeing then that reverend antiquity, eminencie of honour, and due right of merit, bestowed so high a dignity upon [them]'.[156] His confidence on this important point of detail might have been bolstered by the fact that the Drapers had 'procured a patent' to prove that Fitz-Alwin was a member of their company in the same year as this mayoral Show for the Drapers.[157]

Actually, as Pafford points out (and Munday, as we have seen, admits in passing), 'there is in fact no evidence that Fitzailwin [*sic*] was either a Goldsmith or a Draper'.[158] In the context of a Show sponsored by the Drapers, it is perhaps understandable that Munday might choose to represent their own historical archives as totally authoritative and to accentuate their primacy despite the risks. More generally, Munday's evident unwillingness to risk offence to either of these important companies and potential future employers leads inevitably to confusion and chastisement. His own words suggest as much; he concludes his personal preamble with an explanation of his conduct: 'I might well be justly condemned if I should seeke after any other argument of credit for [the Drapers] (when so maine a busines doth necessarilie require it) then their own due deserving, so long time sleeping in oblivion, yet now revived, to their endlesse honor'.[159] Implicit in this is the suggestion that the Goldsmiths' condemnation which he is dealing with here was *unjust*. Negotiating Munday's convoluted prose when he feels himself to be at a disadvantage is often difficult, but it seems to me that he is conceding that only his own interest in putting the best possible gloss on the history of the Drapers ('so maine a busines', as he calls it) justifies the claim about Fitz-Alwin, not any definitive authority. In the same way, ironically, it would certainly have earlier served his immediate short-term purpose to associate Fitz-Alwin, undoubtedly London's first recorded Lord Mayor, with the Goldsmiths in their 1611 pageant, regardless of any future difficulties that lay ahead.

Fidelity to the historical truth was less than a priority when Munday was attempting to put a particular interpretation on the past, especially when it was his own company that was setting the agenda. He may have laid claim to historical credibility in *Metropolis Coronata* by presenting the Show as if it were a truncated version of the more expansive form of chronicle history, such as when he mentions in passing famous Drapers and Staplers about whom 'our Chronicles (at large) do more amply declare', but in practice he struggled to preserve historical consistency, not to mention accuracy.[160] Even in *Himatia-Poleos* itself, despite the labyrinthine apology I have just discussed, Munday could not refrain from making the equally unsubstantiated claims that the Drapers were both the City's oldest and its leading livery company, calling them 'the first Companie of all other in this Citie', 'the first honoured Companie', and 'the first originall' of the livery company system itself, which of course laid him open to the possibility of future humiliating retractions.[161] Evidently he was not able to resist the temptation of replicating both claims of the Drapers' primacy, one in the title page of the following year's pageant, *Metropolis Coronata*, which celebrated 'the truly Honourable Society of Drapers, the first that received such Dignitie in this Citie', and the other in the body of the text, with a reference to 'Drapery ... as being the first and cheefest honoured Society before all other'.[162]

What is more – astonishingly, given the publicity in *Himatia-Poleos* of Munday's embarrassment over his mis-ascription of Fitz-Alwin, the first Lord Mayor – he once more and with considerable emphasis claims this famed worthy for the Drapers. *Metropolis Coronata* actually begins with Munday associating 'the true antiquitie, and primary Honour of Englands Draperie' with the installation of 'that famous noble Gentleman, Sir Henry Fitz-Alwine Knight, in the first dignity of L. Maior of London', since, allegedly, Richard I 'granted' this honour to the Drapers.[163] When one remembers that he barely saved himself from serious error only a year before by explaining belatedly that he meant a different Henry Fitz-Alwin, it is all the more remarkable that Munday should state so explicitly in *Metropolis Coronata* that the honour of the Drapers can be likened directly to the first conferment of the City's highest office. Fitz-Alwin gets more than this passing reference, too; indeed, he has a lengthy speech in which he boldly identifies himself with the Drapers despite Munday's protestation in the previous year's Show that the identity of Fitz-Alwin's guild was 'doubtful'. Furthermore, in this later text one gains the impression that Munday is quite deliberately exploiting this very uncertainty as his representation of Fitz-Alwin is noticeably ambiguous. Fitz-Alwin refers back to *Himatia-Poleos* and the 'borrowed shape' of Fitz-Alwin he himself bore in that Show, suggesting, as was actually the case, that there might be two Henry Fitz-Alwins.[164] Later on, 'Time' (another familiar figure from a previous year for all Munday's talk of 'novelty') alludes to 'our supposed Sir Henry Fitz-Alwine'.[165] The 'borrowed' and 'supposed' guise of this disputed figure might also be a gesture, equally damaging to the pageant's basis in historical truth, towards the feigned theatricality implicit in the impersonation of Fitz-Alwin by an actor. Such equivocation sits uneasily with Munday's stated intention from the Show's very outset to co-opt Fitz-Alwin as one of the Drapers' own, a tactic which Fitz-Alwin himself reiterates at length as his speech proceeds. Munday is in trouble whichever way he chooses to deal with Fitz-Alwin, it would appear: associating him exclusively with any one livery company risks offending the other claimants but being faithful to history and preserving the dubiety might entail offending them all. His solutions, as we can see, were informed by the specific requirements of that year's agenda-setters, with some unfortunate consequences for the hapless pageanter.

Munday's text also twice rehearses the glory that resulted from the fact that *Metropolis Coronata* was the second consecutive pageant in honour of the Drapers, who were 'triumphing', as he puts it, 'a second Yeere'. It was of course not only the Drapers who were in the limelight in both 1614 and 1615, and Munday could not restrain himself from overtly celebrating his own authorial part in these two productions. Reminding his readers that he had in *Himatia-Poleos* 'sufficiently approved the true antiquitie, and primary Honour of Englands Draperie', he then discusses the artistic challenge presented to him of representing the historical and present condition of the Drapers' Company twice in as many years without repeating himself.

'Seeing likewise', he states, 'that Drapery triumpheth now two yeers together ... I held it not fit (finding myself not barren of invention, in a Theame of such scope and large extendure) to runne againe the same course of antique honour'. The Drapers, it would appear, as a subject close to Munday's heart, provide ample material for his creativity, so rather than going over old ground for the second year running, he prefers to offer his audience and readership 'novelty, in a new forme of this second yeeres triumph'.[166] As we have already seen, however, Munday was not altogether comfortable with innovations in pageantry and quickly fell back into his tried-and-tested formula – as his words 'antique honour' indicate – of emphasising 'auncient and most honourable custome'.[167]

For all his obsession with tradition and continuity, Munday was at times uncertain about points of detail in relation to Fitz-Alwin and hence, by implication, about the other facts of London's successive history. Inconsistencies can often be identified between his various texts. In *Metropolis Coronata*, as we have seen, he claims that Fitz-Alwin was established as London's first Lord Mayor by Richard I, an act 'seconded by his brother John'.[168] A few years later, however, in the more comprehensive *Survay*, he is less sure of his ground: 'some hold [the beginning of the Mayoralty] to be in King Johns time; but most maintaine and avouch it, to bee in the first yeere of King Richard the first'.[169] As Marcus comments, as in *Metropolis Coronata*, here Munday once more subordinates the role of the monarch to that of the City's worthies, for the kings he mentions are important only in so far as they advance the City's own liberties.[170] Stow's original text is more categorical: 'in the first yeare of king Richard the first, the Citizens of London ... obtained to have a Maior, to be their principall Governour ... Their 1. Maior was H. Fitz Alwin Fitz Liefstane, Goldsmith, [ap]pointed by the said king, and continued maior from the first of Richard the first.'[171] This, of course, is the mis-identification of Fitz-Alwin as a Goldsmith that was to cause Munday so much trouble in his Shows. Once again, Munday proves shaky on historical data. Not only does he repeat his further error over Fitz-Alwin's livery company in his 1618 edition of the *Survay*, as we have seen; in *Metropolis Coronata* he had not learnt his lesson, for here by a crafty sleight of hand he once more incorrectly ascribes London's first mayor to membership of the Drapers. In *Himatia-Poleos* Munday may well have been motivated more by a desire to gratify (or at least not to offend any further) his own Company than by a sudden attack of historical accuracy, given that he had in 1611 assigned Fitz-Alwin to the ranks of the Goldsmiths.

His account of Fitz-Alwin in the 1614 text is framed less defensively to reflect maximum glory on to the Drapers at the expense of historical truth, let alone at the expense of Munday's own reputation as a writer who could be trusted to represent his city faithfully. The truth of the matter was somewhat more complicated, although despite his later struggles Munday does manage to avoid confusion and/or error, at least about the date of the inception of the mayoralty if not the associated livery company, in his earlier text *Chrysothriambos*. Here it is explained that the office of the Lord Mayor commenced during the reign of Richard, with the important clarification that, although Richard himself nominated the Mayor, it was in the later reign of the usually maligned but in this instance 'gracious' King John that 'the Cittizens of London [gained] absolute power, to elect a Lord Mayor amongst themselves'.[172] The certainty with which Munday pronounces on this subject in 1611 seems to have deserted him, as we have seen, by 1618. It would appear that Munday was fated to misrepresent Fitz-Alwin, such an important founding figure of London's own history, for he erroneously claims Robin Hood, 'Robert de la Hude, sometime the noble Earle of Huntington', to be Fitz-Alwin's son-in-law in this pageant, a curious mistake for him to make given that he had written extensively about Robin Hood as the Earl in the *Huntington* plays some years previously, in which Robin Hood's father-in-law is called 'Lord Fitzwater' (latterly: initially, he is 'Lord Lacy').[173] Munday's desire in this later instance is primarily to recast this famous figure in a civic mould. He clearly felt able to change the details around at whim, for in *Metropolis Coronata* 'Gilbert de la hude', who in the plays was Robin's uncle, becomes 'a most unnatural covetous Brother'. Such intertextuality is a feature of Munday's writing, for in another play, *Sir John Oldcastle*, Harpoole, Oldcastle's steward, owns a book about Robin Hood.[174] Nevertheless, despite these curious inaccuracies in his 1611 pageant, Munday established new traditions of the Robin Hood story, such as the identification of his hero as the real Earl of Huntington.[175]

Munday's personal visibility in all these embarrassing errors is in part entirely characteristic, but it also derives from the unusually 'authored' nature of the city pageants. As Johnson has remarked, in contrast to a large number of plays, 'not a single one of the Lord Mayors' Shows is anonymous; and only one is not by an established professional writer'.[176] Although for most contemporary critics the authorship of playtexts is considerably more important and more interesting than that of civic pageants, as far as Munday's works are concerned it is noticeable that his playwrighting is often in the form of collaboration, with all its consequent uncertainties in terms of his particular contribution. However, in respect of his pageants and prose works he is usually the sole and often highly visible author. Munday, like so many of his pageant-making rivals, first earned his limited literary renown (and personal notoriety, perhaps) in the city theatres; even if the connection was understandably not made overt in the civic context since pageant-writing would there have been the higher-status literary activity, it must surely have been known by the audiences of both forms of entertainment.[177] Johnson argues that the way in which some of Munday's earlier Shows were published points up their theatrical dimensions: with the speeches collected together separately at the end of the text after a prose section describing the scene and properties, 'they read', she states, 'much more like the script of a contemporary play than the account of public experience'.[178]

These writers were identified by their livery company allegiance on the printed versions of the Shows (thus Munday is always called a 'Cittizen and Draper'). Johnson has argued further 'that the name of a recognised poet should appear on the booklet's title page was ... part of the conspicuous consumption reflected in the titles themselves'.[179] Self-advertisement, too, must have formed part of the equation, since these writers were competing amongst themselves for civic business and would have had an eye to lucrative future contracts.[180] Munday, as we have seen, had been for a long time a relentless self-publicist in a wide variety of texts. The 'authorial presence', in Johnson's words, in Munday's pageants differs somewhat from that of, say, Webster, who strives to retain his poetic dignity; Munday, in contrast, as *Himatia-Poleos* demonstrates, struggles not altogether successfully to preserve his *amour propre*.[181]

'A RETURNE TO LONDON': MUNDAY'S SURVAY

An authorial presence can equally be detected in Munday's editions of the *Survay*, not least in the change of the title of the book from *A Survay of London* to the more assertive *The Survay*. I have already noted the absence of any extended reference to the London playhouses, but as well as making omissions Munday also enlarged Stow's text in his own idiosyncratic fashion. The studied indifference to London's theatres does not mean that Munday's theatrical past is not reflected in his editions of Stow; it does make an impact, but in a covert, possibly unconscious way. Munday's extensive additions to the 1618 edition of the *Survay*, 'continued, corrected and much enlarged with many rare and worthie notes', as he himself puts it with typical immodesty, have been characterised somewhat dismissively by Kingsford as consisting 'very largely of copies from monumental inscriptions from churches and extracts from [Stow's] *Summarie* and *Annales*'.[182] The work Munday undertook on Stow's texts reflects what we know to be his especial preoccupations: the history and topography of his civic world. The 1618 edition of the *Survay* reiterates Munday's conclusion to the *Briefe Chronicle*, with its bathetic list of civic posts. Munday's posthumously published 1633 edition adds the coats of arms of all the Mayors and the City Companies from 1189 to the present, plus what Kingsford calls 'a large if somewhat undigested mass of new matter, copies of Acts and Statutes of Parliament and the Common Council, [and] notes on the origin of the City Companies'.[183] These 'notes' probably constitute a reflection of Munday's extensive pageant-writing for a number of the major livery companies over the preceding years. Specifically, Munday extended Stow's chapter on the 'Honor of Citizens, and worthinesse of men in the same', a list of civic benefactors. He did so in a particular fashion by greatly expanding on each of the brief entries in this section which Stow had ended with a curt 'as in my Summarie'. The consequence was not simply a longer book, for by so doing Munday erased the cross-reference to the text's original author's other work, for although the additions were taken from Stow's *Summarie* Munday nowhere acknowledges that fact.[184] As with his use of Stow's texts in his Lord Mayors' Shows, Munday's literary relationship with his forebear is ambivalent.

As one might expect given his ostensible piety and reported friendship with clerics, Munday paid particular attention to ecclesiastical developments when revising Stow's work. In the 1633 edition he proffers an alphabetical appendix of recent rebuildings and other improvements to London churches, together with some details of their benefactors, which he calls 'infinite supplements of Ancient and Moderne Monuments.[185] Appropriately enough, this is the section which he claims to have been specifically requested to put together for the 1618 edition by the Bishop of London, John King, via an unnamed 'Gentleman of much learning and respect'. The material was not ready for the 1618 edition, much to Munday's apologetic regret, but was promised for the forthcoming 'larger Volume'.[186] Indeed, Munday had to negotiate this earlier edition's 'double dutie' to both the City's temporal and religious leaders quite carefully, stating that the dedication to John King 'rightly deserv[ed] to be the first, by reason that Gods cause ought to be preferred before the Worlds'.[187] However, he makes no explanation as to why 'Gods cause' actually appeared second, leaving it to this cynical modern reader to speculate that the motive might be the greater likelihood of monetary recompense from 'the World', i.e. the City, than from God. When the section did materialise in the 1633 edition, Munday celebrated its appearance by stressing the fact that these details 'before this instant were never published'.[188]

Drawing on his previous forays into London history in both dramatic and prose form, he also added to the 1618 edition an much-expanded account of Wat Tyler's rebellion, which was enlarged from three to fourteen pages and focused, as in *Chrysanaleia*, on the role of Walworth in putting down the unrest. He also highlighted the 'Evil May Day' riots of 1517 by inserting an extensive and detailed five-page account of the unrest and its aftermath (rather inappropriately) before Stow's original passing reference in his section on 'Sports and Pastimes'.[189] Like the *Thomas More* playtext, Munday's account of the May Day unrest draws extensively on Edward Hall's chronicle. As the extracts from Hall that I quoted in the introduction indicate, Hall, a civic historian like Stow, took a sympathetic approach to the rioters. Hall's understanding position regarding the London rioters' grievances might be explained, at least in part, by the fact that he himself had been, according to Stow, 'a common Sergeant of London, and one of the Judges in the shiriffes Court'. Perhaps because Hall was too 'a Citizen by birth and office' Stow praises him highly as the writer of a 'famous and eloquent Chronicle'.[190]

Both Munday's plays and pageants have an impact on his editions of the *Survay*. Moore has suggested that the large, twenty-four-page section that Munday added on the Thames might have been prompted by the role played by the river in civic pageantry as the Mayor and Aldermen travelled by barge to Westminster on the day of the conferment of the mayoralty. Compared to Stow's general account of 'the ancient and present rivers ... serving the Citie', Munday's two separate chapters specifically on 'the ancient and famous River of Thames' do indicate a particular interest on his part; his frequent use of the 'argoe' in a number of his works underlines the point. In the same fashion,

Munday added to Stow's text details of recent work to improve London's water supplies.[191] In his Lord Mayors' Shows, too, Munday regularly uses the river and water imagery, such as the 1623 production he shared with Middleton; in the 1610 civic text *Londons Love* there are two woodcuts of ships.[192]

His local associations also permeate the text, for Munday extended Stow's original account of Cripplegate Ward in many respects. For the 1618 edition, Munday attempted to collaborate with John Speed (another St Giles parishioner) but his wish to include a map by Speed of the causeways built to make the swampy Moorfields passable was thwarted and he did not manage to add it to the 1633 edition either.[193] In the lengthy section about the ward of Cripplegate in his versions of the *Survay*, Munday describes his dealings with Speed thus: 'M. John Speed, my especiall kinde friend, acquainted me with the draught of a Mappe ... I purposed to have beene at so much charge, as to have had that map (in some apt and convenient forme) printed in this booke: but that I could not attaine thereto, being promised, that at the next impression I shall have it'.[194] Munday had previously used the same explanation for the non-appearance of Speed's map of Moorfields in the 1618 edition, adding in a marginal note that he hoped 'it [would] be seen in a larger Volume'.[195] Clearly over the course of fifteen years his wishes had been confounded owing to some vaguely worded business involving the Mayor, Aldermen and John Speed. Here, as elsewhere in his revisions to the *Survay*, Munday makes personal interjections which stand out amongst Stow's more objective prose; for instance, he praises those responsible for draining and laying down walks across Moorfields (an area close to his Cripplegate locality) by saying 'I am certainely perswaded, that ... they are no meane cause of preserving health and wholsome ayre to the Citie'.[196] Cripplegate and Moorgate, both places with which Munday would have been very familiar, are mentioned specifically in his pageant *Chrysanaleia*, since they were allegedly built by a Goldsmith and a Fishmonger respectively. The establishment of these two gates is used by Munday to exemplify the long-standing union between these two companies. He writes that 'this league of love and fellowship ... continued ... [by] building the Wall and two North Gates therein, Moore-gate and Criples-gate ... the one performed by Thomas Faulconer, Fishmonger, and the other by William Shaw Goldsmith'.[197] This is Munday's sole topographical reference in his pageants that does not relate directly to places that traditionally featured in the progress of the show itself, such as Baynard's Castle or Soper Lane. Alas, as with Fitz-Alwin before, Munday's enthusiasm to applaud the merits of the livery company in question leads him to make a mistake, since Moorgate was in fact founded by a Mercer, not a Fishmonger; he also mistook the name of the Goldsmith who founded Cripplegate, who was actually called Edmund Shaw or Shaa, a Cripplegate alderman from 1478.[198] The latter seems an unlikely error on the part of such a long-standing Cripplegate resident with a lifelong interest in history.

There are in the *Survay* some quite uncanny moments where Munday revisits not only London's past in his searching after antiquities (especially epitaphs and other memorials) but also his own past. Thus in the 1633 edition, for instance, he mentions – only very briefly – Sir Thomas More's monument 'in the church at Chelsey' but unlike his usual practice he fails to reproduce the tomb's inscription.[199] As Moore has recently noted, Munday also revived an old troubling connection when researching the 1618 edition of this text. In the course of his many visits to London's churches he sought the assistance of local clerics, among whom he thanks especially one 'M. Stephen Gosson', the parson of the church of St Botolph without Bishopsgate.[200] Gosson, once his antagonist in the debate about the stage over forty years previously, gave the now more respectable editor of Stow what Munday calls 'friendly furtherance' when he came to set down the bounds of Gosson's parish.[201] As we can see with this re-emergence of Stephen Gosson into Munday's life, Munday's theatrical past comes back to haunt him elsewhere in the *Survay*. The final part of 'the Remaines', the concluding section of the 1633 *Survay*, is entitled 'A Returne to London'. Here Munday is on home territory, amassing a helpfully alphabetical 'catalogue' of works of repair and beautification to the city's parish churches. He begins his list, however, on a negative note by expressing sorrow at the 'pulling downe, Demolishment and Ruines of a Church … the most ancient', St Alban on Wood Street, which was another Cripplegate church located just the other side of the wall from St Giles.[202] 'The Remaines' also includes a detailed survey of the manor of Finsbury – the location of the Fortune – but it was based on a 1550s–60s survey that preceded the building of the playhouse, although the latter had of course been in existence for quite some time when Munday revised the *Survay*, as he would have known full well having actually worked there.[203] As such, the account of Finsbury is a form of implicit self-censorship and echoes Munday's reluctance to highlight the other London theatres in his editions of

Stow. The consequence is a strange instance of anachronism in a text which is otherwise so carefully updated. There is also an unusual instance of official censorship explicitly presented in the 1633 *Survey*. The second imprint (printed by Nicholas Bourne rather than Elizabeth Purslowe) bears an addendum to 'The Remaines' which states that the text had been scrutinised by Sir Henry Marten, a judge of the Admiralty, on the suspicion that it might contain 'some passages prejudiciall to his Majesties right ... and Derogatory to the just power belonging thereunto'. Any such passages were to be excised or the book in its entirety would be suppressed. Marten instructed the Stationers' Company that 'all the words together with the copy of the Letter, and my answer thereunto, as above ... [had] to be imprinted page 939' – which indeed they were.[204]

Implicit and explicit forms of censorship thus co-exist in Munday's editions of the *Survay*. Another of the most noticeable additions that he made in the 1618 edition was a lengthy description of the annual perambulation by its parishioners around the 'bounds' of the parish of St Giles (the parish, note, rather than the ward, thus the area that included the site of the Fortune).[205] This section stands out not least because the *Survay* is otherwise organised around wards (the City Corporation entities) rather than parishes. 'The Circuit of the Parish of S. Giles without Cripplegate' is also the only account of such a ritual to be found in this text; that it is this particular parish, given the local connections of the writer, surely cannot be a coincidence. This ceremony established the limits of the parish by traversing them, encountering at times obstacles in the perambulators' way. That Munday should have devoted two pages of this text to this Cripplegate ritual only compounds the sense of his local identity which comes across so strongly in his civic works, especially this one. The Cripplegate bounds section of the *Survay* confirms the extended dimensions of the extramural part of the parish, especially at its north-eastern edge, as we have seen in the discussion of the Fortune. It is in fact only the extramural part of the parish that the bounds ceremony is concerned with; the parishioners may walk along the course of the City wall but they do not cross it. They walk up almost as far as Islington towards 'Dame Anne de Clare' (a spring beside Bunhill Fields) to reach the outer limits of their territory, where 'they come within 3 roddes of a little Bridge ... at the lower end of the Close next unto Islington'.[206] Their perambulation is punctuated with markers of geographical integrity and limits, many of which are intended to 'mark off' Cripplegate from its neighbouring parishes. At the intersection of Barbican and Redcross Street, for instance, Munday writes that the parishioners arrive 'ouer against the signe of the Bores Head, [where] they set up their marks upon a great Post (as it seemeth set there for the same purpose)'.[207] The bounds of Cripplegate are contested in places, however. Having bypassed Barbican the parishioners continue towards the northern parish boundary 'where they should crosse over to the North side, right over against the said bounds, thorow certaine Garden Alleys lying on the west side of Willoughby House: but by reason of some contention, that course is of late denied them'.[208] This is a curious echo of a 'contention' that took place 'of late' in Cripplegate involving the name of 'Willoughby' back in 1600 – especially since the street 'where they should cross over' and where their progress is impeded just happens to be Golding Lane, the location of the Fortune playhouse.

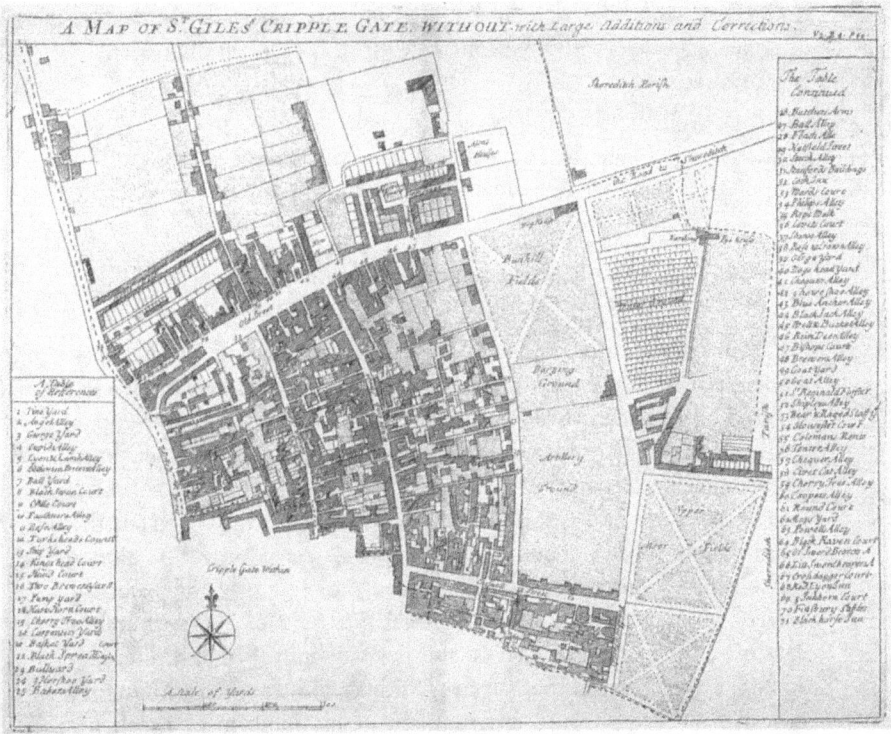

6 Map of the parish of St Giles Cripplegate Without

The description of the Cripplegate 'bounds' ceremony was duplicated with some minor changes in the 1633 edition, where one final uncanny moment occurs in the concluding pages of this, Munday's last and (as far as we know) only posthumous publication, issued four months after his death in August of that year. Whereas in the 1618 edition of the *Survay* Munday himself reproduced a number of Jacobean memorials in the church of St Stephen Coleman Street, in the 1633 text a later contributor adds Munday's own epitaph, without any comment whatsoever, to the entry for St Stephen's. The prose then switches with a curious effect from Munday's still-living voice commenting on various enhancements to the church in the 1620s, to the last word *about* rather than by its ubiquitous editor, summarising his life and achievements as he himself had done throughout the text about other past 'worthies'. In the same fashion (cited, oddly as 'Munday, or Mundy') Munday appears in the index of the book he himself was chiefly responsible for preparing for publication.[209] The inscription from Munday's tomb begins 'To the memory of that ancient servant to the City, with his pen, in divers imployments, especially the Survay of London, Master Anthony Munday, Citizen and Draper of London'.[210] It continues:

> His Tombe
> Claiming (as worthily it may) this roome,
> Among those many Monuments his Quill
> Has so revived, helping now to fill
> A place (with those) in his Survay: in which
> He has a Monument, more faire, more rich,
> Than polisht Stones could make him.

Munday's entries on parish churches, dismissed by Kingsford as trivial, are nothing of the kind: as his epitaph itself indicates, they have in effect preserved for us long-lost historical evidence about the City's buildings (and in the process, its inhabitants, in the case of the names on the monuments and of the church benefactors), so much of which perished during the Great Fire, or, as with St Giles, barely escaped the wartime assault on London.[211] Munday has a place in his text alongside all these other ordinary citizens and the records of their worthy deeds. As St Stephen Coleman Street was one of those churches destroyed during the Great Fire and never rebuilt, Munday's textual epitaph is the only one that survives for him. His traces have therefore moved from the physical environment of his tomb in St Stephen's ('this roome') to a textual 'place' alongside other objects of memory. It is fitting, then, that the epitaph itself twice mentions the work into which it had been copied, as if acknowledging its place there in Munday's valedictory text to his city. As the epitaph seems to foretell, the *Survey*, his most London-centred book and one obsessed, as he was, with the history of the city, had become quite literally Munday's final resting place and his lasting monument.

NOTES

1. Stow, ed. Munday, *The Survay of London*, A4r.
2. Thomas Heywood, ed. Rowland, *Edward IV*, p. lxxix.
3. Sayle, *Lord Mayors' Shows*, pp. 65, 70–2.
4. Munday, *Chruso-thriambos*, sig. B3r. See also Bergeron, *Pageants and Entertainments*, pp. 55 and 70. Conversely, the 1615 edition of Stow's *Annales* cites Munday as an authority on Campion (Turner, *Anthony Mundy*, p. 150).
5. Archer calls Munday's work a 'derivative' of Stow's ('The nostalgia of John Stow', p. 17).
6. Stow, ed. Kingsford, *A Survey of London*, vol. I, p. lxvi.
7. *Ibid.*, p. lxvii. There was a (somewhat belated) redress from James I: two years before Stow's death in 1605 he was granted Letters Patent on account of the fact that this 'very aged and worthy member of our city of London [for] this five and forty yeers hath to his great charge … compiled and published diverse necessary bookes, and Chronicles' (*Ibid.*, vol. I, p. lxvii).
8. Stow, ed. Munday, *The Survay of London*, sig. §2r.
9. *Ibid.*, sig. Ar.
10. See Manley, 'Of sites and rites', p. 54 and *Literature and Culture*, p. 274, Paster, 'The idea of London', pp. 57–8, and Bald, 'Middleton's civic employments', pp. 66–7.
11. Jonson, *Three Comedies*, p. 322.
12. See Stow, ed. Kingsford, *A Survey of London*, vol. I, pp. lxxxii–lxxxiv.
13. Stevenson, *Praise and Paradox*, p. 18.
14. In 1623 Munday dedicated *The theater of honour and knighthood*, a text which bears some resemblances to his *Briefe Chronicle*, to Sir Henry Montague, the Recorder of London, and to the Privy Council (he also dedicated to Montague in 1619). The former work was published by Jaggard, Printer to the City. According to its preface, Montague had seen and approved the draft of Munday's 1618 edition of *The Survay*.
15. Stow, ed. Munday, *The Survay of London*, sig. Ppp4v.
16. Munday, *Chruso-thriambos*, sig. B4r.
17. John Windet had been an apprentice of John Allde's from 1579, thus at around the same time as Munday (see Aldis *et al.*, *A Dictionary of Printers and Booksellers in England*, p. 294, and Turner, *Anthony Mundy*, p. 6).
18. Stevenson, *Praise and Paradox*, p. 108.
19. Beer, *Tudor England Observed*, pp. 17, 23 and *passim*.
20. *Ibid.*, p. 18.
21. See Stow, ed. Kingsford, *A Survey of London*, vol. II, p. 368. Kingsford remarks that Stow's deletion in 1603 of the brief paragraph about the Clerkenwell

theatres was 'intentional', despite the fact that the Theatre had been demolished two years previously.
22 In his *Annales* Stow does, however, give an account of a theatrical entertainment in Utrecht for the Earl of Leicester in 1586: perhaps it was only London theatregoing and/or the professional stage that he disapproved of (MacLean, 'Leicester's Men', p. 265).
23 Manley, *Literature and Culture*, p. 50; see also Dillon, *Theatre, Court and City*, pp. 31 and 155 n. 17.
24 Foster, *The Politics of Stability*, p. 125. In this respect Stow can be contrasted with his perennial antagonist Richard Grafton, a fervent Protestant whose patrons included Thomas Cromwell. Much Elizabethan historiography from Polydore Vergil onwards, of which Stow's own work forms an important part, was driven by the political need to construct a national history grounded on the newly constituted Anglican church (see Alsop, 'William Fleetwood and Elizabethan historical scholarship', pp. 156 and 159). Stow probably used his close acquaintance with the strongly Protestant William Fleetwood, Recorder of London, to gain access to the Guildhall records (*ibid.*, p. 175).
25 Stow, ed. Kingsford, *A Survey of London*, vol. I, pp. 266–7. See also Archer, 'Popular politics', p. 37, and Archer, 'The nostalgia of John Stow', pp. 22–3.
26 See Archer, 'The nostalgia of John Stow', p. 29, and Devereux, 'Empty tuns and unfruitful grafts', pp. 48–9. While employed as a recusant hunter in the 1580s Munday himself would have undertaken the same kind of searches. Stow was interrogated because he owned a copy of a pro-Catholic text by the Duke of Alva. This was the text for the printing of which John Allde (the man who released Munday from his apprenticeship early so that he might make his controversial trip to the continent) was imprisoned in the Poultry Counter in 1568; the connection with Allde has also been cited to prove Munday a Catholic sympathiser, if not convert, in his early days (see Duff, *A Century of the English Book Trade*, p. 2, Turner Wright, 'Young Anthony Mundy again', p. 154, and Hamilton, 'Anthony Munday and *The Merchant of Venice*', p. 91). It also stands, implicitly, as an early moment of intersection between Munday and Stow.
27 Stow, ed. Kingsford, *A Survey of London*, vol. II, p. 339; the reference to Crowley's burial is in vol. I, p. 300. Munday also added to the *Survay* a lengthy digression about godly Bishop Ridley, the famed Marian martyr (Stow, ed. Munday, *The Survay of London*, sigs Pp8v–Qq2r). See also Archer, 'The nostalgia of John Stow', pp. 28–30.
28 Stow, ed. Munday, *The Survay of London*, sig. Mm8r.
29 Hamilton, 'Anthony Munday and *The Merchant of Venice*', p. 91.
30 Stow, ed. Munday et al., *The Survey of London*, sig. Vvv5r; Stow, ed. Munday, *The Survay of London*, sig. N5v.
31 Dillon, *Theatre, Court and City*, p. 144; see also Heinemann, *Puritanism and Theatre*, pp. 123–4, and Marcus, 'City metal and country mettle', p. 28.
32 Bergeron, *Pageants and Entertainments*, p. xiii. It is perhaps not a coincidence that this, Munday's most monarchical (and in many respects least typical) pageant in terms of its subject matter, is one of the most discussed by critics; it is also, perhaps for the same reason, the sole Lord Mayor's Show selected by Arthur Kinney to sit alongside *The Magnificent Entertainment* for his *Renaissance Drama* anthology.
33 Bergeron, *Pageants and Entertainments*, p. xv; see also Withington, *English*

Pageantry, vol. II, pp. 28–9.
34 Marcus, 'City metal and country mettle', p. 27.
35 Bergeron, *Pageants and Entertainments*, p. xiii. Corns has commented that this pageant demonstrates 'how alertly metropolitan ideology aligned itself with the emerging themes of the new regime' ('Literature and London', p. 549).
36 Gordon, 'Performing London', p. 78.
37 Some earlier reader of this text evidently noticed Munday's civic bias, for one copy bears the annotation 'Champion for the City or the City Champion' on its title page (see Kinney, *Renaissance Drama*, p. 370).
38 Munday, *The triumphes of re-united Britania*, sig. B2r.
39 Corns, 'Literature and London', p. 550.
40 Munday, *The triumphes of re-united Britania*, sig. Cv.
41 *Ibid.*, sig. Cv.
42 *Ibid.*, sigs Ciir–v.
43 Dekker repeated Munday's citation of these seven kings in *Troia-Nova Triumphans* in 1612, another Merchant Taylors' Show, but by 1624 in *The Monuments of Honour* Webster felt able to list all eight, including Richard III, although he does comment that Richard was a 'bad man'.
44 *Ibid.*, sig. Ciir. Kinney remarks that 'the pageantry moves directly from Brute to James to Sir Leonard Holliday', the new mayor (*Renaissance Drama*, p. 372).
45 Stow, ed. Munday, *The Survay of London*, sig. Ppp6r.
46 *Ibid.*, sig. Ppp7r.
47 Gordon has noted that John Norden's 1600 map of London features the barge used in the Lord Mayor's Show rather than the *royal* barge, as is the case in the Braun and Hogenberg map. He has argued that, as with Munday's pageants, Norden's map, with its aldermen very much in the foreground, 'suggests a deliberate displacement of the monarchic presence in favour of a reference to … an autonomous mercantile civic space' ('Performing London', p. 81).
48 Munday, *Metropolis Coronata*, sig. B4v.
49 Munday, *Londons Love*, sig. B2v. Prince Henry himself was made free of the Merchant Taylors. Munday's friend and collaborator Michael Drayton was for a while a member of Prince Henry's household (see Parry, 'Patronage and the printing of learned works', p. 181).
50 Munday, *Londons Love*, sig. D2r.
51 *Ibid.*, sig. B2r.
52 Munday had probably ceased to be a Messenger of her Majesty's Chamber by 1596/7; however, his texts proudly if anachronistically call him 'Messenger of her Maiesties chamber' well into the seventeenth century: see *The Third and last part of Palmerin of England* (1602) and the 1616 reprint of *Palmerin of England*.
53 Munday had received two pounds from the Haberdashers' Company for his bid for the 1604 pageant which went to Jonson (see Munday, ed. Pafford, *Chruso-thriambos*, p. 49) and he was once again unsuccessful in competing with Middleton over the Lord Mayor's Show in 1619.
54 See Overall and Overall, *Analytical Index*, p. 410.
55 See Bergeron, *Pageants and Entertainments*, p. xi.
56 Marcus, 'City metal and country mettle', p. 28.
57 Stow, ed. Kingsford, *A Survey of London*, vol. I, p. xcv.

58 Stow, ed. Munday, *The Survay of London*, title page.
59 Manley, *London in the Age of Shakespeare*, p. 179.
60 Manley, 'Of sites and rites', p. 37.
61 Geertz, *Local Knowledge*, p. 124.
62 See Manley, *Literature and Culture*, pp. 239–40.
63 *Ibid.*, p. 108.
64 Stow, ed. Munday, *The Survay of London*, sig. §3v.
65 See Meagher, 'The London Lord Mayor's Show of 1590', p. 94.
66 Withington, *English Pageantry*, vol. II, pp. 13–15 and 23. Lancashire dates the *established* use of pageant stations with costumed performers (as featured in the Midsummer Watch ceremony) in the Lord Mayor's Show to the 1530s–40s, although she does suggest that they may have appeared sporadically from the 1480s onwards (*London Civic Theatre*, p. 184).
67 Bergeron, *Pageants and Entertainments*, p. xii.
68 Johnson, 'Jacobean ephemera', p. 162.
69 Paster, 'The idea of London', p. 58.
70 Sullivan, *The Drama of Landscape*, p. 229.
71 Munday, ed. Meagher, *The Downfall*, lines 19–20.
72 *Ibid.*, line 58. Jonson parodied such simple exposition in his part of *The Magnificent Entertainment*.
73 Munday, *Chruso-thriambos*, sig. A3r; see also Lobanov-Rostovsky, 'The Triumphes of Golde', p. 881, and Kipling, 'Triumphal drama', p. 39. The illustrations for *Chrysanaleia* indicate that some of the figures in the mayor's procession were dressed in Roman-style attire.
74 See, for example, the dedication to George Bolles and his 'Brethren-Senatours' in Munday's 1618 *Survay* (Stow, ed. Munday, *The Survay of London*, sig. §2r). Meagher calls the description of the Corporation as a Senate an 'affectation' on the part of the City ('The London Lord Mayor's Show of 1590', p. 102).
75 Paster, 'The idea of London', p. 56.
76 Gordon, 'Performing London', p. 81.
77 Marcus, 'City metal and country mettle', p. 31. In the 1630s the Privy Council tried to establish the 'Incorporation of Westminster', which would have taken over the City Corporation's previous economic autonomy over freemen and trade, and would also have included the extant liberties. The proposed new system of governance was disputed and more or less defunct by 1640 (Sheppard, *London: A History*, p. 191).
78 See Dutton, *Jacobean Civic Pageants*, pp. 170 and 173.
79 *Ibid.*, p. 175; see also Johnson, 'Jacobean ephemera', pp. 168–9.
80 Munday, *Chruso-thriambos*, sigs. Br and C2r.
81 Bergeron comments that 'Time' is 'essential, both dramatically and thematically, in Munday's pageant' ('The restoration of Hermione', p. 128). The character had previously appeared more briefly in the 1609 pageant *Camp-Bell* (see Bergeron, *Pageants and Entertainments*, p. 28) and he reappears in *Metropolis Coronata* (see below).
82 Munday, *Chruso-thriambos*, sig. B2v.
83 *Ibid.*, sig. C2r.
84 *Ibid.*, sig. C3v. Jenstad has demonstrated the extent to which this rhetorical munificence disguises a reluctance on the part of some members of the Company to pay their share of the cost ('Institutional uses of pageantry', p. 14).

85 Johnson, 'Jacobean ephemera', p. 161.
86 Munday, *Chruso-thriambos*, sig. C3r; see also Marcus, 'City metal and country mettle', p. 33. If Munday's obsequiousness towards these city dignitaries seems excessive, it is worth remembering that, in Manley's words, 'the Lord Mayor of Tudor-Stuart London was, on the death of a monarch, the highest ranking officer in the kingdom' until the appointment of a royal successor (*London in the Age of Shakespeare*, p. 31). In London's small pond, mayors and aldermen were big fish indeed.
87 Munday, *Chruso-thriambos*, sig. C3r.
88 See Munday, ed. Pafford, *Chruso-thriambos*, pp. 55–6. For the complete contemporary transcript of the memorial compiled by Munday himself in the *Survay* see Stow, ed. Munday, *The Survay of London*, sigs Nn8v–Oov.
89 Stow, ed. Munday, *The Survay of London*, sig. Oor.
90 Munday, *Metropolis Coronata*, sig. A4r.
91 Ibid., sig. A4v. Manley comments that such mythological diversity was chiefly exhibited in the water show and that pagan deities like Neptune did not appear in the land-based 'pageant stations' (*Literature and Culture*, p. 285).
92 Munday, *Metropolis Coronata*, sigs. A3r-v.
93 Ibid., sig. A3v.
94 Ibid., sig. A4v. Marcus says that in *Sidero-Thriambos* Munday re-used material 'with the express intention of recalling the earlier pageant [*Chruso-thriambos*] to the minds of his spectators' ('City metal and country mettle', p. 44). Similarly, in the 1618 edition of the *Survay* Munday may have added an allusion to one of his pageants in a short addition to Stow's original entry on Walworth: when he writes 'as before hath been related' he may be directing his readers towards *Chrysanaleia* (see Stow, ed. Munday, *The Survay of London*, sig. M3v). Bergeron has commented that Munday and Heywood's pageants 'presuppose a reading public conversant with [their] other texts' ('Stuart civic pageants', p. 179). It is perhaps only to be expected of Munday that here the implied memory might benefit him personally as much as the City more generally.
95 Munday, *Metropolis Coronata*, sig. A3v.
96 Lobanov-Rostovsky, 'The Triumphes of Golde', p. 884. See also Bergeron, 'Actors in English civic pageants', p. 26.
97 Stow, ed. Munday, *The Survay of London*, sig. Cr; my emphasis. See also Withington, *English Pageantry*, vol. II, p. 38.
98 See Lobanov-Rostovsky, 'The Triumphes of Golde', pp. 886–8.
99 Cited in Manley, *London in the Age of Shakespeare*, p. 105; see also p. 116 n. 7.
100 See Manley, *Literature and Culture*, p. 129, Withington, *English Pageantry*, vol. II, p. 24, and Meagher, 'The London Lord Mayor's Show of 1590', p. 104.
101 Stow, ed. Kingsford, *A Survey of London*, vol. I, p. 215; see also Manley, 'Of sites and rites', p. 49.
102 Stow, ed. Kingsford, *A Survey of London*, vol. I, pp. 220–1. Interestingly, a dagger has been displayed for many years in a case in Fishmongers' Hall on the pretext that it was the actual dagger used by Walworth to kill Tyler; like the story about Walworth's dagger and the City arms this is no doubt apocryphal, but according to the Fishmongers' archivist it *is* possible that the former dagger was the one used during Munday's pageant to impersonate Walworth's.

103 Munday, *Chrysanaleia*, sig. C3v. As Bergeron states, 'Munday is confused' about the provenance of London's dagger (*Pageants and Entertainments*, p. 122).
104 Munday, *Chrysanaleia*, sig. B3r.
105 See, for example, sigs B3r and C2r.
106 *Ibid.*, sig. B3v.
107 Leinwand, 'London triumphing', p. 150.
108 Munday, *Chrysanaleia*, sigs B4v and B3v.
109 Stow, ed. Munday, *The Survay of London*, sig. §4r.
110 *Ibid.*, sig. §4v.
111 *Ibid.*, sig. §2v.
112 *Ibid.*, sig. Ar.
113 Corns notes similarly that 'Munday, by foregrounding continuities, averts the watchers' gaze from the plain evidence of economic transformations ... suggesting that the City carries on much as the City always has carried on – and always will' ('Literature and London', p. 551).
114 Sullivan, *The Drama of Landscape*, pp. 211–12.
115 Cited in Doolittle, *The City of London*, p. 6. In 1614 James I tried with an equal lack of success to limit the city's expansion.
116 Archer, 'The nostalgia of John Stow', pp. 24–5.
117 Manley, *Literature and Culture*, pp. 47–8.
118 See Sayle, *Lord Mayors' Pageants*, pp. 70 and 72.
119 Stow, ed. Munday et al., *The Survey of London*, sig. Eee3v.
120 Bergeron, *English Civic Pageantry*, p. 146. In later years Middleton's civic pageants too were criticised for 'abuses and badd workmanship' (see Middleton, *Women Beware Women*, p. xiii).
121 See Bergeron, *Pageants and Entertainments*, pp. 31–2; see also Withington, *English Pageantry*, vol. II, p. 30.
122 Bergeron, *Pageants and Entertainments*, p. 29.
123 *Ibid.*, p. 29.
124 *Ibid.*, p. 46.
125 *Ibid.*; see also Withington, *English Pageantry*, vol. I, p. 231.
126 Manley, *London in the Age of Shakespeare*, p. 209; see also pp. 337–8.
127 Heinemann, 'Rebel lords, popular playwrights, and political patronage', p. 83.
128 Manley, *London in the Age of Shakespeare*, p. 136.
129 See *ibid.*, p. 210.
130 See *ibid.*, p. 334.
131 *Ibid.*, p. 335.
132 *Bartholmew Fair*, induction, 59–62. The Smithfield liberty of St Bartholomew's was added to the City's jurisdiction under the terms of the 1608 charter, thus *before* Jonson's play was produced (see Birch, *The Historical Charters*, pp. xxxvi and 139–50). In *Epicoene*, Morose links the Lord Mayor's Show and the civic unrest dramatised in *Sir Thomas More* when he calls some rowdy guests 'you sons of noise and tumult, begot on an ill May Day, or when the galley-foist [the Lord Mayor's barge] is afloat to Westminster' (IV.ii.108–10).
133 A statue of Fitz-Alwin stands today (opposite one of William Walworth) high up in a niche overlooking the Holborn viaduct, still guarding the now invisible portals of the City.
134 See also Manley, 'Of sites and rites', p. 50, and Bergeron, 'Anthony Munday: pageant poet to the City of London', p. 360.
135 Munday, *Chruso-thriambos*, sig. B2r.

136 Ibid., sig. B3r.
137 As we have seen, one of Munday's anti-Catholic tracts was corrected, possibly by Robert Crowley; another such text was attacked in the same way, this time by George Ellyot, Munday's erstwhile colleague (see my '"This is as true as all the rest is"'). Withington, somewhat unfairly to my mind, calls Munday's apology one of 'the only noteworthy things' in this pageant (*English Pageantry*, vol. II, p. 36).
138 Bergeron, 'Stuart civic pageants', pp. 167-8.
139 Ibid., p. 177.
140 Munday, *Himatia-Poleos*, sig. A4r.
141 Munday, *Chruso-thriambos*, sig. B3r.
142 Munday, *Himatia-Poleos*, sig. A4r.
143 See, for instance, Stow, ed. Kingsford, *A Survey of London*, vol. II, p. 149, and *passim*. Stow himself had some years earlier criticised his enemy Richard Grafton for plagiarising his own work, and then to exacerbate the offence, mistaking 'the names & yeres of the bayleys maiors & shrives ... whiche by great labour, & not without great costes I had gathered' (cited in Devereux, 'Empty tuns and unfruitful grafts', p. 50). Like Munday, Stow regarded correctness in civic history to be no small matter. He returned to his quarry in the *Survay* (ibid., p. 56 n. 70).
144 Stow, ed. Munday, *The Survay of London*, sig. 3r.
145 Ibid.
146 Munday, *Himatia-Poleos*, sig. A4v.
147 Stow, ed. Munday, *The Survay of London*, sig. Oov.
148 See Stow, ed. Kingsford, *A Survey of London*, vol. I, p. 306.
149 Stow, ed. Munday, *The Survay of London*, sig. Nnn2r. Munday reproduces the 1618 entry in his later edition of the *Survey* (sig. Zz4v).
150 Stow, ed. Kingsford, *A Survey of London*, vol. II, p. 149; my emphasis.
151 Munday, *Himatia-Poleos*, sig. Br. Unfortunately for Munday, even Faringdon's history is not altogether uncontested. In the 1618 *Survay* Munday tasks Stow with possibly being 'much wronged in information' over the granting of a deed to Faringdon in 1277; in this text, however, Munday is unwilling to criticise Stow too harshly and he asks of John Speed, who actually saw the deed in question, that he bear witness 'that herein I doe no way deprave M. Stowe but set downe the truth' (sigs Pp2r-v). Munday also claims in *Chruso-thriambos* that Nicholas Faringdon gave his name to the London ward, when in fact this honour belongs to Faringdon's father (see Munday, *Chruso-thriambos*, sig. B4r, and Munday, ed. Pafford, *Chruso-thriambos*, p. 16).
152 Munday, *Himatia-Poleos*, sig. A4v.
153 Ibid., sig. Br. This 'especiall Gentleman' and his 'no meane paines' have unfortunately left no mark in the Goldsmiths' archives; David Beesley, their Librarian, is of the view that someone from the Company 'probably had a quiet word' with Munday after *Chruso-thriambos* took place.
154 Ibid., sig. A4r.
155 Ibid., sig. A3v.
156 Ibid., sig. Br.
157 See Johnson, *A History of the Worshipful Company of the Drapers*, p. 11 n. 1.
158 Munday, ed. Pafford, *Chruso-thriambos*, p. 15. The Drapers' historian concedes that there is no 'conclusive proof' that Fitz-Alwin was a Draper

(Johnson, *A History of the Worshipful Company of the Drapers*, p. 11 n. 1).
159 Munday, *Himatia-Poleos*, sig. Br.
160 Munday, *Metropolis Coronata*, sig. A4v.
161 Munday, *Himatia-Poleos*, sigs A3v and C3v. See also Bergeron, *Pageants and Entertainments*, pp. 82–3.
162 Munday, *Metropolis Coronata*, sigs A2r and B4r.
163 *Ibid.*, sig. A3r.
164 *Ibid.*, sig. A4v.
165 *Ibid.*, sig. B4v.
166 *Ibid.*, sigs A3r–v.
167 *Ibid.*, sig. A3v.
168 *Ibid.*, sig. A3r.
169 Stow, ed. Munday, *The Survay of London*, sig. A4r.
170 Marcus, 'City metal and country mettle', p. 32.
171 Stow, ed. Kingsford, *A Survey of London*, vol. II, pp. 149–50. Kingsford points out that the London Chronicles date the City's first mayor to the tenth year of King John's reign (*ibid.*, vol. II, p. 384).
172 Munday, *Chruso-thriambos*, sig. A4r.
173 Bergeron describes this as Munday's 'own special corruption of the legend' (*Pageants and Entertainments*, p. 99). See also Dobson and Taylor, 'The legend since the Middle Ages', p. 163. Both Sir (Robert) Fitzwater and his daughter Matilda were historical figures from the reign of King John (see Stow, ed. Kingsford, *A Survey of London*, vol. 1, pp. 61–2). Other errors of historical fact occur in *The Death of Robert, Earle of Huntington*, such as Fitzwater himself mistaking Harold Harefoot, son of King Canute, for Harold Godwin, but in this case it would appear that the confusion is deliberate on Munday's part (lines 377–83).
174 Munday *et al.*, *Sir John Oldcastle*, IV.iii.1.958; see also Barton, 'The king disguised', p. 111.
175 See Knight and Ohlgren, *Robin Hood*, p. 299.
176 Johnson, 'Jacobean ephemera', p. 158.
177 See Kipling, 'London triumphing', p. 38.
178 Johnson, 'Jacobean ephemera', pp. 162–3.
179 *Ibid.*, p. 158.
180 See *ibid.*, p. 159.
181 See *ibid.*, p. 169.
182 Stow, ed. Kingsford, *A Survey of London*, vol. 1, p. xlii.
183 *Ibid.* Twyning has commented that *The Survay* demonstrates bourgeois writers' 'obsession with completeness' (*London Dispossessed*, p. 66).
184 One can contrast, for instance, Stow's short account about Sir Thomas White (Stow, ed. Kingsford, *A Survey of London*, vol. I, p. 113) with Munday's detailed three-page entry for the same man (Stow, ed. Munday, *The Survay of London*, sigs M7r–8r).
185 Stow, ed. Munday *et al.*, *The Survey of London*, sig. A4v. See also Schofield, 'The topography and buildings of London', p. 308.
186 Stow, ed. Munday, *The Survay of London*, sig. A2r.
187 *Ibid.*, sig. Av.
188 Stow, ed. Munday *et al.*, *The Survey of London*, sig. A4v.
189 See Stow, ed. Munday, *The Survay of London*, sigs L4r–7r.
190 Stow, ed. Kingsford, *A Survey of London*, vol. I, p. 113.

191 See, for example, Stow, ed. Munday, *The Survay of London*, sig. C2r.
192 Manley characterises the water-borne part of the Lord Mayor's Show as 'the roughest and most boisterous of the pageants' (*Literature and Culture*, p. 271).
193 John Speed died in 1629; his memorial inscription in St Giles Cripplegate is reproduced in Munday's 1633 *Survey* (sig. Vvv3v).
194 Stow, ed. Munday et al., *The Survey of London*, sig. Ddv.
195 Stow, ed. Munday, *The Survay of London*, sig. Ll6r.
196 *Ibid.*
197 Munday, *Chrysanaleia*, sig. A4v.
198 See Bergeron, *Pageants and Entertainments*, p. 120, and Gordon and Dewhirst, *The Ward of Cripplegate*, p. 158. It is possible that Munday's first mistake was the result of a misreading of Stow, since it *was* a Fishmonger who was responsible for 'reedifying' Moorgate at a later date (see Stow, ed. Kingsford, *A Survey of London*, vol. I, p. 32). Stow writes that Cripplegate, also, was *rebuilt* rather than built by 'Edmond Shaw Goldsmith', so Munday may well have been wrong about this too (*ibid.*, p. 34). In his 1618 edition of Stow's work Munday changes Shaw's name yet again, to 'Edward' (sig. M5r).
199 Stow, ed. Munday et al., *The Survey of London*, sig. Xxx2r. The brevity of Munday's citation of More's monument is a retrospective echo of the ellipses and omissions one finds in Munday's *More* play (see my 'Marked down for omission'). More is also cited as one of the 'authors of reverend antiquitie' to whom Munday's 1618 *Survay* is indebted (sig. A2r).
200 Moore, 'Another link between Anthony Munday and Stephen Gosson', p. 255.
201 Stow, ed. Munday, *The Survey of London*, sig. X7v.
202 Stow, ed. Munday et al., *The Survey of London*, sig. Zzz6r. Only the tower of St Alban survives today, standing incongruously in the middle of Wood Street just below the Barbican complex.
203 See Holmes, 'A source-book for Stow?', pp. 279–80. This section's title page is in full 'The Remaines or Remnants of divers worthy things, which should have had their due place and honour in this Worke, if promising friends had kept their words. But they failing, and part of them coming into my hands by other good meanes, they are here inserted, to accompany my Perambulation foure miles about London' (sig. Sss6r). Here we find another allusion, as with Speed's map of Moorfields, to the difficulties Munday experienced in bringing this work to completion.
204 Stow, ed. Munday et al., *The Survey of London*, sig. Kkkk6r. I am grateful to Ian Gadd for drawing my attention to this detail.
205 Rowland has noted Stow's *Survay*'s interest in the boundaries of the City and the 'vulnerability' of its 'walls, bridges and gates' (Heywood, ed. Rowland, *Edward IV*, p. lxxxv).
206 Stow, ed. Munday, *The Survay of London*, sig. Nn3v.
207 *Ibid.* Two other playhouses have a spectral presence in this text: the place called the 'Bores Head' recalls the Whitechapel theatre at the eastern boundary of the City limits, and the perambulators go past Holy Well near Shoreditch, in the close vicinity of the Curtain (which, as in Stow's 1603 edition of this text, is not mentioned).
208 *Ibid.*
209 See Stow, ed. Munday et al., *The Survey of London*, sig. Nnn5r.
210 *Ibid.*, sig. Eeeer.

211 St Gregory by St Pauls, where Munday was baptised, was also ruined in the Fire. In the same fashion, as Cynthia Wall has noted, the maps drawn up in the 1660s were an attempt to 'make known the lost [and] the destroyed' features of London (cited in Gordon, 'Performing London', p. 85 n. 8).

Bibliography

WORKS BY ANTHONY MUNDAY

The mirrour of mutabilitie (London 1579)
'Anglo-phile Eutheo', *A second and third blast of retrait from plaies and theaters* (London 1580)
A courtly controversie, betweene loove and learning (London 1581)
A breefe aunswer made unto two seditious pamphlets (London 1582)
A breefe and true reporte, of the execution of certain traytours at Tiborne (London 1582)
A discoverie of Edmund Campion, and his confederates (London 1582)
The English Romayne lyfe (London 1582)
Two godly and learned sermons (London 1584)
A watch-woord to Englande to beware of traytours and tretcherous practices (London 1584)
Fedele and Fortunio (London 1585)
The true image of Christian love (London 1587)
A banquet of daintie conceits (London 1588)
The famous, pleasant, and variable historie, of Palladine of England (London 1588)
Palmerin D'Oliva. The mirrour of nobilitie (London 1588)
The declaration of the Lord de la Noue (London 1589)
The honorable, pleasant and rare conceited historie of Palmendos (London 1589)
The coppie of the Anti-Spaniard (London 1590)
The first book of Amadis of Gaule (London ?1590)
Archaioplutos. Or the riches of elder ages (London 1592)
Gerileon of England (London 1592)
The masque of the League and the Spanyard discovered (London 1592)
The first booke of Primaleon of Greece (London 1595)
Anthony Munday/Lazarus Pyott (asc.), *The orator: handling a hundred severall discourses, in forme of declamations* (London 1596)
The [first] seconde part, of the no lesse rare historie, of Palmerin of England (London 1596)
The second booke of Primaleon of Greece (London 1596)
The first part of the honourable historie, of Palmerin d'Oliva (London 1597)

A breefe treatise of the vertue of the crosse (London 1599)
A womans woorth, defended against all the men in the world (London 1599)
Anthony Munday et al., *The first part of the true and honorable historie, of the life of Sir John Oldcastle, the good Lord Cobham* (London 1600)
The strangest adventure that ever happened: either in the ages passed or present (London 1601)
Anthony Munday and Henry Chettle, *The Death of Robert, Earle of Huntington* (London 1601)
The Downfall of Robert, Earle of Huntington (London 1601)
The Heaven of the Minde, or The myndes Heaven (BL MS Add. 33304)
The third and last part of Palmerin of England (London 1602)
The true knowledge of a mans owne selfe (London 1602)
A true and admirable historie, of a mayden of Consolens (London 1603)
The dumbe divine speaker (London 1605)
Falshood in friendship, or unions vizard: or Wolves in lambskins (London 1605)
The triumphes of re-united Britania (London 1605)
The admirable deliverance of 266. Christians (London 1608)
(asc.) *The conversion of a most noble lady of Fraunce* (London 1608)
Camp-bell, or the Ironmongers Faire Field (London 1609)
The first part of the no lesse rare, then exellent [sic] and stately Historie, of the famous and fortunate Prince, Palmerin of England (London 1609)
Londons Love, to the Royal Prince Henrie (London 1610)
A briefe chronicle, of the successe of times (London 1611)
Chruso-thriambos. The triumphes of golde (London 1611)
Himatia-Poleos. The triumphes of olde draperie (London 1614)
Metropolis coronata, the triumphes of ancient drapery (London 1615)
Chrysanaleia: the golden fishing (London 1616)
The first part of the no lesse rare, then excellent and stately historie, of the famous and fortunate Prince Palmerin of England (London 1616)
Palmerin d'oliva the first [second] part (London 1616)
Sidero-Thriambos. Or Steele and iron triumphing (London 1618)
The third booke of Amadis de Gaule (London 1618)
The ancient, famous and honourable history of Amadis de Gaule (London 1619)
The famous and renowned historie of Primaleon of Greece (London 1619)
Archontorologion, or The diall of princes (London 1619)
(asc.) *The theater of honour and knight-hood* (London 1623)
The triumphs of the Golden Fleece (London 1623)
ed. P. Simpson, *Fidele and Fortunio* (Malone Society Reprints, Oxford, 1909)
The paine of pleasure, describing in a perfect mirror, the miseries of man (Cambridge 1938)
ed. J. Pafford, *Chruso-thriambos. The Triumphs of Gold* (London: J. Pafford, 1962)
ed. Jack Stillinger, *Anthony Munday's Zelauto: the Fountaine of Fame* (Carbondale: Southern Illinois University Press, 1963)
ed. J. C. Meagher, *The Downfall of Robert, Earle of Huntington* (Oxford: Oxford University Press, 1965)
Anthony Munday and Henry Chettle, ed. J. C. Meagher, *The Death of Robert, Earle of Huntington* (Oxford: Oxford University Press, 1967)
The Defence of Contraries (Amsterdam: Da Capo Press, 1969)
ed. Arthur E. Pennell, *John a Kent and John a Cumber* (Garland, New York and London, 1980)

ed. Hans Peter Heinrich, *A mirrour of mutabilitie* (Frankfurt: Peter Lang, 1990)
Anthony Munday *et al.*, ed. V. Gabrieli and G. Melchiori, *Sir Thomas More* (Manchester: Manchester University Press, 1990)
The Triumphs of Reunited Britannia, in Richard Dutton, ed., *Jacobean Civic Pageants* (Keele: Ryburn Publishing, Keele University, 1995), 117–36
ed. Russell Peck, *The Downfall of Robert, Earle of Huntington* (available at www.lib.rochester.edu/camelot/teams/dowdeint.htm. Accessed 5 December 2001)
ed. Russell Peck, Excerpts from *The Death of Robert, Earle of Huntington* (available at www.lib.rochester.edu/camelot/teams/death.htm. Accessed 5 December 2001)

OTHER WORKS

Ackroyd, Peter, *London: The Biography* (London: Chatto and Windus, 2000)
Agnew, Jean-Christophe, *Worlds Apart: The Market and the Theater in Anglo-American Thought, 1550–1750* (Cambridge: Cambridge University Press, 1988)
Aldis, H. G., Robert Bowes, E. R. McC. Dix, E. Gordon Duff, Strickland Gibson, G. J. Gray, R. B. McKerrow, Falconer Madan and H. R. Plomer (eds), *A Dictionary of Printers and Booksellers in England, Scotland and Ireland, and of Foreign Printers of English Books 1557–1640* (London: The Bibliographical Society, 1910)
'Alfield, Thomas', *A true reporte of the death and martyrdome of M. Campion Iesuite and preiste* (London 1582)
Alsop, J. D., 'William Fleetwood and Elizabethan historical scholarship', *Sixteenth Century Journal*, 25:1 (1994), 155–76
Anderson, Randall, 'The rhetoric of paratext in early printed books', in John Barnard and D. F. McKenzie (eds), *The Cambridge History of the Book in Britain*, vol. IV, 1557–1695 (Cambridge: Cambridge University Press 2002), 636–44
Anglo, Sydney, *Spectacle, Pageantry, and Early Tudor Policy* (Oxford: The Clarendon Press, 1969)
Anon., ed. W. W. Greg, *Fair Em* (Oxford: The Malone Society, 1927)
Anon., 'Some hostile "true reports" of the martyrs', *Miscellanea*, 15, Catholic Record Society, no. 32 (London 1932), 390–8
Arber, Edward, (ed.), *A Transcript of the Registers of the Company of Stationers 1554–1640 AD*, 5 vols (London and Birmingham: privately printed, 1875–94)
Archer, Ian, *The Pursuit of Stability: Social Relations in Elizabethan London* (Cambridge: Cambridge University Press, 1991)
Archer, Ian, 'The nostalgia of John Stow', in David Smith, Richard Strier *et al.* (eds), *The Theatrical City* (Cambridge: Cambridge University Press, 1995), 17–34
Archer, Ian, 'Popular politics in the sixteenth and early seventeenth centuries', in Paul Griffiths and Mark S. R. Jenner (eds), *Londinopolis: Essays in the Cultural and Social History of Early Modern London* (Manchester: Manchester University Press, 2000), 26–46
Archer, Ian, Caroline Barron and Vanessa Harding (eds), *Hugh Alley's Caveat: The Markets of London, 1598* (London: London Topographical Society, 1988)

Ashley, Leonard R. N., 'Munday, Anthony', in *A Reference Guide to English Literature*, vol. II (Chicago and London: St James Press, 1991), 1005–6
Ashton, Robert, *The City and the Court* (Cambridge: Cambridge University Press, 1979)
Ashton, Robert, 'Popular entertainment and social control in later Elizabethan and early Stuart London', *The London Journal*, 9:1 (1983), 3–19
Ayres, P. J., 'Anthony Munday: "Our best plotter"?', *English Language Notes*, 18:1 (1980), 13–15
Bald, R. C., 'Middleton's civic employments', *Modern Philology*, 31 (1933), 65–78
Baldwin, T. W., *The Organization and Personnel of the Shakespearean Company* (Princeton: Princeton University Press, 1927)
Baldwin, T. W., *On the Literary Genetics of Shakspere's Plays* (Urbana: University of Illinois Press, 1959)
Barnard, John, and D. F. McKenzie (eds), *The Cambridge History of the Book in Britain*, vol. IV, *1557–1695* (Cambridge: Cambridge University Press, 2002)
Barton, Anne, 'The king disguised: Shakespeare's *Henry V* and the comical history', in Joseph G. Price (ed.), *The Triple Bond* (Philadelphia and London: Pennsylvania State University Press, 1975), 92–117
Barton, Anne, 'London comedy and the ethos of the city', *London Journal*, 4:2 (1978), 158–80
Beaumont, Francis, ed. Michael Hattaway, *The Knight of the Burning Pestle* (London: A. & C. Black, 1991)
Bednarz, James P., 'Representing Jonson: *Histriomastix* and the origins of the Poets' War', *Huntingdon Library Quarterly*, 54 (1991), 1–30
Beer, Barrett L., 'London and the rebellions of 1548–1549', *Journal of British Studies*, 12:1 (1972), 15–38
Beer, Barrett L., *Rebellion and Riot: Popular Disorder in England During the Reign of Edward VI* (Kent, Ohio: Kent State University Press, 1982)
Beer, Barrett L., 'John Stow and Tudor rebellions, 1549–1569', *Journal of British Studies*, 27 (1988), 352–74.
Beer, Barrett L., *Tudor England Observed* (Stroud: Sutton, 1998)
Beier, A. L., 'Social problems in Elizabethan London', *Journal of Interdisciplinary History*, 9:2 (1978), 203–21
Beier, A. L., and Roger Finlay (eds), *London 1500–1700: The Making of the Metropolis* (London: Longman, 1986)
Bennett, H. S., *English Books and Readers, 1558 to 1603* (Cambridge: Cambridge University Press, 1965)
Bentley, G. E., 'Records of players in the parish of St Giles, Cripplegate', *P.M.L.A.*, 44 (1929), 789–826
Bergeron, David, 'Anthony Munday: pageant poet to the City of London', *Huntingdon Library Quarterly*, 30 (1967), 345–68
Bergeron, David, 'Jack Straw in drama and pageant', *The Guildhall Miscellany*, 2:10 (1968), 459–63
Bergeron, David, 'Prince Henry and English civic pageantry', *Tennessee Studies in Literature*, 13 (1968), 109–16
Bergeron, David, 'Anthony Munday's son, Richard', *Notes and Queries*, 7 (1969), 115–17
Bergeron, David, *English Civic Pageantry* (London: Edward Arnold, 1971)
Bergeron, David, 'Actors in English civic pageants', *Renaissance Papers*, (1973), 17–28

Bergeron, David, 'The restoration of Hermione in *The Winter's Tale*', in Carol McGinnis Kay and Henry E. Jacobs (eds), *Shakespeare's Romances Reconsidered* (Lincoln: University of Nebraska Press, 1978), 125–33

Bergeron, David (ed.), *Pageants and Entertainments of Anthony Munday: A Critical Edition* (New York and London: Garland, 1985)

Bergeron, David (ed.), *Pageantry in the Shakespearean Theatre* (Athens: University of Georgia Press, 1985)

Bergeron, David, 'Thomas Middleton and Anthony Munday: artistic rivalry?', *Studies in English Literature*, 36 (1996), 461–79

Bergeron, David, 'Stuart civic pageants and textual performance', *Renaissance Quarterly*, 51:1 (1998), 163–83

Berlin, Michael, 'Civic ceremony in early modern London', *Urban History Yearbook*, 19 (1986), 15–27

Berry, Herbert, 'The player's apprentice', *Essays in Theatre*, 1:2 (1983), 73–80

Birch, Walter de Gray (ed.), *The Historical Charters and Constitutional Documents of the City of London* (London: Whiting and Co., 1887)

Blackstone, Mary A., 'Patrons and Elizabethan dramatic companies', *The Elizabethan Theatre*, 10 (1988), 112–32

Blayney, Peter, *The Bookshops in Paul's Cross Churchyard* (London: The Bibliographical Society, 1990)

The Booke of Sir Thomas More, ed. W. W. Greg (Oxford: The Malone Society, 1911)

Booty, John, 'Tumult in Cheapside: the Hacket conspiracy', *Historical Magazine of the Protestant Episcopal Church*, 42 (1973), 293–317

Boynton, Lindsay, 'The Tudor provost-marshal', *English Historical Review*, 77 (1962), 437–55

Breight, Curtis, 'Duelling ceremonies: the strange case of William Hacket, Elizabethan messiah', *Journal of Medieval and Renaissance Studies*, 19:1 (1989), 35–67

Brigden, Susan, *London and the Reformation* (Oxford: The Clarendon Press, 1989)

Brooks, Douglas A., *From Playhouse to Printing House: Drama and Authorship in Early Modern England* (Cambridge: Cambridge University Press, 2000)

Bruster, Douglas, *Drama and the Market in the Age of Shakespeare* (Cambridge: Cambridge University Press, 1992)

Burnett, Mark Thornton, *Masters and Servants in English Renaissance Drama and Culture* (Basingstoke: Macmillan, 1997)

Butler, Martin, 'Literature and the theatre to 1660', in David Loewenstein and Janel Mueller (eds), *The Cambridge History of Early Modern English Literature* (Cambridge: Cambridge University Press, 2002), 565–602

Byrne, Muriel St Clare, 'Anthony Munday and his books', *The Library*, 1 (1920), 225–56

Carson, Neil, 'Literary management in the Lord Admiral's Company, 1596–1603', *Theatre Research International*, 2 (1977), 186–97

Carson, Neil, 'Production finance at the Rose theatre', *Theatre Research International*, 4 (1979), 172–83

Carson, Neil, *A Companion to Henslowe's Diary* (Cambridge: Cambridge University Press, 1988)

Cerasano, S. P., '"More elbow roome, but scant better aire": the Fortune playhouse and its surroundings', *Indiana Social Studies Quarterly*, 35:1 (1982), 70–84

Cerasano, S. P., 'Edward Alleyn: 1566–1626', in Aileen Reed and Robert Maniura (eds), *Edward Alleyn: Elizabethan Actor, Jacobean Gentleman* (London: Dulwich Picture Gallery, 1995), 11–31

Cerasano, S. P., 'The patronage network of Philip Henslowe and Edward Alleyn', *Medieval and Renaissance Drama in England*, 13 (2001), 82–92

Chambers, E. K., *The Eliabethan Stage*, vols II and IV (Oxford: The Clarendon Press, 1965)

Chapman, George, ed. Jonathan Hudson, *Plays and Poems* (Harmondsworth: Penguin, 1998)

Chettle, Henry, *Kind-Harts Dreame* (1592). (Renascence Editions. Available at: www.darkwing.uoregon.edu/~rbear/kind.html. Accessed 23 July 2002)

Clare, Janet, *'Art Made Tongue-tied by Authority': Elizabethan and Jacobean Dramatic Censorship* (Manchester: Manchester University Press, 1990)

Clark, Peter, and Paul Slack (eds), *Crisis and Order in English Towns 1500–1700* (London: Routledge and Kegan Paul, 1972)

Clark, Peter, and Paul Slack, *English Towns in Transition 1500–1700* (Oxford: Oxford University Press, 1976)

Clegg, Cynthia, *Press Censorship in Elizabethan England* (Cambridge: Cambridge University Press, 1997)

Clegg, Cynthia, *Press Censorship in Jacobean England* (Cambridge: Cambridge University Press, 2001)

Cockagne, G. E., *The Lord Mayors and Sheriffs of London* (London: Phillimore and Co., 1857)

Collinson, Patrick, 'Calvinism with an Anglican face: the stranger churches in early Elizabethan London and their superintendent', in Derek Baker (ed.), *Reform and Reformation* (Oxford: Blackwell, 1979), 71–102.

Collinson, Patrick, 'Saints on Sundays, devils all the week after', *London Review of Books* (19 September 2002), 15–16

Conway, Eustace, *Anthony Munday and Other Essays* (New York: Privately printed, 1927)

Corbin, Peter, and Douglas Sedge (eds), *The Oldcastle Controversy* (Manchester: Manchester University Press, 1991)

Corns, Thomas N., 'Literature and London', in David Loewenstein and Janel Mueller (eds), *The Cambridge History of Early Modern English Literature* (Cambridge: Cambridge University Press, 2002), 544–64

Corporation of London, the, *The Corporation of London: Its Origin, Constitution, Powers and Duties* (Oxford: Oxford University Press, 1950)

Dasent, J. R., *Acts of the Privy Council*, vols I and II (London: HMSO, 1890)

Denkinger, Emma Marshall, 'Actors' names in the registers of St Botolph Aldgate', *P.M.L.A.*, 41 (1926), 91–109

Devereux, E. J., 'Empty tuns and unfruitful grafts: Richard Grafton's historical publications', *Sixteenth Century Journal*, 21:1 (1990), 33–56

Dillon, Janette, *Theatre, Court and City* (Cambridge: Cambridge University Press, 2000)

Dobb, Clifford, 'London's prisons', *Shakespeare Survey*, 17 (1965), 87–100

Dobson, R. B., and J. Taylor, 'The legend since the Middle Ages', in Stephen Knight (ed.), *Robin Hood: An Anthology of Scholarship and Criticism* (Cambridge: D. S. Brewer, 1999), 155–84

Doolittle, I. J., *The City of London and Its Livery Companies* (Dorchester: The Gavin Press, 1982)

Dorsten, Jan van, 'Literary patronage in Elizabethan England: the early phase', in Guy Fitch Lytle and Stephen Orgel (eds), *Patronage in the Renaissance* (Princeton: Princeton University Press, 1981), 191–206

Duff, E. Gordon, *A Century of the English Book Trade* (London: The Bibliographical Society, 1905)

Dutton, Richard, 'King Lear, The Triumphs of Reunited Britannia and the "matter of Britain"', *Literature and History*, 12:2 (1986), 139–51

Dutton, Richard, *Mastering the Revels: The Regulation and Censorship of English Renaissance Drama* (Basingstoke: Macmillan, 1991)

Dutton, Richard (ed.), *Jacobean Civic Pageants* (Keele University: Ryburn Publishing, 1995)

Dutton, Richard, *Licensing, Censorship and Authorship in Early Modern England* (Basingstoke: Palgrave, 2000)

Dyce, Alexander (ed.), *Kemps Nine Daies Wonder* (New York and London: AMS Press, 1968)

Eccles, Mark, 'Anthony Munday', in Josephine Bennett *et al.* (eds), *Studies in the English Renaissance Drama* (New York: Peter Owen/Vision Press, 1959), 95–105

Eccles, Mark, 'Elizabethan actors III: K–R', *Notes and Queries*, 237 (1992), 293–303

Ekwall, Eilert, *Street-Names of the City of London* (Oxford: The Clarendon Press, 1965)

Ellyot, George, *A very true report of the apprehension and taking of that Arche Papist Edmond Campion ... Conteining also a controulment of a most untrue former booke set out by one A.M. alias Anthonie Munday* (London 1581)

Fehrenbach, Robert J., 'When Lord Cobham and Edmund Tilney "were att odds": Oldcastle, Falstaff and the date of *1Henry IV*', *Shakespeare Studies*, 18 (1986), 87–101

Ferdinand, C. Y., 'Towards a demography of the Stationers' Company 1601–1700', *Journal of the Printing Historical Society*, 21 (1992), 51–69

Finlay, Roger, *Population and Metropolis: The Demography of London 1580–1650* (Cambridge: Cambridge University Press, 1981)

The first part of the true & honourable history, of the Life of Sir Iohn Old-castle, the good Lord Cobham (London: printed for T.P., 1600)

Fisher, F. J., ed. P. J. Corfield and N. B. Harte, *London and the English Economy, 1500–1700* (London: The Hambledon Press, 1990)

Foakes, R. A., 'Henslowe and the theatre of the 1590's', *Renaissance Drama*, 6 (1963), 4–6

Foakes, R. A., and R. T. Rickert (eds), *Henslowe's Diary* (Cambridge: Cambridge University Press, 1961)

Foakes, R. A., (ed.), *Henslowe's Diary* Second Edition (Cambridge: Cambridge University Press, 2002)

Forker, Charles R., 'Two notes on John Webster and Anthony Munday: unpublished entries in the records of the Merchant Taylors', *English Language Notes*, 6 (1968), 26–34

Forse, James H., *Art Imitates Business: Commercial and Political Influences in Elizabethan Theatre* (Bowling Green: Bowling Green State University Popular Press, 1993)

Foster, Frank Freeman, 'Merchants and bureaucrats in Elizabethan London', *The Guildhall Miscellany*, 4 (1971–73), 149–60

Foster, Frank Freeman, *The Politics of Stability: A Portrait of the Rulers in Elizabethan London* (London: Royal Historical Society, 1977)

Freedman, Barbara, 'Elizabethan protest, plague, and plays: rereading the "Documents of Control"', *English Literary Renaissance*, 29 (1996), 17–45

Freeman, Arthur, 'Marlowe, Kyd, and the Dutch Church libel', *English Literary Renaissance*, 3 (1973), 44–52

Gadd, Ian Anders, 'Early modern printed histories of the London Livery Companies', in Ian Anders Gadd and Patrick Wallis (eds), *Guilds, Society and Economy in London 1450–1800* (London: Centre for Metropolitan Research, 2002)

Gadd, Ian, 'Hunting down John Wolfe for the new *DNB*', in Robin Myers, Michael Harris and Giles Mandelbrote (eds), *Lives in Print: Biography and the Book Trade from the Middle Ages to the 21st century* (London: British Library Publishing, 2002), 193–201

Geertz, Clifford, *Local Knowledge* (London: Fontana, 1993)

Gibbons, Brian, *Jacobean City Comedy* (London: Methuen, 1980)

Gordon, Andrew, 'Performing London: the map and the city in ceremony', in Andrew Gordon and Bernhard Klein (eds), *Literature, Mapping, and the Politics of Space in Early Modern Britain* (Cambridge: Cambridge University Press, 2001), 69–88

Gordon, Caroline, and Wilfred Dewhirst, *The Ward of Cripplegate in the City of London* (London: The Cripplegate Ward Club, 1985)

Graves, Thornton S., 'Notes on Puritanism and the stage', *Studies in Philology*, 18:2 (1921), 141–69

Greg, W. W. (ed.), *Henslowe Papers* (London: A. H. Bullen, 1907)

Greg, W. W., 'Autograph plays by Anthony Munday', *Modern Language Notes*, 8 (1913), 89–90

Greg, W. W., *Dramatic Documents from the Elizabethan Playhouses* (Oxford: The Clarendon Press, 1931)

Greg, W. W., and E. Boswell (eds), *Records of the Court of the Stationers' Company. 1576–1602* (London: The Bibliographical Society, 1930)

Greenblatt, Stephen, 'Loudon and London', *Critical Inquiry*, 12:2 (1986), 326–46

Greenblatt, Stephen, *Shakespearean Negotiations* (Oxford: The Clarendon Press, 1990)

Greenblatt, Stephen, et al. (eds), *The Norton Shakespeare* (New York and London: Norton 1997)

Griffiths, Paul, 'Politics made visible: order, residence and uniformity in Cheapside, 1600–45', in Paul Griffiths and Mark S. R. Jenner (eds), *Londinopolis: Essays in the Cultural and Social History of Early Modern London* (Manchester: Manchester University Press, 2000), 176–96

Gurr, Andrew, *The Shakespearean Stage* (Cambridge: Cambridge University Press, 1987)

Gurr, Andrew, *The Shakespearian Playing Companies* (Oxford: The Clarendon Press, 1996)

Gurr, Andrew, 'The authority of the Globe and the Fortune', in Lena Cowen Orlin (ed.), *Material London, ca. 1600* (Philadelphia: University of Pennsylvania Press, 2000), 251–67

Gurr, Andrew, 'Privy Councilors as theatre patrons', in Paul Whitfield White and Suzanne R. Westfall (eds), *Shakespeare and Theatrical Patronage in Early Modern England* (Cambridge: Cambridge University Press, 2002), 221–45

Gurr, Andrew, and Mariko Ichikawa, *Staging in Shakespeare's Theatres* (Oxford: Oxford University Press, 2000)
Haaker, Ann, 'Anthony Munday', in Terence P. Logan and Denzell S. Smith (eds), *The Popular School* (Lincoln: University of Nebraska Press, 1975)
Hadfield, Andrew (ed.), *Literature and Censorship in Renaissance England* (Basingstoke: Palgrave, 2001)
Halasz, Alexandra, *The Marketplace of Print: Pamphlets and the Public Sphere in Early Modern England* (Cambridge: Cambridge University Press, 1997)
Hamilton, Donna B., 'Anthony Munday and *The Merchant of Venice*', *Shakespeare Survey*, 54 (2001), 89–99
Hamilton, Donna B., 'Munday, Anthony (1560–1633)', in Arthur F. Kinney and David W. Swain (eds), *Tudor England: An Encyclopedia* (New York: Garland Publishing, 2001), 504–5
Hamilton, Donna B., and Richard Strier (eds), *Religion, Literature, and Politics in Post-Reformation England, 1540–1688* (Cambridge: Cambridge University Press, 1996)
Handover, P. M., *Printing in London from 1476 to Modern Times* (London: Allen and Unwin, 1960)
Harding, Vanessa, 'The population of London 1550–1700', *The London Journal*, 15:2 (1990), 111–28
Harris, P. R., 'William Fleetwood, Recorder of the City, and Catholicism in Elizabethan London', *Recusant History*, 7 (1963), 106–22
Harris, Tim, 'The problem of "popular political culture" in seventeenth-century London', *History of European Ideas*, 10:1 (1989), 43–58
Harrison, G. B., *Elizabethan Plays and Players* (Ann Arbor: University of Michigan Press, 1956)
Hawkes, David, 'Idolatry and commodity fetishism in the antitheatrical controversy', *Studies in English Literature*, 39:2 (1999), 255–73
Hayes, Gerald R., 'Anthony Munday's romances of chivalry', *The Library*, 6 (1925), 57–81
Hayes, Gerald R., 'Anthony Munday's romances: a postscript', *The Library*, 4:7 (1926), 31–8
Heal, Felicity, and Clive Holmes, *The Gentry in England and Wales, 1500–1700* (Basingstoke: Macmillan, 1994)
Heinemann, Margot, *Puritanism and Theatre* (Cambridge: Cambridge University Press, 1980)
Heinemann, Margot, 'Rebel lords, popular playwrights, and political patronage: notes on the Jacobean patronage of the Earl of Southampton', *Yearbook of English Studies*, 21 (1991), 63–86
Helgerson, Richard, 'The land speaks: cartography, chorography, and subversion in Renaissance England', *Representations*, 16 (1986), 50–85
Helgerson, Richard, *Forms of Nationhood: The Elizabethan Writing of England* (Chicago: University of Chicago Press, 1992)
Henning, Standish (ed.), *Fair Em* (New York and London: Garland Publishing, 1980)
Heywood, Thomas, ed. Richard Rowland, *Edward IV* (Manchester: Manchester University Press, forthcoming)
Hill, Christopher, 'Robin Hood', in Stephen Knight (ed.), *Robin Hood: An Anthology of Scholarship and Criticism* (Cambridge: D. S. Brewer, 1999), 285–95

Hill, Tracey, '"He hath changed his coppy": anti-theatrical writing and the turncoat player', *Critical Survey*, 9:1 (1997), 59–77

Hill, Tracey, '"This is as true as all the rest is": religious propaganda and the representation of truth in the 1580s', *Critical Survey*, 11:1 (1999), 48–65

Hill, Tracey, 'Marked down for omission: censorship and *The Booke of Sir Thomas More*', *Parergon*, 17:1 (1999), 63–87

Hodges, C. Walter, *The Globe Restored: A Study of the Elizabethan Theatre* (London: Oxford University Press, 1968)

Holmes, Martin, *Elizabethan London* (London: Cassell, 1969)

Holmes, Martin, 'A source-book for Stow?', in A. E. J. Hollaender and William Kellaway (eds), *Studies in London History* (London: Hodder and Stoughton, 1969), 275–85

Hosking, G. L., *The Life and Times of Edward Alleyn* (London: Cape, 1952)

Hosley, Richard, 'Anthony Munday, John Heardson, and the authorship of "Fedele and Fortunio"', *Modern Language Review*, 40 (1960), 564–5

Hosley, Richard, 'The date of "Fedele and Fortunio"', *Modern Language Review*, 57 (1962), 385–6

Hotson, Leslie, 'Anthony Munday's birth-date', *Notes and Queries*, 6 (1959), 2–4

Howard, Jean E., *The Stage and Social Struggle in Early Modern England* (London: Routledge, 1994)

Huffman, Clifford Chambers, *Elizabethan Impressions: John Wolfe and his Press* (New York: AMS Press, 1988)

Hughes, Paul L., and James F. Larkin (eds), *Tudor Royal Proclamations*, vols II and III (New Haven and London: Yale University Press, 1969)

Ingram, William, *A London Life in the Brazen Age* (Cambridge, Mass.: Harvard University Press, 1978)

Ingram, William, 'The Globe playhouse and its neighbors in 1600', *Essays in Theatre*, 2 (1984), 63–72

Ingram, William, *The Business of Playing: The Beginnings of the Professional Theatre in Elizabethan London* (Ithaca: Cornell University Press, 1992)

Ingram, William, 'What kind of future for the theatrical past: or, what will count as theater history in the next millennium?', *Shakespeare Quarterly*, 48:2 (1997), 215–225

Jack, Sybil M., 'The revels accounts: this insubstantial pageant leaves not a wrack behind?', *Renaissance Studies*, 9:1 (1995), 1–17

Jenner, Mark S. R., 'From conduit community to commercial network? Water in London, 1500–1725', in Paul Griffiths and Mark S. R. Jenner (eds), *Londinopolis: Essays in the Cultural and Social History of Early Modern London* (Manchester: Manchester University Press, 2000), 250–72

Jenstad, Janelle Day, 'Institutional uses of pageantry: the case of the Goldsmiths' (unpublished conference paper, March 2002)

Jenstad, Janelle Day, '"The City cannot hold you": social conversion in the Goldsmith's shop', *Early Modern Literary Studies*, 8:2 (2002) (Available at: www.shu.ac.uk/emls/08-2/jensgold.html. Accessed 4 November 2002)

Johnson, A. H., *A History of the Worshipful Company of the Drapers of London*, vol. III (Oxford: Clarendon Press, 1922)

Johnson, David J., *Southwark and the City* (London: Oxford University Press, 1969)

Johnson, Gerald D., 'The Stationers versus the Drapers: control of the press in the late sixteenth century', *The Library*, 6th series, 10:1 (1988), 1–17

Johnson, Paula, 'Jacobean ephemera and the immortal word', *Renaissance Drama*, 8 (1977), 151–72
Johnson, Robert Carl (ed.), *Elizabethan Bibliographies Supplements IX: Minor Elizabethans* (London: The Nether Press, 1968)
Jones, Ann Rosalind, and Peter Stallybrass, *Renaissance Clothing and the Materials of Memory* (Cambridge: Cambridge University Press, 2000)
Jonson, Ben, ed. Michael Jamieson, *Three Comedies* (Harmondsworth: Penguin, 1969)
Jonson, Ben, ed. G. A. Wilkes, *The Complete Plays of Ben Jonson*, vols I–II (Oxford: The Clarendon Press, 1981–82)
Jonson, Ben, ed. Peter Happé, *The Devil Is an Ass* (Manchester: Manchester University Press, 1996)
Kahan, Jeffrey, 'Henry Chettle's *Romeo* Q1 and *The Death of Robert Earl of Huntingdon*', *Notes and Queries*, 43 (1996), 155–6
Kalb, Eugénie de, 'Robert Poley's movements as a Messenger of the Court, 1588 to 1601', *Review of English Studies*, 9 (1933), 13–18
Kastan, David Scott, 'Opening gates and stopping hedges: Grafton, Stow, and the politics of Elizabethan history writing', in Elizabeth Fowler and Roland Greene (eds), *The Project of Prose in Early Modern Europe and the New World* (Cambridge: Cambridge University Press, 1997), 66–79
Kay, W. David, *Ben Jonson: A Literary Life* (Basingstoke: Macmillan, 1995)
Keene, Derek, and Vanessa Harding, *A Survey of Documentary Sources for Property Holdings in London before the Great Fire* (London: London Record Society, 1985)
Kenny, R. W., 'Notes on the "Catholicism" of Charles Earl of Nottingham', *Notes and Queries*, 16 (1969), 461–4
King, John N., *English Reformation Literature* (Princeton: Princeton University Press, 1982)
Kinney, Arthur F., ed., *Renaissance Drama: An Anthology of Plays and Entertainments* (Oxford: Blackwell, 2002)
Kipling, Gordon, 'Triumphal drama: form in English civic pageantry', *Renaissance Drama*, 7 (1977), 37–56
Knight, Stephen (ed.), *Robin Hood: An Anthology of Scholarship and Criticism* (Cambridge: D. S. Brewer, 1999)
Knowles, James, 'The Spectacle of the Realm: civic consciousness, rhetoric and ritual in early modern London', in J. R. Mulryne and Margaret Shewring (eds), *Theatre and Government under the Early Stuarts* (Cambridge: Cambridge University Press, 1993), 157–89
Knutson, Roslyn L., 'Play identifications', *Huntingdon Library Quarterly*, 47:1 (1984), 1–11
Knutson, Roslyn L., *The Repertory of Shakespeare's Company 1594–1613* (Fayetteville: University of Arkansas Press 1991)
Knutson, Roslyn L., *Playing Companies and Commerce in Shakespeare's Time* (Cambridge: Cambridge University Press, 2001)
Kuhl, Ernest, 'The Stationers' Company and censorship (1599–1601)', *The Library*, 9 (1928–9), 388–94
Lake, Peter, with Michael Questier, *The Antichrist's Lewd Hat: Protestants, Papists and Players in Post-Reformation England* (New Haven and London: Yale University Press, 2002)
Lancashire, Anne, *London Civic Theatre* (Cambridge: Cambridge University Press, 2002)

Lang, R. D. (ed.), *Two Tudor Subsidy Assessment Rolls for the City of London: 1541 and 1582* (London: London Record Society, 1993)

Langbein, John H., *Torture and the Law of Proof* (Chicago: University of Chicago Press, 1977)

Larkin, James F., and Paul L. Hughes (eds), *Stuart Royal Proclamations*, vol. I (Oxford: The Clarendon Press, 1973)

Lefebvre, Henri, trans. Donald Nicolson-Smith, *The Production of Space* (Oxford: Blackwell, 1999)

Leinwand, Theodore B., 'London triumphing: the Jacobean Lord Mayor's Show', *Clio*, 11:2 (1982), 137–53

Leinwand, Theodore B., *Theatre, Finance and Society in Early Modern England* (Cambridge: Cambridge University Press, 1999)

Levin, Carole, *Propaganda in the English Reformation* (Lewiston: Edwin Mellen, 1988)

The Life of Sir John Oldcastle, ed. Percy Simpson (London: The Malone Society, 1908)

Lloyd, Bertram, 'Anthony Munday, dramatist', *Notes and Queries*, 152 (1927), 98

Loades, D. M., 'The press under the early Tudors', *Transactions of the Cambridge Bibliographical Society*, 4 (1964–5), 29–50

Loades, D. M., 'The theory and practice of censorship in sixteenth-century England', *Transactions of the Royal Historical Society*, 24 (1974), 141–57

Lobanov-Rostovsky, Sergei, 'The Triumphes of Golde: economic authority in the Jacobean Lord Mayor's Show', *English Literary History*, 60 (1993), 879–98

Longstaffe, Stephen, 'What is the English history play and why are they saying such terrible things about it?', *Renaissance Forum*, 2:2 (1997) (Available at: www.hull.ac.uk/renforum/v2no2/longstaf.htm. Accessed 1 April 1998)

Longstaffe, Stephen, '"A short report and not otherwise": Jack Cade in *2 Henry VI*', in Ronald Knowles (ed.), *Shakespeare and Carnival: After Bakhtin* (Basingstoke: Macmillan, 1998), 13–35

Longstaffe, Stephen, 'Carnival versus London: regional risings and the English history play, 1593–1607' (unpublished conference paper, April 1999)

Lytle, Guy Fitch, and Stephen Orgel (eds), *Patronage in the Renaissance* (Princeton: Princeton University Press, 1981)

MacLean, Sally-Beth, 'Leicester's Men: patronage of a performance troupe', in Paul Whitfield White and Suzanne R. Westfall (eds), *Shakespeare and Theatrical Patronage in Early Modern England* (Cambridge: Cambridge University Press, 2002), 246–71

MacLure, Millar, *Register of Sermons Preached at Paul's Cross, 1534–1642* (Ottawa: Dovehouse Editions, 1989)

McEachern, Claire, *The Poetics of English Nationhood* (Cambridge: Cambridge University Press, 1996)

McKenzie, D. F., 'Apprenticeship in the Stationers' Company, 1555–1640', *The Library*, 13:4 (1958), 292–9

McLuskie, Kathleen, *Dekker and Heywood* (Basingstoke: Macmillan, 1994)

McMillin, Scott, *The Elizabethan Theatre and 'Sir Thomas More'* (Ithaca: Cornell University Press, 1987)

McMillin, Scott, 'Building stories: Greg, Fleay, and the Plot of *2 Deadly Sins*', *Medieval and Renaissance Drama in England*, 4 (1989), 53–62

McMillin, Scott, and Sally-Beth MacLean, *The Queen's Men and Their Plays* (Cambridge: Cambridge University Press, 1999)

McMillin, Scott, Lawrence Manley, Roslyn L. Knutson and Mark Bayer, 'Reading the Elizabethan acting companies', *Early Theatre*, 4 (2001), 111–48

McRae, Andrew, '"On the famous voyage": Ben Jonson and civic space', *Early Modern Literary Studies*, 4:2 (1998) (Available at: www.shu.ac.uk/emls/04-2/mcraonth.htm. Accessed 4 November 2002)

Manley, Lawrence (ed.), *London in the Age of Shakespeare: An Anthology* (London: Croom Helm, 1986)

Manley, Lawrence, *Literature and Culture in Early Modern London* (Cambridge: Cambridge University Press, 1995)

Manley, Lawrence, 'Of sites and rites', in David Smith, Richard Strier et al. (eds), *The Theatrical City* (Cambridge: Cambridge University Press, 1995), 35–54

Manley, Lawrence, et al., 'Fictions of settlement: London 1590', *Studies in Philology*, 88 (1991), 201–24

Mann, David, 'Sir Oliver Owlet's Men: fact or fiction?', *Huntingdon Library Quarterly*, 54 (1991), 301–11

Marcus, Leah S., 'City metal and country mettle: the occasion of Ben Jonson's *Golden Age Restored*', in David Bergeron (ed.), *Pageantry in the Shakespearean Theatre* (Athens: University of Georgia Press, 1985), 26–47

Marcus, Leah S., *Puzzling Shakespeare: Local Reading and its Discontents* (Berkeley: University of California Press, 1988)

Marks, Stephen Powys, *The Map of Mid Sixteenth Century London* (London: London Topographical Society, 1964)

Marston, John (asc.), *Histrio-Mastix. Or, the player whipt* (London 1610)

Masters, Betty R. (ed.), *Chamber Accounts of the Sixteenth Century* (London: London Record Society, 1984)

Meagher, John C., 'Hackwriting and the Huntingdon plays', in John Russell Brown (ed.), *Elizabethan Theatre* (London: Edward Arnold, 1966), 197–219

Meagher, John C., 'The London Lord Mayor's Show of 1590', *English Literary Renaissance*, 3 (1973) 94–104

Mehl, Dieter, 'Forms and functions of the play within a play', *Renaissance Drama*, 8 (1965), 41–61

Middleton, Thomas, ed. Roma Gill, *Women Beware Women* (London: Ernest Benn Ltd., 1968)

Miller, William E., 'Printers and stationers in the parish of St Giles Cripplegate 1561–1640', *Studies in Bibliography*, 19 (1966), 15–38

Moore, Helen, 'Jonson, Dekker, and the discourse of chivalry', *Mediaeval and Renaissance Drama in England*, 12 (1999), 121–65

Moore, Helen, 'Another link between Anthony Munday and Stephen Gosson', *Notes and Queries*, 49:2 (2002), 254–6

Moretti, Franco, *Atlas of the European Novel* (London: Verso, 1999)

Mullaney, Steven, *The Place of the Stage* (Chicago: University of Chicago Press, 1988)

Mundy, Percy D., 'Anthony Munday, dramatist', *Notes and Queries*, 9 (1914), 181–3

Myers, Robin, and Michael Harris (eds), *Censorship and the Control of Print in England and France 1600–1910* (Winchester: St Paul's Bibliographies, 1992)

Nashe, Thomas, ed. R. B. McKerrow, *The Works of Thomas Nashe*, vols I and III (Oxford: Blackwell, 1966)

Nashe, Thomas, ed. J. B. Steane, *The Unfortunate Traveller and Other Works* (Harmondsworth: Penguin, 1978)

Nichols, J. G. (ed.), *Chrysanaleia, the Golden Fishing* (London: printed for the Worshipful Company of Fishmongers, 1844)

Oakley-Brown, Liz, 'Framing Robin Hood: temporality and textuality in Anthony Munday's Huntington plays', in Helen Phillips (ed.), *Robin Hood Traditions: Medieval and Postmedieval* (Woodbridge: Boydell and Brewer, forthcoming)

Orlin, Lena Cowen (ed.), *Material London, ca. 1600* (Philadelphia: University of Pennsylvania Press, 2000)

Overall, W. H., and H. C. Overall (eds), *Analytical Index to the Series of Records Known as the Remembrancia* (London: E. J. Francis and Co., 1878)

Parry, Graham, 'Literary patronage', in David Loewenstein and Janel Mueller (eds), *The Cambridge History of Early Modern English Literature* (Cambridge: Cambridge University Press, 2002), 117–40

Parry, Graham, 'Patronage and the printing of learned works for the author', in John Barnard and D. F. McKenzie (eds), *The Cambridge History of the Book in Britain*, vol. IV, *1557–1695* (Cambridge: Cambridge University Press 2002), 174–88

Paster, Gail Kern, *The Idea of the City in the Age of Shakespeare* (Athens: University of Georgia Press, 1985)

Paster, Gail Kern, 'The idea of London in masque and pageant', in David Bergeron (ed.), *Pageantry in the Shakespearean Theatre* (Athens: University of Georgia Press, 1985), 48–64

Patterson, Annabel, *Censorship and Interpretation: The Conditions of Writing and Reading in Early Modern England* (Madison: University of Wisconsin Press, 1984)

Pearl, Valerie, 'Social policy in early modern London', in Hugh Lloyd-Jones *et al.* (eds), *History and Imagination: Essays in Honour of H. R. Trevor-Roper* (London: Duckworth, 1981), 115–31

Pettegree, Andrew, *Foreign Protestant Communities in Sixteenth-Century London* (Oxford: The Clarendon Press, 1986)

Pitcher, John, 'Literature, the playhouse and the public', in John Barnard and D. F. McKenzie (eds), *The Cambridge History of the Book in Britain*, vol. IV, *1557–1695* (Cambridge: Cambridge University Press 2002), 351–75

Poole, Kristen, 'Facing Puritanism: Falstaff, Martin Marprelate and the grotesque Puritan', in Ronald Knowles (ed.), *Shakespeare and Carnival: After Bakhtin* (Basingstoke: Macmillan, 1998), 97–122

Potter, Lois (ed.), *Playing Robin Hood* (Newark: University of Delaware Press, 1998)

Power, H. J., 'A "crisis" reconsidered: social and demographic dislocation in London in the 1590s', *The London Journal*, 12:2 (1986), 134–45

Prideaux, W. S., *Memorials of the Goldsmiths' Company*, vol. I (London: Eyre and Spottiswoode, 1896–7)

Prior, R., 'Anthony Munday as father and grandfather', *Notes and Queries*, 20 (1973), 453–4

Prockter, Adrian, and Robert Taylor (eds), *The A to Z of Elizabethan London* (Lympne Castle: Harry Margary, 1979)

Rankins, William, *A Mirrour of Monsters: wherein is plainely described the manifold vices and spotted enormities, that are caused by the infectious sight of playes* (London 1587)

Rappaport, Steven, *Worlds Within Worlds: Structures of Life in Sixteenth-Century London* (Cambridge: Cambridge University Press, 1989)

Robertson, James, 'Stuart London and the idea of a royal capital city', *Renaissance Studies*, 15:1 (2001), 37–58

Robertson, Jean and D. J. Gordon (eds), *A Calendar of Dramatic Records in the Books of the Livery Companies of London 1485–1640* (Oxford: The Malone Society, 1954)
Rollins, Hyder E., 'William Elderton: Elizabethan actor and ballad-writer', *Studies in Philology*, 17 (1920), 199–245
Rutter, Carol Chillington (ed.), *Documents of the Rose Playhouse* (Manchester: Manchester University Press, 1999)
Salgādo, Gāmini (ed.), *Four Jacobean City Comedies* (Harmondsworth: Penguin 1975)
Sayle, R. T. D., *Lord Mayors' Pageants of the Merchant Taylors Company in the 15th, 16th and 17th Centuries* (Privately printed, 1931)
Scanlon, P. A., 'Munday's *Zelauto*: form and function', *Cahiers Elisabéthains*, 18 (1980), 11–17
Schlauch, Margaret, *Antecedents of the English Novel, 1400–1600* (London: Oxford University Press, 1965)
Schmidgall, Gary, '*The Tempest* and *Primaleon*: a new source', *Shakespeare Quarterly*, 37:4 (1986), 423–39
Schofield, John, 'The topography and buildings of London, ca. 1600', in Lena Cowen Orlin (ed.), *Material London, ca. 1600* (Philadelphia: University of Pennsylvania Press, 2000), 296–321
Schrickx, Willem, 'Anthony Munday in the Netherlands in October 1595', *Notes and Queries*, 44: 4 (1997), 484–5
Scoufos, Alice-Lyle, *Shakespeare's Typological Satire: A Study of the Falstaff-Oldcastle Problem* (Athens: Ohio University Press, 1979)
Seaver, Paul S., *The Puritan Lectureships: The Politics of Religious Dissent 1560–1662* (Stanford: Stanford University Press, 1970)
Seaver, Paul S., 'The artisanal world', in David Smith, Richard Strier et al. (eds), *The Theatrical City* (Cambridge: Cambridge University Press, 1995), 87–100
Shapiro, Michael, 'Patronage and the companies of boy actors', in Paul Whitfield White and Suzanne R. Westfall (eds), *Shakespeare and Theatrical Patronage in Early Modern England* (Cambridge: Cambridge University Press, 2002), 272–94
Sheppard, Francis, *London: A History* (Oxford: Oxford University Press, 1998)
Sidney, Sir Philip, ed. Richard Dutton, *Selected Writings* (Manchester: Carcarnet, 1987)
Siebert, Fredrick S., *Freedom of the Press in England 1476–1776* (Urbana: University of Illinois Press, 1952)
Simeone, William E., 'Renaissance Robin Hood plays', in Horace P. Beck (ed.), *Folklore in Action* (Philadelphia: The American Folklore Society, 1962), 184–99
Singman, Jeffrey L., 'Munday's unruly Earl', in Lois Potter (ed.), *Playing Robin Hood* (Newark: University of Delaware Press, 1998), 63–76
Sir Thomas More, a Play, ed. Alexander Dyce (London: The Shakespeare Society, 1844)
Sisson, C. J., *The Boar's Head Theatre* (London: Routledge and Kegan Paul, 1972)
Stevenson, Laura, *Praise and Paradox: Merchants and Craftsmen in Elizabethan Popular Literature* (Cambridge: Cambridge University Press, 1984)
Stow, John, ed. Anthony Munday, *The Survay of London* (London 1618)
Stow, John, ed. Anthony Munday et al., *The Survey of London* (London 1633)
Stow, John, ed. C. L. Kingsford, *A Survey of London*, 2 vols (Oxford: The Clarendon Press, 1971)

Streitberger, W. R., 'Some new specimens of Edmond Tyllney's hand', *The Library*, 28:2 (1973), 151–5

Sugden, E. H., *A Topographical Dictionary to the Works of Shakespeare and his Fellow Dramatists* (Hildesheim and New York: Georg Olms Verlag, 1969)

Sullivan, Garrett A., *The Drama of Landscape* (Stanford: Stanford University Press, 1998)

Thompson, Edward, 'The autograph manuscripts of Anthony Mundy', *Transactions of the Bibliographical Society*, 14 (1915–17), 325–53

Thompson, Elbert N. S., *The Controversy Between the Puritans and the Stage* (New York: Russell and Russell, 1966)

Thomson, Patricia, 'The literature of patronage', *Essays in Criticism*, 2 (1952), 267–84

Tribble, Evelyn, *Margins and Marginality: The Printed Page in Early Modern England* (Charlottesville: University Press of Virginia, 1993)

Twyning, John, *London Dispossessed: Literature and Social Space in the Early Modern City* (Basingstoke: Macmillan, 1998)

Turner, Celeste, *Anthony Mundy: An Elizabethan Man of Letters* (Berkeley: University of California Press, 1928)

Turner Wright, Celeste, 'Young Anthony Mundy again', *Studies in Philology*, 56 (1959), 150–68

Turner Wright, Celeste, 'Anthony Mundy, "Edward Spenser", and E.K.', *P.M.L.A.*, 76 (1961), 34–9

Turner Wright, Celeste, 'Mundy and Chettle in Grub Street', *Boston University Studies in English*, 5:3 (1961), 129–38

Turner Wright, Celeste, untitled review of Jack Stillinger (ed.), *Zelauto*, *Journal of English and Germanic Philology*, 58 (1964), 151–60

Unwin, George, *The Gilds and Companies of London* (London: Methuen, 1908)

Ward, A. W., and A. R. Waller (eds), *The Cambridge History of English Literature*, vol. V (Cambridge: Cambridge University Press, 1910)

Weinreb, Ben, and Christopher Hibbert (eds), *The London Encyclopaedia* (London: Macmillan, 1993)

Wells, Susan, 'Jacobean city comedy and the ideology of the city', *English Literary History*, 48 (1981), 37–60

White, Paul Whitfield, 'Shakespeare, the Cobhams, and the dynamics of theatrical patronage', in Paul Whitfield White and Suzanne R. Westfall (eds), *Shakespeare and Theatrical Patronage in Early Modern England* (Cambridge: Cambridge University Press, 2002), 64–89

White, Paul Whitfield, and Suzanne R. Westfall (eds), *Shakespeare and Theatrical Patronage in Early Modern England* (Cambridge: Cambridge University Press, 2002)

Wickham, Glynne, Herbert Berry and William Ingram (eds), *English Professional Theatre, 1530–1660* (Cambridge: Cambridge University Press, 2000)

Williams, Franklin B., *Index of Dedications and Commendatory Verses in English Books before 1641* (London: The Bibliographical Society, 1962)

Williams, Sheila B., 'The Lord Mayor's Show in Tudor and Stuart times', *Guildhall Miscellany*, 1:10 (1959), 3–18

Wilson, Richard, *Will Power: Essays on Shakespearean Authority* (Hemel Hempstead: Harvester Wheatsheaf, 1993)

Winger, Howard W., 'Regulations relating to the book trade in London from 1357–1586', *The Library Quarterly*, 26:3 (1956), 157–95

Withington, Robert, 'The Lord Mayor's Show for 1623', *P.M.L.A.*, 30 (1915), 110–15

Withington, Robert, *English Pageantry: an historical outline*, 2 vols (New York: Arno Press, 1980)

Wolf, William D., 'Anthony Munday as popular artist', *Journal of Popular Culture*, 13:4 (1980), 659–62

Worden, Blair, 'Which play was performed at the Globe theatre on 7 February 1601?', *London Review of Books* (10 July 2003), 22–4

Worden, Thomas, 'The rhetoric of place in Ben Jonson's "Chorographical" entertainments and masques', *Renaissance Forum*, 3:2 (1998) (Available at: www.hull.ac.uk/renforum/v3no2/worden.htm. Accessed 27 February 2003)

Wright, Louis B., *Middle-Class Culture in Elizabethan England* (Chapel Hill: University of North Carolina Press, 1935)

Index

Note: 'n' after a page reference indicates the number of a note on that page.

Ackroyd, Peter 10
Admiral's Men, the 6, 20, 30, 47, 88, 89, 103n125, 104n171, 116, 121–7, 131–5, 141n105, 141n111
Agnew, Jean-Christophe 11, 53
Alfield, Thomas 29, 32, 56, 66n61, 122–3
Allde, Edward 32, 41n81
Allde, John 20, 28, 29, 32, 40n57, 41n81, 48, 116, 122, 183n17, 184n26
Alleyn, Edward 30, 37n6, 40n56, 40n66, 72, 116, 127–8, 133
An Almond for a Parrat 61
Amadis de Gaule 70
Andrewes, Launcelot 42n86, 160
antitheatricality 72, 80–1, 95, 106–20 *passim*, 132, 136n11, 166, 179
Archer, Ian 163
Ashton, Robert 90
A-Z of Elizabethan London 6

Baldwin, T. W. 74, 77
Barber Surgeons' Company, the 92–3
Bayer, Mark 131
Beer, Barrett 146–7
Bell, Thomas 42n91
Bell Inn, the (Gracechurch Street) 118
Bel Savage Inn, the (Ludgate Hill) 118
Bergeron, David 28, 78, 79–80, 116, 117–19, 149, 153, 164, 167

Berlin, Michael 148
Bertie, Peregrine, 9th Lord Willoughby d'Eresby 132, 181
Blackfriars, the 80, 100n77, 119, 123, 125, 130
Blagrave, Thomas 110
Boar's Head, the 142n129, 191n207
Bolles, George 186n74
Bourne, Nicholas 180
Braithwait, Richard 165
Branche, Sir John 38n14
Brooke, Henry, 8th Lord Cobham 122, 138n46
Bruster, Douglas 115
Buckle, Sir Cuthbert 113
Bull Inn, the (Bishopsgate Street) 118
Burbage, James 109, 114, 115
Burbage, Richard 27, 117–18, 164
Burnett, Mark Thornton 72
Butler, Martin 73

Calvin, Jean 85–6
Camden, William 147, 148
Campbell, Thomas 89, 163–4
Campion, Edmund 34, 88, 102n108, 103n135, 183n181
Carey, George, 2nd Lord Hunsdon 111, 114, 122, 134
Carson, Neil 124, 131
Catholicism 21, 41n81, 65n22,

101n107, 139n88, 140n96, 147–8, 165; Munday and 3, 22, 34–6, 48, 51, 57–8, 60–1, 85–90 *passim*, 102n107, 102n108, 103n135, 104n149, 148, 184n26, 189n137
Cecil, Robert Lord, Viscount Cranbourne 134
Cecil, William, 1st Lord Burghley 96, 148
Cerasano, S. P. 133
Chamberlain, John 131
Chamberlain's Men, the 111, 122, 125, 135, 141n112
Chambers, E. K. 121
Chapel Children, the 123, 140n100
Chapman, George 77
Charlewood, John 30, 32, 41n77, 41n80, 41n81, 48, 49, 65n22
Chaucer, Geoffrey 69, 97n3
Chettle, Henry 26, 28, 41n81, 56, 63, 64, 67n66, 68n114, 74–5, 88–9, 122
Chomley, John 115, 121
Cicero 49, 65n25, 97n11, 156, 165
Clerkenwell 131, 142n138, 183n21
Cockpit, the 80
Coke, Edward 27
Collinson, Patrick 108
Corns, Thomas 150
Corporation of London, the 21–4, 31, 86, 91, 128, 138n48, 151–4, 159–61, 180, 186n74, 186n77, 188n113, 188n132
Craven, Sir William 89, 90, 103n130
Creede, Thomas 30, 32
Cripplegate, parish of St Giles Without 8–9, 30–4, 40n64, 127–34, 142n129, 142n130, 143n151, 179–82
Cripplegate, ward of 14, 31, 38n14, 40n64, 40n70, 42n86, 42n87, 91, 129–31, 142n129, 178–9, 180
Cromwell, Thomas 184n24
Cross Keys Inn, the (Gracechurch Street) 111, 118, 133, 139n75
Crowley, Robert 31, 33–4, 42n86, 42n87, 42n89, 65n22, 66n50, 148, 167, 184n27, 189n137
Curtain, the 36, 129, 135, 143n162, 147, 191n207

Danter, John 30, 32, 41n81

Davies, Sir John 58
Day, John (playwright) 88
Day, John (printer) 40n62
Defoe, Daniel 41n73
Dekker, Thomas 4, 16n2, 16n8, 16n13, 41n74, 65n5, 74, 79, 80, 88, 91–2, 104n152, 116, 119, 122, 124, 126, 149; *The Gull's Hornbook* 45; *Old Fortunatus* 131; *The Seven Deadlie Sins of London* 38n22; *Troia Nova Triumphans* 12, 17n33, 159, 185n43
Derby's Men 103n125, 121, 137n26
Devereux, Robert, 2nd Earl of Essex 90
Devereux, Walter, 1st Earl of Essex 66n27, 86, 98n14, 122
Dillon, Janette 19–20, 116, 127–8, 135–6, 148–9
Don Quixote 98n19
van Dorsten, Jan 96
Drapers' Company, the 6, 19–20, 27–30, 33, 38n14, 72, 77, 79, 87, 100n59, 100n60, 102n123, 124, 131, 136, 137n19, 157, 166–74, 189n158
Drayton, Michael 69, 74–5, 88, 124, 185n49
Dudley, Robert, Earl of Leicester 86, 89, 97, 184n22
Dutton, Richard 78, 114, 119, 131–2

Eccles, Mark 22
Edward III, king of England 150
Elizabeth I, queen of England 1, 18n60, 42n94, 53, 71, 85, 87, 97, 103n124, 103n135, 148, 150
Ellyot, George 60–1, 189n137
'Evil May Day' riot (1517) 10, 12–15, 17n46, 18n55, 18n67, 35, 177

Fair Em 31, 32, 40n68, 42n81, 67n91, 72, 76–7, 97n8
Faringdon, Nicholas 169, 189n151
Finsbury 129, 132–3, 143n151, 179
Fishmongers' Company, the 23–5, 82–3, 104n163, 120, 156, 160–1, 166, 169, 178–9, 187n102, 191n198
Fitz-Alwin, Henry 144, 158, 166–74, 179, 188n133, 189n158
Fleetwood, William 114, 148, 184n24
Foakes, R. A. 115, 125

Ford, Thomas 35
Forker, Charles 31
Fortune, the 2, 7, 8, 14, 32, 47, 78, 80, 89, 119, 121, 124–36, 137n25, 141n105, 142n129, 142n130, 143n147, 143n152, 143n162, 143n163, 147, 179, 181
Foster, Frank Freeman 147
Foxe, John 41n73, 42n87, 125, 147, 148
Freedman, Barbara 5, 9, 113

Gadd, Ian 48
Geertz, Clifford 152
Gibson/Gybson, Anthony 52–3, 90, 97n6
Globe, the 125, 127, 141n111, 141n112, 143n147, 143n162
Goldsmiths' Company, the 12, 27, 28, 43n95, 81–2, 101n94, 117, 156, 166–74 *passim*, 178–9, 186n84, 189n153
Gordon, Andrew 130, 149, 155
Gosson, Stephen 95–6, 109, 137n15, 140n94, 179
Grafton, Richard 127, 147, 184n24
Greenblatt, Stephen 5
Greene, Robert 31, 40n68, 55, 72, 76–7
Gresham, Sir Thomas 115
Grindal, Edmund, Bishop of London 148
Grinkin, John 26, 78
Grocers' Company, the 39n40
Gurr, Andrew 122, 123, 126

Haberdashers' Company, the 185n53
Halasz, Alexandra 37
Hall, Edward 10, 17n46, 18n55, 18n67, 177
Hamilton, Donna 51, 85–6
Harrison, William 28
Hathaway, Richard 88, 124, 141n105
Haughton, William 88
Haunse, Everard 42n89
Hawkes, David 46–7, 111
Hayes, Gerald 45
Heardson, John 87
Heardson, Thomas 87
Heinemann, Margot 4, 72, 165
Henry, Prince of Wales 116, 119, 151, 152, 164, 185n49
Henry VI, king of England 150

Henslowe, Philip 19–20, 30, 37n6, 39n54, 40n56, 115–16, 124–5, 127–8, 133–4; Henslowe's *Diary* 62, 68n105, 68n114, 121, 122, 124, 131, 141n105, 141n122
Heywood, Thomas 3, 4, 16n2, 100n59, 116, 124, 125, 187n94; *Edward IV* 103n125, 126, 162
Histrio-Mastix 26–7, 56, 76, 99n50, 99n52
Hog Hath Lost His Pearl, The 103n145
Holinshed, Raphael 10, 159
Holland, Hugh 34, 42n91
Holliday, Sir Leonard 149, 185n44
Hollyband, Claudius 102n107
Holmes, Martin 11
Hope, the 165–6
Hosley, Richard 87
Howard, Charles, 1st Earl of Nottingham 47, 96, 101n107, 114, 121–2, 133–5, 138n48, 140n92

Ingram, William 2, 6, 19, 110–12, 135
Ironmongers' Company, the 164

Jaggard, William 32, 41n80, 183n14
James I, king of England 1, 12, 25, 38n29, 93, 97, 116–17, 135, 148–51, 155, 183n7, 185n44, 188n115
Jenner, Mark 14
Jenstad, Janelle Day 78, 80–1, 82, 120
John, king of England 173–4, 190n171, 190n173
John, St John, Baron of Bletso 140n92
Johnson, A. H. 81
Johnson, Paula 153–4, 157, 174–5
Jones, Ann Rosalind 117
Jonson, Ben 4, 26, 29, 39n56, 41n74, 65n5, 70, 98n28, 100n60, 115, 116, 119, 124, 157, 185n53, 186n72; *Bartholmew Fair* 165–6, 188n132; *The Case is Altered* 75–6, 99n42, 99n46, 99n47; *The Devil is an Ass* 6–7; *Epicoene* 97n7, 188n132; *The Golden Age Restored* 152; (with Nashe) *The Isle of Dogs* 36, 43n104

Keysar, Sir Robert 119, 139n79
King, John, Bishop of London 81, 162, 176

INDEX—213

Kingsford, C. L. 6, 176, 182
King's Men, the 117, 125, 164
Kirbie, Luke 34–5
Knack to Know a Knave, A 121
Knight, Stephen 63
Knight of the Burning Pestle, The 71–2, 98n18, 119
Knutson, Roslyn 122

Langley, Francis 2, 19, 135
Leake, William 103n139
Lee, Sir Robert 91
Lefebvre, Henri 130
Leicester's Men 109
Leinwand, Theodore 15, 47, 118, 161
Leman, Sir John 24–5, 38n27, 160
livery companies, the 7, 45, 80–1, 110, 112, 115, 120, 145, 149, 153, 162–5; *see also individual companies*
Lobanov-Rostovky, Sergei 55–6, 80–1, 117, 119, 158–9
local knowledge 5, 9–10, 166
Lord Howard's Men 123
Lord Mayors' Shows 55–6, 75, 80–1, 112, 116–20, 137n16, 147–75 *passim*, 185n47, 186n66, 188n132, 191n192; publication of 100n79, 175; route of 15, 18n64
Low Countries, the 7, 59, 104n171
Lowin, John 27, 117, 139n63
Luther, Martin 48
Lyly, John 70, 71, 84, 140n97

MacLean, Sally-Beth 114, 123
McLuskie, Kathleen 4, 55
McMillin, Scott 114, 121, 123
McRae, Andrew 7
Magnificent Entertainment, the 37n11, 116–17, 149, 184n32, 186n72
Mandeville, Lord Viscount, President of the Privy Council 81
Manley, Lawrence 12, 15, 25, 55, 73, 96–7, 147, 152, 163, 165
Mann, David 5, 56
Marcus, Leah 10, 149, 152, 155, 173
Marlowe, Christopher 102n119
Marprelate controversy, the 33, 48, 57, 61, 77, 113, 121, 139n75, 140n101
Marston, John 4, 76, 99n49

Marten, Sir Henry 180
Martin, Sir Richard 35–6, 43n95, 43n96, 43n98, 89–90, 113
Massinger, John 4
Meagher, John 57, 63
Mehl, Dieter 63, 64
Mercers' Company, the 169, 179
Merchant Taylors' Company, the 19, 28, 32, 39n55, 81, 90–1, 119, 144, 150, 163, 185n43, 185n49
Meres, Francis, *Palladis Tamia* 72, 75, 76
Middlesex 42n92, 107, 111, 129, 132–5
Middleton, Thomas 4, 33, 39n40, 42n86, 77–80, 83, 91, 100n60, 101n83, 116, 124, 145; as pageant-writer 80, 100n59, 119–20, 138n59, 153, 155, 185n53, 188n120; *A Chaste Maid in Cheapside* 139n79; *Civitatis Amor* 120, 139n81; *The Triumphes of Love and Antiquity* 78; *The Triumphs of Integrity* 79; *The Triumphs of Truth* 12, 26, 38n30, 77–9, 159
Milles, Thomas 10
Milton, John 40n64
Montague, Sir Henry 183n14
Moore, Helen 74, 75–6, 86, 118, 177, 179
Moorgate 8, 178, 191n198
More, Sir Thomas 35, 179, 191n199
Moretti, Franco 6–8, 130
Morris, William 55
Mostyn, Sir Roger 140n99
Mullaney, Steven 108, 112, 118, 128, 131
Munday, Anthony, *The admirable deliverance of 266 Christians* 99n43, 104n165; *Amadis of Gaul* 97n7, 98n19, 104n155; *Archaioplutos* 48, 49; *A Banquet of Dainty Conceits* 37; (with Dekker, Heywood *et al.*) *The Booke of Sir Thomas More* 10–14 *passim*, 43n104, 56, 121, 123, 125, 126, 139n88, 177, 188n132, 191n199; *A breefe and true reporte, of the Execution of certain Traytours* 35, 37n9; *A breefe Aunswer made unto two Seditious Pamphlets* 29,

32, 43n98, 102n108; *A breefe Treatise of the vertue of the Crosse* 86, 88; *A Briefe Chronicle, of the Successe of Time* 32, 38n20, 81–2, 90, 144–6, 153, 154, 176, 183n14; (with Middleton) *Caesar's Fall* 78, 124; *Camp-bell* 78, 89, 164, 186n81; *Chruso-thriambos* 12, 38n22, 68n114, 78, 82, 90, 98n12, 98n18, 117, 144, 146, 154, 156–7, 166–71, 174, 187n94, 189n151, 189n153; *Chrysanaleia* 23–5, 80, 83, 94, 120, 160–1, 177, 178, 186n73, 187n94, 187n102; *The Conversion of a most Noble Lady of Fraunce* 103n140; *The Coppie of the Anti-Spaniard* 93; (with Chettle) *The Death of Robert, Earle of Huntington* 60–4, 68n105, 126–7, 141n122, 174, 190n173; *The declaration of the Lord de la Noue* 104n155; *The Defence of Contraries* 75, 121; *A Discoverie of Edmund Campion, and his Confederates* 65n25; *The Downfall of Robert, Earle of Huntington* 54, 58–64, 68n98, 68n105, 83, 118, 122, 126–7, 141n122, 154, 174; *The English Romayne lyfe* 85, 86; *Fedele and Fortunio* 74, 87, 122, 123, 140n94; (with Chettle) *The Funeral of Richard Coeur de Lion* 64, 68n114; *Galien of Fraunce* 84; *Gerileon of England* 49, 87; *A Godly exercise for Christian families* 34; *The Heaven of the Mynde* 90, 103n139; *Himatia-Poleos* 130, 158, 167–75; (with Dekker) *Jephtha* 124; *John a Kent and John a Cumber*; 56, 123, 140n99, 140n101; *Londons Love* 32, 107, 117–18, 139n81, 151, 164, 178; *The Masque of the League and the Spanyard discovered* 49; *Metropolis Coronata* 94, 151, 157–8, 171–4, 186n81; *The Mirrour of Mutabilitie* 46, 48, 51–2, 65n25, 69, 75, 83–5, 98n12, 102n107, 103n136, 123, 124; ('Lazurus Pyott') *The Orator* 140n92; *The paine of pleasure* 54–5, 75, 94; *Palladine of England* 32, 49, 66n27, 72, 74, 86, 98n14, 99n45, 102n119; *Palmendos* 32; *Palmerin d'Oliva* 37n9, 45–6, 49, 72, 74, 84, 98n19, 98n20; *Primaleon of Greece* 26, 41n81, 69, 74–5, 102n107, 105n171; *A second and third blast of retrait from plaies and Theaters* 22, 46–7, 55–8, 81, 94, 106–9, 111–12, 118, 122, 127, 136n11, 147; *The [first] Seconde Part, of the ... Historie, of the ... Princes Palmerin of England* 45, 49, 98n19; *A Set at Tennis* 124; *Sidero-Thriambos* 11, 17n39, 30, 79, 107, 159, 187n94; (with Drayton, Hathaway and Wilson) *Sir John Oldcastle* 60, 122, 124, 126, 138n46, 174; *The strangest adventure that ever happened* 88–9; (with Middleton) *The Sun in Aries* 79; *The Survay of London* (1618) 11, 20–4, 81, 101n94, 145–8, 152–3, 157, 161–2, 166, 168–9, 173–81 *passim*, 183n14, 184n27, 186n74, 187n88, 187n94, 189n151, 190n184, 191n198, 191n199, 191n203, 191n207; *The Survey of London* (1633) 11, 21, 23, 83, 101n83, 148, 163–4, 178–80, 182–3, 189n149, 191n193; *The theater of honour and knighthood* 183n14; *The Third and last part of Palmerin of England* 38n18, 52, 54, 69–70, 74, 77, 86–7, 90, 97n6, 104n152, 185n52; *The Triumphes of re-united Britania* 28, 104n160, 149–51, 155, 184n32, 185n35; *The Triumphs of the Golden Fleece* 79, 94, 136; *A True and admirable Historie, of a Mayden of Consolens* 32, 91–3, 102n119; *The True Image of Christian Love* 34–5, 89; *The True knowledge of a mans owne selfe* 70–1, 90–1; *A View of Sundry Examples* 84, 146; *A Watch-woord to Englande* 87–8; 'The Woodman's Walk' 54; work for the Corporation of London 81,

96, 106–9, 117–18, 151–2, 177; *A Womans Woorth* 49, 52–3; *Zelauto* 11, 45, 49–51, 54, 57, 69–71, 75, 84–6, 93–6, 97n8, 101n107, 140n97
Munday, Christopher (father) 28
Munday, Gillian (wife) 31, 33, 83, 101n83
Munday, Priscilla (daughter) 31
Munday, Richard (son) 29–30, 33, 39n36, 40n60, 101n94
Munday, Susan (step-daughter) 86
Mundy, William 39n45

Nashe, Thomas 26, 36, 43n103, 50, 70, 72–3, 77, 98n23, 99n47, 115, 147
Nelson, Thomas 160–1, 166
Newington Butts playhouse, the 123
Nichols, Humphrey 39n40, 78
Norden, John 185n47
Nowell, Thomas 86

Oakley-Brown, Liz 59, 61
Orlando Amareso 48
Orlando Furioso 48
Oxford's Boys 140n97, 140n100
Oxford's Men 20, 47, 116, 123

Pafford, J. 90, 170
Painter Stainers' Company, the 39n36
Palsgrave's Men 119
Parry, Graham 69, 86
Paster, Gail Kern 154
patronage 3, 7, 23–4, 26, 34–7, 37n6, 44, 47–8, 53–4, 76, 83–97 *passim*, 98n20, 103n136, 103n140, 120
Paul's Children 123, 140n96
Peck, Russell 64, 126
Pemberton, Sir James 82, 157
Pennell, Arthur 2–3, 56
Poley, Robert 102n119
Privy Council, the 8, 36, 40n66, 96, 97, 103n135, 111–15, 132–6, 142n130, 151, 163, 183n14, 186n77
Prynne, William 17n36
Pullison, Sir Thomas 87
Purslowe, Elizabeth 180

Queen Anne's Men 142n138
Queen's Men, the 123, 137n26, 140n100

Rainolds, John 96
Raleigh, Sir Walter 159
Rankins, William 55, 141n105
Red Bull, the 125, 129
Red Lion, the 115, 123, 127
Rice, John 117, 164
Richard I, king of England 171, 173–4
Richard II, king of England 150
Richard III, king of England 150, 151, 185n43
Rickert, R. T. 115
Rider, Sir William 89
Ridley, Nicholas, Bishop of Rochester 184n27
Rising of Cardinal Wolsey, The 124
Roberts, Francis 42n89
Roberts, James 30, 32, 41n80
Robinson, Richard 101n97
Rome 7, 34, 85–6, 122
Rose, the 2, 7, 8, 14, 27, 30, 32, 47, 58, 75, 76, 88, 99n49, 115, 121–6 *passim*, 134, 141n112, 143n147
Royal Exchange, the 94, 115
Rutter, Carol Chillington 115, 122, 133–4

de Sales, Francis 86
Salgādo, Gāmino 4
Scanlon, Paul 50–1, 94
Scott, William 58
Seccombe, Thomas 2, 27
Seven Deadlie Sinns, The 27, 123
Shaa, Robert 36
Shakespeare, William 125, 141n112; *Measure for Measure* 10
Shank, John 19
Sherwin, Ralph 34
Sidney, Sir Philip 70
Simeone, William 59, 63
Simpson, Richard 79
Singman, Jeffrey 58, 62–3
Skinners' Company, the 82, 87
Smith, Wentworth, *The Hector of Germanie, or, the Palsgrave* 119
Smythe, William 153
Soame, Sir Stephen 88–9
Sotherne, Nicholas 79
Southwark 30, 118, 127–31, 134, 162, 165–6
Southwell, Robert 43n101, 48

Sparkes, Thomas 143n163
Speed, John 42n87, 178, 189n151, 191n193, 191n203
Spelman, Henry 42n87
Spenser, Gabriel 36, 40n56
Spigurnel, Thomas 69
Stallybrass, Peter 117
Standard, the (Cheapside) 7, 10, 11–15
Stanley, Ferdinando, Lord Strange 101n106, 121, 139n88
Stationers' Company, the 27, 29–30, 40n62, 41n81, 116, 180
Statute of Artificers, the 40n57
Stephens, John 55
Stevenson, Laura 146, 153, 165
Stillinger, Jack 49, 50, 86
Stow, John 7, 22–3, 73, 98n28, 101n83, 144–7, 166, 183n7, 184n24, 184n26, 189n143, 189n151; *The Annales of England* 160, 176, 183n4, 184n22; *Memoranda* 148; *A Summarie of English Chronicles* 141n123, 146, 176; *A Survay of London* 6–15 passim, 17n53, 37n12, 41n73, 44, 144, 146, 152–4, 162–3, 168–70, 175–80, 183n21, 184n27, 187n94, 189n143, 190n183, 190n184, 191n198, 191n205
Strange's Men 27, 72, 121, 123, 139n75
Straw, Jack 160–1
Street, Peter 127, 131
Sullivan, Garrett 3, 154, 162–3
Surrey 107, 111, 135, 166
Swan, the 19, 36, 135
Swynnerton, Sir John 12, 33, 38n18, 87, 90–1, 97, 103n140, 103n145, 119, 157, 159

Talbot, Gilbert, 7th Earl of Shrewsbury 48
Tarleton, Dick 67n69
Theatre, the 2, 36, 123, 127, 129, 137n20, 147, 183n21
Tilney, Edmund 110, 113, 114, 123, 135, 137n20, 138n46
Topcliffe, Richard 36–7, 43n101, 43n103, 43n105, 87
translation 8, 52–4, 66n38, 73–5, 92–3, 104n149, 104n152

Turner (Wright), Celeste 1, 85, 93
Twyning, John 25, 45
Tyburn 2, 11
Tyler, Wat 160, 177, 187n102
Tylers' and Bricklayers' Company, the 29, 39n56

de Vere, Edward, 17th Earl of Oxford 51, 54, 70–1, 74, 75, 84–6, 96, 98n20, 101n107, 103n136, 123, 140n97
de Vere, Henry, 18th Earl of Oxford 102n107
Vergil, Polydore 184n24

Walsingham, Sir Francis 89, 102n108
Walworth, Sir William 24–5, 80, 159–61, 166, 169, 177, 187n94, 187n102, 188n133
Weavers' Company, the 19
Webster, John 19, 69–70, 77, 90, 100n59, 104n152, 116, 175; *Monuments of Honour* 143n166, 155–6, 167, 185n43
Westcott, Sebastian 140n96
Westminster 1, 7, 97, 112, 158, 159, 186n77
West Smithfield 165–6, 188n132
White, Paul Whitfield 122, 126
White, Sir Thomas 190n184
Whitefriars, the 103n145, 119
Whitgift, John 33, 57, 61, 113
Whittington, Dick 165
Wickham, Glynne 110–11
Wigginton, Giles 48, 57
Wilson, Robert 32, 40n68, 41n75, 68n114, 88, 124
Windet, John 146, 183n17
Wise Men of Westchester, The 123
Wither, George 48
Withington, Robert 79
Wolf, William 59
Wolfe, John 30, 40n62, 48, 52, 93, 104n155, 146
Wotton, Sir Henry 104n145
Wriothesley, Elizabeth, Countess of Southampton 52–3

Young, Richard 34–6, 42n92

EU authorised representative for GPSR:
Easy Access System Europe, Mustamäe tee 50,
10621 Tallinn, Estonia
gpsr.requests@easproject.com

www.ingramcontent.com/pod-product-compliance
Lightning Source LLC
Chambersburg PA
CBHW070942230426
43666CB00011B/2526